YOU KNOW

C000118472

Does a word mean what it says? Sometimes – but not always. Everyone thinks that meaning is contained within words – like sardines in a tin, or milk in a bottle. After all, words are nice stable things that you can look up in a dictionary aren't they? But dictionaries only take us so far …

If you eavesdropped on a teenage conversation, rushing to a dictionary – with its definitions frozen in time – wouldn't help much. Who's using a word and to whom, in what context, for what purpose – all these influence the meaning of the language we use. The word's origins and history (its 'genetics') also help.

Try teaching yourself another language from a phrase-book and you'll soon learn that you can be correct, in the formal sense, but still way behind the times in reality.

In this book Ruth Wajnryb explores how and why our language works the way it does.

Dr Ruth Wajnryb is an applied linguist, researcher and writer, with a weekly column, 'WORDS', in *The Sydney Morning Herald*. She has written many books on language, typically using a linguistic lens to look at social interaction. She is currently writing a detective novel about a forensic linguist.

YOU KNOW WHAT I MEAN?

WORDS, CONTEXTS AND COMMUNICATION

RUTH WAJNRYB

CAMBRIDGE
UNIVERSITY PRESS

CAMBRIDGE UNIVERSITY PRESS
Cambridge, New York, Melbourne, Madrid, Cape Town, Singapore,
São Paulo, Delhi

Cambridge University Press
The Edinburgh Building, Cambridge CB2 8RU, UK

Published in the United States of America by Cambridge University Press,
New York

www.cambridge.org
Information on this title: www.cambridge.org/9780521703741

First published 2005 by ABC Books for the Australian Broadcasting Corporation
GPO Box 9994, Sydney, NSW 2001, Australia
This edition published in 2008 by Cambridge University Press
Not for sale in Australia or New Zealand

Printed in the United Kingdom at the University Press, Cambridge

A catalogue record for this publication is available from the British Library

Library of Congress Cataloguing in Publication data

Wajnryb, Ruth.
You know what I mean : words, contexts, and communication / Ruth Wajnryb.
p. cm.
Includes bibliographical references and index.
ISBN 978-0-521-87885-2 (hardback) – ISBN 978-0-521-70374-1 (paperback)
1. English language – Idioms. 2. English language – Usage. 3. Lexicology.
4. English language – Spoken English. I. Title.

PE1460.W215 2008
428 – dc22 2008019388

ISBN 978-0-521-87885-2 hardback
ISBN 978-0-521-70374-1 paperback

To the memory of my parents

Sine quibus nihil

CONTENTS

NUTS AND BOLTS

It's usual to think that meaning is contained in words, the way sardines come in tins, or milk in bottles. Words are things you can look up in a dictionary. If you don't know what 'iconoclastic' means, a dictionary will help. But even though I do love dictionaries, I'm the first to admit that they'll only take you so far. Meanings also reside – perhaps even more essentially – in the grammar of the language, what some like to call its nuts and bolts. Here a dictionary is less helpful (try looking up 'it') and a grammar reference is needed, though such books tend to be *über*-unfriendly. This is a pity because grammar embeds meaning in centrally important ways. Take pronouns for instance – 'I', 'you', 'he', 'she', etc. – which furnish one small example of grammatical nuts and bolts. One function of pronouns is to impart a sense of ourselves and our relationship with others, a crucial element of the social function of language, arguably its most important. All the sections in this chapter show how pronouns manage the nexus of grammar and meaning.

In the kingdom of we

Let's talk about 'we'. I mean the pronoun 'we', as in plural subject: 'you and me'. Not the 'wee' that explains the temperature of the paddling pool. Nor the endearing 'wee' that Scots are wont to add to nouns: 'Come on in for a wee moment and have a wee cup of tea.'

As a pronoun, 'we' stands in for any plural subject (either previously named, or implicit) to give the first person plural perspective. Here's Napoleon to his minders, about himself and Josephine: 'We're staying in tonight so you boys can have the night off.'

And here's Winston Churchill rallying a nation to war: 'We shall fight on the beaches, we shall fight on the landing grounds, we shall fight in the fields and in the streets, we shall fight in the hills; we shall never surrender.'

And here's George W. Bush immediately after September 11 speaking for 250 million Americans: 'We will not rest until their deaths are avenged.'

So 'we', like any pronoun, is a handy little device, saving one from clumsily having to repeat the subject; and at the same time holding together, into a cohesive whole, a larger text that might otherwise crumble away.

Despite its diminutive stature, 'we' has a range of uses. There is the now-almost-obsolete 'royal we', once used by a single royal person to refer to herself – for instance Queen Victoria's 'We are not interested in the possibilities of defeat.' The sense here is that a royal personage would compromise her dignity by referring to herself in the naked 'I'. Also, as the throne is larger than the singularity of the person currently in office, 'we' conveys the weight of tradition. While young Wills or Harry Windsor are far removed from 'we' behaviour, I suspect Prince Charles, especially when miffed, might not be beyond the old fallback.

Nor is the 'royal we' limited to royalty. Many a school principal has aped it – 'We are not amused' – in punitive contexts. Here too, plurality conveys the force of authority of those who hold the reins of power.

There's the so-called 'editorial we'. This term is reserved for a single speaker or writer who is prompted to eschew the singular 'I' to avoid the charge of egotism. In academe, the use of 'I' is discouraged as part of the more general pursuit of an impersonal tone. Thus a lecturer might say, 'As we [not 'I'] showed a moment ago.' Overused, of course, avoiding 'I' warrants the charge of pomposity. Funnily enough, the term 'editorial we' is not applied to the fully justified use of 'we' which refers to the consensus of a collective body, such as a committee or editorial board – for example, a newspaper editorial that includes 'we deplore the current wave of terrorism'.

Sometimes 'we' seeks to avoid a separation of self and reader/audience. Such a 'we' can be very serviceable when there is a desire to identify the speaker/writer and listener/reader in a joint enterprise. Compare 'We [or 'Let's'] now turn to a different problem' with 'You now turn to a different problem.' Counsellors of various persuasions use this 'we' to gently manage and steer their discourse. Sometimes 'we' (standing for 'you') can serve as encouragement: 'We should soon start thinking about ways in which we might end the marriage.' At other times, depending on tone, context and power relations, the intention approximates cajolery: 'We can do better than that, can't we?' Or condescension masquerading as forced conviviality – 'And how are we feeling today?' – a form much beloved in nursing homes and among those who wait on tables.

In a recent critique of Australian TV, gardening show *Burke's Backyard* was commended for establishing the genre of 'we-dom'. This, I infer, is the Kingdom of We, where the backyard, as the great Australian leveller, renders irrelevant all other distinctions – age, gender, social class, suburb, sexual preference. Everything is happily subordinated to the backyard altar.

Finally, there's the 'universal we' – this establishes a lofty solidarity across a shared humanity. Never better illustrated than in these lines of T. S. Eliot's from 'Little Gidding':

> We shall not cease from exploration
> And the end of all our exploring
> Will be to arrive where we started
> And know the place for the first time.

The Queen's we

The Queen's 2001 Christmas Message (QCM) contained thirty instances of first person plural pronouns ('we', 'us', 'our'), only five first person singulars ('I', 'my') and four second person pronouns ('you', 'your'). This makes for a maximum of solidarity (usness) and a minimum of distance (them-and-usness).

Yes, I confess, I was counting. A closet QCM aficionado, I watch, record, re-watch, analyse and, yes, I count. In uncertain times, the QCM offers great dollops of comfort. There's a predictability in the cadences, sequence, inclusions and exclusions, dress, colours, hats, horses, corgis, medals, photography, palaces, the studied casualness of some shots, the frozen poise of others, and, most particularly, the language.

From Christmas to Christmas not much changes in the QCM. It's a ten-minute broadcast from Buckingham Palace, sandwiched between a bit of pomp, ceremony and anthem at start and end. Indeed, so very distinctive is the text-type of the QCM that if you stumbled across one while blindfolded in the Sudanese desert, you'd still recognise it: 'Ah, the Queen's Xmas Message', you'd say, wiping some sand from your eyes, 'fancy running into it out here!'

Within moments of the opening, you're being lulled into a hypnotically peaceful, fairyland sensibility. Ho hum, here we are, the Queen and me, sharing this day, again. So little separates us. Oceans, accents, belief systems, socioeconomic status. Nothing comes between. For these brief minutes, we can forget that she lives in a palace or three, the richest woman in the world, with the power to choose how much tax to pay. Trifling matters. What really counts is what we share.

Enter the 'we's. 'We' is a marvellous device for accentuating our common humanity. Or for pretending there is some, when there plainly isn't. 'We' is small and inconspicuous and slips in innocuously. It spreads itself around disguised as 'us' or 'our'. It's subliminal. Without knowing why, we feel warm, gooey. It's the pronominal counterpart to 'Kumbaya'.

'We' also serves by being slippery. The Queen's 'we' can mean lots of things, many things at the same time, some things and not others, different things to different people. But precisely because it *is* slippery, pinning down the meaning is not easy.

The Queen's 'we' sometimes means 'British' ('our farmers and rural communities'). Sometimes 'we Christian Britons' ('we look to the Church to bring us together'). Sometimes 'we of any faith' ('so many of us, whatever our religion, need our faith more than ever'). Sometimes it means 'Britons as distinct from (mostly) Americans' ('we in this country have tried to bring comfort to all those who were bereaved'). But mostly it embraces the widest possible agency – 'ordinary common humanity' ('we all have something to learn from one another').

The one thing 'we' does *not* mean in this QCM is 'I' – which rather ironically, and as already mentioned, is a circumstance known as 'the royal we'. Nor does the Queen's 'we' include Prince Philip in any specific way other than as part of the throbbing humanity to which we must presume he belongs. And it doesn't refer to the Windsors per se, that particular group of special folk whose antics the Queen is seasonally at pains to sanitise.

Supporting 'we' in the QCM is the usual collection of anodyne abstract nouns. They too slip in unremarkably, meaning whatever you want them to mean – hardship, anxiety, wanton acts, grief, evil, commemoration, tribute, horror, experience, support, hope, distress, comfort. All motherhood words. Hypnotically, we nod in agreement. Just as we embrace the Queen's themes of community and belonging. No contest. It's inoffensively platitudinous and effectively so.

But be not beguiled. There's a PR dimension at work, disguised under the veneer of humanity and stability. In speaking out against excesses ('wanton acts of . . . terror') the Queen implicitly offers the strength and decency of the *status quo* as bulwark – a message reinforced by her syntax. She balances 'the storms and droughts' with 'epidemics and famine.' Natural disasters are balanced with man-made ones. There are 'times of tragedy' alongside 'occasions of celebration'. It's almost Ecclesiastical, in the literal sense.

Clichés get in on the balancing act. We 'enjoy moments of great happiness' and 'suffer times of profound sadness'. And just when we're lulled into a compliant state of non-contest, the simple plea is made for 'a fair and ordered society'. In this way, slippery 'we' blurs the boundaries between Queen/throne/monarchy/goodness/truth.

By the end, we have Queen & Co. lined up on the side of common decency.

The final scene – Queen on doorstep, *mit* corgis, receiving passing carollers' good wishes – clinches the just-like-any-of-us myth. Nice.

Flexible you

A piece of advice: if you must have a cross-cultural marriage, I suggest you don't blend two languages with different pronoun systems. Believe me when I say that this can capsize even the best of intentions, overturn goodwill, and leave shattered pieces of metaphorical wedding cake all over the floor.

I'm thinking in particular of mixing a T/V (*tu/vous*) language with a non-T/V one. A T/V language (like French, German, Italian, Spanish) allows you the flexibility of differentiating in your choice of 'you' to show friendly familiarity or respectful deference, depending on whether you're patting your dog or your mother-in-law. A non-T/V language (like English) is one where 'you' covers everything from familial and friendly, to formal, from singular to plural. Dogs and mothers-in-law get lumped together, for better or for worse.

Speakers of a T/V language are wont to criticise English for the bluntness of its all-purpose 'you'. Now I can see why they might come to this conclusion. However, what they fail to appreciate is that our little 'you' is an amazingly flexible and context-sensitive creature with subtleties and nuances oft overlooked. Far from being gross, overworked, unrefined, impoverished and under-differentiated, 'you' is subtle, supple, versatile. In short, 'you' sports range, scope and richness. If this little pronoun were a dancer, it would do classical square-toe ballet, the waltz, 'The Pride of Erin', the foxtrot, Latin salsa, funk and the Argentine tango.

Like a traditional Japanese garden, 'you' has the elegance of the minimally bare. It is confident that context will always fill out the semantic corners and render it unambiguous. Look at a person and use 'you' and s/he will know who you mean. Speak to a room of 'you's and spread your eye contact around the room, they'll all know you mean all of them.

'You' can mean you-and-other-people-in-your-circumstance. This is impersonal but not as distantly snotty as 'one'. Perfect for the commercial relationship calling for pseudo-formality tempered by mock-friendliness. You're at the travel agent's, wanting to know how to get to Laos: 'Well, you could fly to Bangkok and travel a bit around the country. Then you could take a train across the border, or if you wanted to get there faster, you could fly direct from Bangkok.' Here 'you' locates the other as separate from the speaker but not distant or unreachable. Politicians are fond of this 'you', using it to engender and invest a personal touch: 'This election is about security and stability. You want to know that you're safe and your savings are safe.'

There's another 'you' that epitomises 'otherness'. Its range of reference is 'people over there' or People Not Like Us. You're talking about the restaurants that dump huge quantities of uneaten food and over-orders in garbage bins at the end of the night: 'You'd think they could spare a thought for the hungry and homeless.'

And between these poles of friendly people-like-you and distancing people-not-like-you is 'neutral you'. The water board wants to tell me about social responsibility: 'If you want to save water, there are some simple steps you can follow.' This is personal but neutral: 'you' is placed in the subject position, giving it agency and standing.

But when we move 'you' to the object (or Kitchener) position ('Your country needs you'), we have something closer to the 'in-your-face you', also known as 'New York you'. One New Yorker says to another, 'What's the time please?' The other retorts with, 'Do I wear a watch for you?'

But if abrasion is what you seek to avoid, you're likely to insert any number of 'you's through the 'you know' device. This 'you' is massively exploited in social interactions where dialogue is co-constructed and talking turns are shared about equitably. Like the 'eh?' you hear in regional Australia and in the speech of some New Zealanders, there's a lubricating function designed to blur the borders between 'I', 'we', 'you' and people-in-general. It's akin to the far more formal 'nostalgic you' that is heard in statements like this: 'We lived in the country when I was growing up. You'd wake with the birds early each morning. The rooster would be your alarm clock.'

'You' can hold its own among the best. So it's quite pointless worrying about whom the bell tolls for. It tolls for thee.

Avoiding you

It was in the Ladies' in an office block leased mostly to the professional class – doctors, lawyers, pathologists, accountants, financial advisers and other people like that. Spotless premises. Sparkling surfaces. Pristine. Lots of glass and metal. In all, a studied, elegant minimalism. A controlled undecoration. Sometimes less is definitely more.

It was in the cubicle, above the cistern, that I saw the sign. It said: 'There's a toilet brush next to the bowl in case it is needed.'

A masterpiece, I thought; a veritable study in linguistic politeness. I was immediately struck by how much energy had been invested in the avoidance of 'you'.

And no wonder. Consider any one of a multitude of nasty inferences that would flow from wording like this: 'If you dirty the bowl, you should/could/must use the brush.' Unpacking these inferences is not a nice business, but here we go. You're the type to dirty bowls. You're the type to fail to clean up after yourself. At the very least, you're the type to need reminding. We suspect you might also have dirty inside-collars, old socks, belly button fluff, and ragged toenails. We don't like your type in this building, but if you must be here, try to play by the rules.

The way to circumvent these nasty inferences is to lose the 'you'. Enter a construction known in some circles as 'the existential "there"' (as in 'there's a toilet brush next to the bowl'). It is sometimes called 'the dummy subject', but I for one find this a disparaging label for what can be an extremely useful device. In our current example, the existential 'there' serves the larger goal of you-avoidance by effectively enabling a shift of focus from nastily constructed 'you' to calm, impassive, inert, waiting-on-the-sidelines toilet brush.

And isn't there something innocuous and unblaming about the fact that the toilet brush is mentioned only insofar as its proximity to the toilet is concerned? This controlled casualness – 'next to the toilet' – is disingenuous. It's there to provoke an assurance of anonymity. Just between me and you and the goalpost, or me and you and the toilet brush...Shhh! No one will know. Our brush is the very soul of discretion.

The feat of you-avoidance is achieved through an amalgam of grammatical collusion. 'There', for instance, is far from being on its ownsome. It has some valuable help. Take the cleverly loaded conjunctive device 'in case'. This construction is nothing if not indeterminate. 'When' would have been a matter of surety, so too 'whenever', while 'if' would have offered a theoretical provision of condition. But 'in case' bespeaks the off-chance. There's nothing definite or inevitable or even likely about 'in case'. No logical sequence of events, no predetermined segues. Just a vague possibility, a circumstance that might happen to anyone. It's a 'with impunity' kind of thing.

And notice the passive 'in case it is needed'. If 'in case' serves to distance the possibility of a nasty occurrence to some remote, unlikely eventuality, the passive is even more effective in depersonalising the circumstance. It allows the sign not to say 'in case you need it', which, in the context of this painstaking crafting of you-avoidance, would be awfully in-your-face.

Indeed, in the toolkit of strategies for avoiding 'you', the passive construction must rank at or near the top. This is because, unlike the active form ('you need the toilet brush'), where the subject/agent of the verb is one of the obligatory elements in the sentence, in a passive construction the subject/agent can be conveniently sidestepped – even deleted.

The passive works largely through inference. We know that 'is needed' assumes the existence of a phrase of agency ('by you'), but it doesn't need spelling out. Indeed, from a stylistic point of view, the 'by you' is much more elegant as an omitted-but-understood component, rather than a cumbersome and unnecessary tack-on. In our case of oopsy toilet occurrences, the passive serves the goal of you-avoidance supremely well. Exit 'you', and all its nasty accoutrements.

There's no doubt that sometimes the effort of avoiding 'you' is an exercise in walking on eggshells – a kind of grammatical callisthenics. Fortunately for all of us 'you's out there, the language scores high in flexibility and fitness.

Youse

Language serves two masters – Identity and Intelligibility. Sometimes we use it to highlight who we want the world to think we are. Sometimes it's more about reaching out to someone else. Mostly, Identity and Intelligibility are compatible. But occasionally there's a collision of goals.

The case of the second person pronoun 'youse' (or 'yous') is just such an instance where, often, the advantage of functionality is sacrificed to protect our image of ourselves. In other words, we'd rather risk momentary ambiguity than tamper with our public face.

'Youse' is a word that the self-appointed custodians of English love to hate. And not only literary types. Apparently, research into small businesses uncovered the fact that many people would withdraw their custom if staff with the 'youse' habit spoke to them. It just 'clangs', they said. So too does 'hi guys', 'yep', 'nah', 'like', 'ain't' and 'we haven't got none'.

I've sat across a desk from a refined, dictionary marketing man as he shuddered in horror while recounting his nephew's occasional use of 'youse'. He looked visibly pained at the thought of this young boy's bringing such disgrace to the family. I tried to tease out the issues – essentially a kind of 'rankism' ('rankist' being a recent super-ordinate term for 'classist') – but he wasn't interested. No nephew of his 'was gonna use "youse"'. While tempted to point out his own 'gonna', I decided, for once, to bite my lip.

Prejudice dies slowly, if ever. It's a long time that poor 'youse' has been maligned and hounded. Initially, its associations with the lowly status of Irish English in Australia made it substandard for those committed to their own superiority. Then it became a class thing, and linked up with rough hands, coarse tongue, minimally educated, unreliable, socially dysfunctional, going nowhere fast.

If I thought it would make an iota of difference, I'd start up a Defence of Youse Society. But while a handful of lexicographers and linguists might be supportive ideologically, I expect they'd be wholly indisposed to street activism. In any case, as *Macquarie Dictionary*'s Sue Butler puts it, 'prescriptivism' is not necessarily a dirty word, any more than 'descriptivism' means an indiscriminate approach to lexicography: 'Both words get bandied around but the words themselves lose illumination as they gain heat.'

As far as 'youse' goes, its disrepute is a pity, given the word's ubiquity and utility. There's no doubt that it's needed. Ever since 'thou' faded from use, 'you' has been massively overworked. It's had to service the functions of singularity, plurality, familiarity and for-mality. That's a big job description for a little pronoun that hasn't had a salary review for ages.

Think about it – many languages employ a whole different pro-noun to differentiate the familial or friendly status from the more formal, distant, respectful. Think of French, Spanish, German. But not good old democratic, egalitarian, non-nepotistic English. It's 'you' whether you're speaking to the dog or the Queen. 'You' pre-emptively cuts down poppies with any ill-conceived pretensions of being tall; it slashes everyone to one-size-fits-all uniformity; it reminds us that we all go out feet first.

One way we are able to get around the problem of 'you' serv-ing as both singular and plural is to substitute the pronoun with something that performs its vocative function (calling or addressing another) and, in doing so, clarifies your intention as regards number. For instance, you can use a personal name ('Come here, Mary') or a kin term ('Over here, Aunt Mildred'), a status term ('Your Honour'), an occupational term ('officer', 'doctor', 'waiter', 'nurse'), a conventional term ('ladies and gentlemen', 'members of the jury'), a term of endearment ('darling', 'buddy', 'mate', 'my dear'), or a derogatory term ('fatso', 'slowcoach', 'nitwit').

Despite these options, the English 'you' has long worked overtime. The truth is, it was only with the advent of 'youse' for plural that 'you' achieved its sorely needed R and R. The brief was clear. 'Youse' is friendly, inclusive, all-embracing and unambiguously so, even through its variants: 'youse-all', 'y'arl', 'yez' and 'y'all'. I'm not suggesting a blanket substitution of 'youse' for 'you', for that would simply create another overworked pronoun. We could still keep 'you' for the dog and the Queen, try to work those vocative substitutes a little harder ('here boy!', 'your Majesty'), but adopt 'youse' for the friendly, plural context, say, when the whole House of Windsor plus corgis drop over for pizza.

It

One thing we all know is that Coke is it. When we buy Coke, when we drink it and share it about, we know it's it. But one thing no one seems to care about is, what exactly 'it' is.

It's not an easy matter to research. I asked some regular Coke-drinkers what they thought 'it' was. One said 'it' was 'being cool'. A second said 'it' was 'everything'. A third said: 'Whatever you want it to be'. A fourth just looked at me.

Hundreds of thousands, nay, millions of people drink it. With China opening up, make that trillions. All into it. But beyond a wild guess, does anyone outside of coke.com know the nature of 'it'?

What a ploy. Link desirability to a perception of need. Associate the brand with a word to which any meaning can accrue. Add a full cup of desirability. And lo, people will flock in droves, equating the quenching outcome with their particular neediness. So, yes, after all, 'it' is anything you want it to be. Funny that.

'It' has served Coke well, but not only Coke. It's a useful device when a certain *je ne sais quoi* quality needs naming. Take the 'it girl'. She's the one all the other girls want to be like, and all the boys (think they) want to hang out with. Whatever the milieu, she's the avatar, the trendsetting leader of the pack. The poise is instantly recognisable. If she's the Coke of cool, then Coke's the 'it girl' of colas.

'It' holds disquiet – an uneasy ambivalence. Remember the children's games when one player becomes 'it'? That kid has to chase the rest – run, tag, capture or subdue. All attention is on 'it'. It's scary, but it's also everyone's secret wish. Being 'it' is where the power is.

'It' pops up where we need a label for a non-specific function: 'There's no getting away from it'; 'I've got it covered'; 'You can depend on it'; 'It's a question of trust'. Similarly, we have the ubiquitous 'empty it', which serves a proxy role in the subject position: 'It's raining'; 'It's a pity'; 'It's a coincidence'; 'It's amazing'; 'It sucks.' And also in the object position: 'Watch it'; 'Forget it'; 'Go for it'; 'Give it up'; 'Damn it.'

Tempting it is to think 'it' a loathsomely vague word. However, it's worth remembering that language is only as vague as we want it to be. When we choose it to be vague, it's usually because it serves us. Vague has a quality of built-in retreatability. 'Is that what you thought I meant?! No, not at all, I didn't mean that. You've misunderstood me.' Vague offers impunity. Prospective deniability is the *sine qua non* of civilised life: without 'it', and other vagueness devices, we'd have no ambassadors, longer queues at the dispute centre, and fewer date rapists.

'It' also plays a vital role in the distribution of information, especially where rules exist for the allocation of new and old. Take the question: 'Where are you going?' The complete answer might be 'I'm going to the beach', and there's a reason it's ordered in this way and not, say, 'To the beach I am going.' Conventionally, in English, old information (or facts we can take as given) comes first – in this case, the fact that a person is going somewhere. And new information – in our case, where the person is going – comes later.

Now 'it' has a role to play in these informational shenanigans. Sometimes we want to locate our information in the position of 'new' in order to take advantage of its prominence. That's where we use a handy construction called 'anticipatory it' which allows the subject to be postponed until the focal end position. Hence the melodrama of: 'It was for you that all our lives we suffered and toiled.' Much more effective than in the reverse position. All brought about and made possible by 'it'.

Now, remember the Coke advertisement-cum-slogan – 'Coke is it'? In this case, our 'it' serves not as the postponer, as in the 'anticipatory it', but rather as the thing postponed. Bottom-line meaning: by the time we get to 'it', we're even thirstier.

It does

I returned home from a writers' festival swankily sporting a very nice publisher's black canvas carry bag which I thought would come in handy for many a carrying need. No, I'm not short of bags, that's true. But this one appealed and seemed likely to emerge as the flavourful bag of the month.

Which is why I immediately noticed the moment it disappeared. It quickly re-emerged in my teenage daughter's room, and on many a subsequent occasion I noticed it perched over her shoulder or on her hip, filled with her things, and serving her in the handy way I had perhaps naively imagined it was going to serve me. Subtly, imperceptibly and in the total absence of language, 'my' bag had switched its possessive adjectives and become 'her' bag. Funny that.

I'm a generous soul but I do prefer things to be explicit. So, as Daughter sat, with bag, in the front passenger seat while I drove her to some event, I commented, not wholly without pointed irony, nodding at the bag, on how handy the bag was for a wide variety of schlepping functions.

Here's what followed in the Mother–Daughter exchange, during which both parties invest considerable effort in the avoidance of markers of possessiveness:

M: I see the bag's working out rather nicely for you.
D: It does.
M: 'It does'? (*rising tone*)
D: Yeah. (*long pause*) You know, like, 'it'll do'.
M: Just 'it'll do'? That's it?
D: Yeah (*further pause*), it's not very flash, like.
M: N-o-o. It's more 'handy' than 'flashy', I'd say. But...it's not 'it'll do', is it? Because you're using it, here and now. It's not a comment on projected utility in the future. We're talking about now; like, there's the bag, on your lap, right now.
D: Yeah, well, like, OK, that's why I said, 'it does'.

Notice how I start out deliberately using the definite article 'the' before 'bag'. This allows me to begin on apparently neutral ground, so as to appear to be innocently inquiring about Daughter's perception of said bag's utility value. I could have said: 'I see my bag's working out rather nicely for you.' But had I done so, my subtext would have capsized my main text in a single blow. Daughter duly picks up on my distancing mechanism and continues it, referring vaguely to what might be the bag or the situation or the bag mixed in with the situation as 'it'.

At the time, two aspects of Daughter's language struck me. One is the nonchalance of 'it'll do'. Here's a girl who's appropriated my bag, commandeered it the way governments take over private vehicles for military transport in times of martial law, and the best she can say is that 'it'll do'.

'It'll do' means a kind of base-line functionality – a borderline pass, if it were an assignment; a barely satisfactory, if it were an annual performance review. It's a maybe, a couldn't really care less, a 'whatever' kind of expression, betraying an irritating shoulder-shrugging nonchalance that only a mother would see. I suspect I'd have been a whole lot happier to have given up my bag if Daughter had truly valued it. But 'it'll do' seemed to fall a good way beneath the required amount of value that would have made my sacrifice worthwhile.

The second aspect of Daughter's response was the novel adaptation of 'it'll do' to 'it does'. In hindsight I reject her explanation that the switch from future projection to present tense was meant to denote a here-and-now time sense. Instead, I strongly suspect that 'it does' was a subtle assertion of ownership. It meant: 'this is my bag now'. It had an in-your-face defiance about it, a surety that is the hallmark of youth, a smugness that bespeaks 'finders keepers, losers weepers', a cavalier quality of the 'possession is nine-tenths of ownership' or whatever, and the drop-dead arrogance of an implied 'get a life'.

Her parting shot, of whose irony she seemed quite oblivious, an oblivion that was itself a considered part of the pose: 'But hey, Mum, any time you want to borrow it, consider it yours.'

New girl in the kitchen

It's Saturday afternoon. Laptop and I are in the kitchen. We're waiting for the delivery men to arrive with our new fridge. As you never can tell just when they will show up, may as well use the time productively.

Today I'm thinking about gender. One of the great things about modern English, from the perspective of a foreign learner, is the fact that nouns, for the most part, lack gender. So the grammatical distinction of gender draws largely on the natural distinction of sex – giving us masculine, feminine and neuter. This means that, in English, things in the natural world that we know to be masculine (from a particular horse, say, to a particular Prime Minister) will be grammatically masculine, too. This is nice. The congruence means you can use your knowledge of the world to help with grammar. Even if it means bending down and having a good look – I'm thinking of the horse, more than the PM.

Conversely, an English speaker attempting a noun-gendered language confronts a world subdivided into logic-defying categories. In French, the word *table*, you're told, is feminine, and so is *voiture* (car), but *chemin* (road) is masculine. German has the perversity of *das Mädchen* (the girl) and *das Kind* (the child), both being grammatically neuter. I realise that every language is supremely logical to its own users. But this surely is a case of 'What the...?'

Where's the logic in the French word for 'love' being masculine in the singular, but often feminine in the plural? Why is a French cloud masculine, a German one feminine? German has spoon (masculine), fork (feminine), knife (neuter). Make sense of that if you will, I dare you.

With English gender so laid-back, it's not surprising our determiners ('a', 'the') are unmarked for gender. Nor are our adjectives obliged to agree with their nouns – it's all-round nice across the board. When my foreign students used to complain to me about the English spelling system, I'd remind them about tables, cars and clouds in other languages, and urge them to count their lucky stars. Of course, they got stumped on the idiom, but what can you do?

Arguably, one reason English is the world's lingua franca is that it's so easy to reach a basic mastery. You're not blocked at every turn by opaque inflections, illogical gender distribution and the requisite rules of agreement, crazy subjunctives and all the rest. But, arguably, language dominance is less about grammar than military/economic conquest. And just as arguably, English has its oddities ('am', 'was', 'have been', for instance).

Lost in reverie, I'm shaken out of it by the phone ringing. It's the delivery men. They'll be here in thirty minutes, they say.

Of course, English has eccentricities. Machines and vehicles are figuratively feminine. Of a boat: 'She runs well before the wind.' Of a car: 'She goes like a dream.' Chris Forde, writing in *The Sydney Morning Herald*, suggests that vehicles are feminine 'because they never stop costing you money; more as they get on in years...You never stop loving them in spite of this. You knew this when you went into the partnership and your first one always holds the fondest memories.' A material, albeit tender, attitude to women. Could always be worse.

Perhaps it's a control thing. According to this hypothesis, men attribute feminine gender to boats, cars and machines because they can turn them on and off at will. This does not work for public transport vehicles – no one would say: 'Take the 378. She goes along Oxford Street' – which serves to bolster the control theory.

Or maybe the 'she' is a boys-only term of endearment targeting something perceived to be 'of service'. After all, we talk about 'maintaining the car' while the payment to an ex-wife is 'maintenance'. And 'handling' goes with cars and, if you're lucky, wifely sexual favours. Certainly, there's something folksy, friendly, hierarchy-flattening and team-building about the allocation of 'she' in these inanimate contexts.

The dog barks moments before the doorbell rings. Two overalled men with 'John Lewis' written on their backs. A trolley bearing the shiny new refrigerator. 'So where do you want her?' they ask, manoeuvring their way into my kitchen.

S/He'll be right

Anyone who writes for a living, or more likely for a non-living, regularly encounters the conundrum of what to do about the third person singular pronoun (TPSP). Because English lacks a sex-indefinite singular pronoun, comparable to the plural 'they', historically the male pronoun has served a generic function.

Thus, in the sentence 'The doctor begins by asking questions about the patient's current health and then he takes a medical history', we're forced to subsume all doctors, male and female, under the 'he' umbrella. For males this is both invisible and natural; for females, it's both obtrusive and unnatural, like seeing all those dark suits in Parliament. One more evidentiary piece in the patriarchal mosaic.

But 'sexist he' is no longer the norm and we're seeing fewer sentences like 'The applicant should fill in the document using his own handwriting.' The search has been on for some time now for a more equitable linguistic representation and an end to the subsuming and marginalising of the female. The truth is we're a bit sick of the obtrusive, unnatural 'he' standing in for all of us. Might be neat, but it sucks.

You'll often find a note in a book's preface explaining the author's position on the TPSP. Where there's no recognition of the problem, one can expect the all-embracing 'he' to pervade. Sometimes a writer will say that 'he' and 'she' have been used randomly through the book so as not to persist with the sexist use of 'he'. Sometimes the writer will limit the use of 'he' and 'she' to different participant groups. For example, it's not uncommon in educational literature for teachers to be 'she' and students to be 'he'. Given that teaching is a female-intensive profession, this makes reasonable sense.

The preface of Adam Phillips's *On Kissing, Tickling, and Being Bored* ends with the following: 'Throughout the text, I have observed the economical but obviously unsatisfactory convention of using the masculine pronoun.' This confession is clever, if also somewhat cynical and overwhelmingly pragmatic. It allows Phillips to subsume all third person singular referents under the all-embracing 'sexist he'. The only difference between Phillips's stance and that of others who make the same choice is that Phillips has owned up to the problem. Lip service, but hey, it's something.

Several options exist for avoiding the 'sexist he'. One way is: 'The applicant should fill in the document using his/her handwriting.' Similarly, you'd use 'he or she' (or 'she or he' – a feminist version, foregrounding the female). Then there's the reduced 's/he' which isn't too ugly when used sparingly.

More cumbersome is the tactic of repeating the generic referent-noun: 'The applicant should fill in the document using the applicant's handwriting.' Elegant, it isn't. Then there's the inanimate version: 'Fill in the document by hand', or 'Use handwriting to fill in the document.' And the old standby is the passive: 'The document should be filled in by hand / using handwriting.' And if you don't mind sounding like Prince Charles, there's always 'One should use one's own handwriting to fill in the document.'

But passives don't serve stylistically. It's then that I turn to 'they' and make it work overtime as the stand-in sex-indefinite pronoun, alongside 'he'/'she'/'it': 'The applicant should fill in the form by hand. They can ask for pens at the counter.' There's no ambiguity here, and it's just a question of time, I like to think, before editors cease getting a blood pressure spike when confronted with the singular 'they'. It's time editors began to recognise 'they' for what it is – an avoidance of pronoun tyranny – and not what they suspect – sloppy habits. There's a nice distinction made by Huddleston and Pullum, in their *Cambridge Grammar of the English Language*, between 'they' as a 'referring pronoun' which must have a plural antecedent ('The holidays arrived and they were dismal') and 'they' as a 'bound pronoun' which has no such restriction ('Name me a teenager who worries about their mother!').

Even more creative – though I concede to being on thin ice here – is the pronoun 'themself': 'The applicant should fill the form in themself, using pens that are available at the counter.' I admit to finding more and more opportunities to slip in this third person singular pronominal solution to 'sexist he'. It's hard to beat 'themself' for clarity and neutrality.

Over the top, you say? Too cutting edge? There'll be blood in the streets? Is it any worse than 'man breastfeeds his young' – an encyclopaedia entry on mammals and such, where 'sexist he', intoxicated by power unchecked, surges to the dizzy heights of absurdity?

They

'They'. Personal pronoun. Third person. Plural (also sometimes singular). Subject. Stands in place of animate or inanimate nouns. Object form is 'them'. Possessive form is 'their'.

Put like that, the pronoun 'they' seems quite benign, if also rather opaque and unreal, removed from the daily currency of ordinary life. In this, it is no different from most grammatical information, which at first (and even at second) glance seems as prosaic and indifferent as a maths formula. I mean, when was the last time a maths formula seemed to have a pulsating heart?

A pronoun is a word that acts for (*pro*) a noun or a noun phrase. It allows us to knit together our utterances to create cohesive text, because few of us (excepting the likes of Marlon Brando and Sylvester Stallone) speak in units of sentences, words or grunts. Normal folk (people like us) create discourse, which means connected text beyond a single utterance.

Take 'I went down to the shop and bought some bananas. The bananas were from Costa Rica.' If we want our English to sound remotely native-like, there's no argument that we need 'they' to substitute for 'the bananas'. It's not something we do with conscious consideration, any more than we give our attention to other conventions of the grammatical system. We just do it. That's the nature of language habit.

In fact, though, 'they' is much more powerful. In combination with 'say', 'they' cuts to the chase of social intercourse, especially social constraint.

So, who are 'they', why are they so garrulous and why do we – the ones who listen to what 'they say' – take any notice? These are the concerns of Douglas Rushkoff, author of *Coercion*, a book about the techniques of manipulation used by what he calls 'the persuasion professionals'. His book begins thus:

They say human beings use only ten per cent of their brains. They say polyunsaturated fat is better for you than saturated fat. They say that tiny squiggles in a rock prove there once was life on Mars. They say our children's test scores are declining. They say Jesus was a direct descendant of King David. They say you can earn $15,000 a week in your spare time. They say marijuana leads to LSD, and LSD can lead to suicide. They say the corner office is a position of power. They say the elderly should get flu shots this season. They say homosexuality is an environmentally learned trait. They say there's a gene for homosexuality. They say people can be hypnotised to do anything. They say people won't do anything under hypnosis that they wouldn't do when conscious. They say Prozac alleviates depression. They say mutual funds are the best long-term investment. They say computers can predict the weather...

Et cetera, et cetera. Sound familiar? Now let's personalise the concept. Consider one or two things you (yeah, you) subscribe to in your life – like vitamin supplements or hair conditioner – that you do largely because of what 'they' have said... (Mmm, now that was easy.)

The flip side of 'they say' is 'trust'. The reality is that we take information on an assumed authority all the time. The fact that we now have laws prescribing food content descriptions on packaging indicates in part that the trust so long handed over has eroded, and in places worn very, very thin.

Mostly we attend uncritically to what 'they' say. All through our lives, 'they' are present. Starting out, they're our parents. Gradually add significant others of various assortments – grandparents, aunts, carers, teachers. By the time our shoe size has stabilised, it's bosses, experts, authorities of all shapes and persuasions. Celebrities bleed across their proper domain and lend their putative authority to areas quite outside their jurisdiction – like William Shatner's endorsement of a breakfast cereal.

In all the years I gave lectures in linguistics, only once did anyone ask me for evidence of the claims I made as a routine matter of course. That was a great moment. The woman who asked said (or rather meant, and note I've removed all the politeness markers): 'Who said that? On what evidence? How valid and reliable is that evidence?'

All good questions, all rightly asked, all tangibly answerable. Sadly, it was just the once.

WORD BEHAVIOURS

This chapter contains ten sections that variously illustrate the complex behaviours to which words are subject. Many are the shaping influences that motivate how words behave. Sometimes the influences are historical, and here etymology and word borrowings can explain a lot. Sometimes it is a word's morphology (the shape of the word, seen as a total of its meaningful bits), such as the role of affixes (prefixes and suffixes), which determines meaning. Sometimes, as in the case of euphemisms, we see how social attitudes shape the perception of acceptability and necessitate alternative expressions, at least for a while, until the stigma catches up. Sometimes certain aberrant behaviours (for example, backformations) can break all the rules and generate their own new subset of patterned behaviour.

Either a borrower or a lender be

While it is in the nature of language to change, people can feel varying levels of discomfort when they encounter shifts and nuances with which they're not familiar. Linguist David Crystal in *The Cambridge Encyclopedia of the English Language* urges upon us the metaphor of the tides – a gently constant and inevitable ebbing and flowing, where change is intrinsic, not to be derided or feared, nor even, indeed, wondered at.

Many are the faces of change. One is found in semantic shifts over time, with words having meanings today that are different from those they had in the past. A 'villain' used to mean a farm labourer; 'sly' once meant wise; 'vulgar' once meant ordinary. When I lived in

Argentina I met a boy who'd taught himself English from the plays of Shakespeare. We conversed in Spanish because his English was off-the-planet. If you see yourself being cryogenically preserved, your first purchase in your brave new thawed life should be a dictionary.

Semantic shifts have multiple shapes. One such is an extension of meaning: 'virtue' used to be a male-only quality, from the Latin word for male strength or virility. Some words narrow in meaning over time: 'meat' used to mean food in general – and at an Argentine barbeque you may well wonder if anything's changed.

Words also shift in their domains of use. A 'navigator' used to apply only to boating craft; now it's something I (try to) be in the car. New meanings come through figurative applications. A 'crane' used to be a bird; now, by visual extension, it's the machine. Sometimes words lose their frowning sense: 'mischievous' has moved from disastrous to playful. And the opposite can happen: 'notorious' used to mean famous, though with celebrities, fame/notoriety can blur.

Change also comes in the shape of new words. Some are 'borrowed' – which word, of course, is a misnomer. After all, the words are taken from other languages with no intention of returning them when we're finished with them. Maybe it's more a matter of loosely 'swapping': we borrowed 'chic' and 'savoir faire' from the French, while they borrowed 'parking' and 'weekend' from us – though heaven knows, the act of adopting happened with much less fuss and bother from French to English than vice versa.

Sometimes the borrowing is shameless, a complete importation of foreign spelling or pronunciation. This applies to words like 'blitzkrieg', 'kibbutz' and 'spaghetti'. Other words are borrowed and naturalised from their original form to something more comfortably mouthed in English: 'coach' (Hungarian), 'tycoon' (Japanese), 'sofa' (Arabic), 'kiosk' (Turkish).

A special kind of borrowing is a loan translation. Here, a word is not borrowed whole. Instead, its parts are translated and a new word formed. German produced the equivalent of 'telephone' in *Fernsprecher* (literally, 'distant' + 'speaker'). Similarly, 'boyfriend' and 'girlfriend' were loan-translated into Chinese as *nan pengyu* and *nu pengy*. In Japanese they were borrowed and then adapted to the local sound system as *boifurendo* and *garufurendo*.

Some borrowings reveal an eccentric development. Euphemistically, we borrowed *double entendre* from French, just as we have other less-than-fully decorous terms, but the French have ceased to use the term in the way that we use it in English. Both English and French borrowed *quid pro quo* from Latin, yet they each use the expression in very different ways.

Word borrowings in English reflect its history. We see the various strata of influences, like the Germanic tribes, the Vikings and the Normans. Then the results of the Renaissance's classical infatuation. And then as English ventured further afield, through conquest and empire, new words were imported from local contexts: like 'chipmunk', 'chutney', 'lychee' and 'kangaroo'. Where a domain of expertise is appreciated, English borrows its words as a mark of respect: musical terms from the Italian (*concerto, soprano*), culinary terms from the French (*sauté, purée, au gratin*).

Professions have sought to mark off their supposed erudition by dipping into other languages. The law dips into Latin (*bona fide, prima facie*), medicine dips into Greek (*bronchitis, paediatrics, vasectomy*).

Every decade adds its touch. What worlds of association are conjured up for you as you hear *perestroika* or *paparazzi* or *jihād* or *intifada*?

It's hard to tell how long the English language will be in Baghdad – probably long enough for some new words to come on board. Stay tuned.

A place for ruthful

Although you probably have less reason than some to look up 'ruth' in the dictionary, doing so can be a learning experience.

You'll find it is an archaic common noun meaning 'pity', 'mercy' or 'compassion'. It derives from the Middle English 'rue' (pity), which we still use for the odd curse, as in 'you'll rue the day you were born'. Granted, this is not heard a lot these days, probably because in a comparable circumstance we're more likely to pull out a handgun than invoke the powers of a curse.

These days 'ruth' is mostly recognisable in 'ruthless'. It's rather sad, don't you think, to be present only through negation? It wasn't always so.

Remember Biblical Ruth? She who worked the fields by day and spent nights sleeping at the foot of Boaz's bed, waiting for him to make a move. Which he did, though not before she'd got through a lot of wheat. That story, told to me as a child, has left me grudgingly respectful of the unrapacious Boaz, guided as he was by ethics rather than opportunism.

Now, you will no doubt have noticed my 'unrapacious'. There's no such word, of course, but my meaning is pretty transparent, I bet. After all, rapacious is a hit-you-in-the-eye kind of word, and 'un' is the conventional semantic reverser. You don't need a huge imaginative leap to place Boaz closer to the 'New Man' end, rather than the Genghis Khan end, of the pillaging and rampaging barometer.

As a reverse marker, 'un' is less than totally dependable. We can use it to reverse 'happy', 'cooperative', 'lucky', 'sure' and 'realistic' (among many more), but not 'sad', 'solemn', 'serious' and 'savage' (among others).

Verbs are equally unpredictable. We can uncage, unbutton, unbrace, unfasten and unbind, but we can't 'unbreak' (even hearts), 'uncalculate', 'unsteal' or 'unspeak' (even Nixon). Some things, once done, cannot be undone. Then there are words where the verb is disallowed ('unbreak') but the related adjective works ('unbroken'). Similarly, we have 'uncensored' but not 'uncensor', 'unloved' but not 'unlove', 'unrivalled' but not 'unrival'.

The suffixes '-ful' and '-less' have their own pattern. Take a noun (such as 'hope'), add '-ful' for *plus* quality or '-less' for *minus* ('hopeful/hopeless'). So too 'useful/useless', 'cheerful/cheerless', 'remorseful/remorseless', 'mindful/mindless' and thousands more.

But of course exceptions exist; indeed they thrive. A room may be windowless but not 'windowful'. We can be limbless or limbed, but not 'limbful' (unless perhaps we're particularly leggy). We have 'awful', but not 'awless', though there's always 'awesome'. One may be mournful but not 'mournless'. We say 'a handful' of coins, but not 'handless', unless we're speaking of an amputee, and then we'd probably search for a euphemism, like 'manually challenged'. We have 'shedful' for a vague large-quantity marker but 'shedless' has little currency, except for a category of male persons deprived, perhaps because of apartment living, of the standard Australian solution to the testosterone-based need for a tool-storage place.

My father used to have great fun creatively adding '-fuls' and '-lesses' wherever he thought they might have something to offer. He'd add '-ful' to an adjective like 'patient', making 'patientful', with the intention of creating a meaning of bonus-quality patience. Ironically, his foreign accent gave him privileges denied the native speaker. Oblivious to the twinkle in his eye, people would let such usages slide, probably thinking, 'poor migrant, doesn't know better'.

Perhaps this biographical remnant accounts for my being inordinately bothered by the fact that the quality of compassion in 'ruth' is used today only to mark its absence. We've lost both 'ruth' and 'ruthful', no doubt casualties to the only-bad-news-is-newsworthy mindset. Granted, governments, armies and cyclones perform ruthless acts. But what about nuns in ruthful bids to save souls? Or researchers toiling ruthfully for cures? Or politicians seeking ruth for human rights?

Some say our words shape our perceptions, and without a word like ruthful we'd probably not recognise ruthfulness, even under our noses. Others say our words expand to accommodate our needs. Accordingly, the hill tribes of Papua New Guinea will develop their own words for 'email' and 'download' if and when the need arises. The logic here would have it that if we don't have ruthful or ruth, it's because we don't need them, or because there's not enough of the quality of ruth around to warrant its own word.

Now there's a depressingful thought.

Working backwards

'I'm reverse-parkingly challenged', said the interviewee, and the TV studio audience laughed sympathetically. They knew exactly what she meant, calling liberally though subliminally on their grammatical resources as well as their experiential reservoir.

We all get playful with language, at times stretching grammatical rules to fit our intentions. And we mostly get away with it, because we generously grant each other this licence (and expect to be granted it in return) and we collaborate in extracting meaning from each other's utterances.

Children are naturally enthusiastic players with language, as evidenced by cultural artefacts like nursery rhymes, knock-knock jokes, Dr Seuss books and Pig Latin. But if children are natural players, then school is their natural enemy. Institutionalism usually nips such playfulness in the bud – it's as if all those prefabricated lesson portions and curriculum bits deaden the playful spirit.

Nonetheless, vestiges of playfulness can seep into ordinary language. One device that displays these characteristics is called 'backformation'. This is a reversal of the usual way new words grow out of old ones – on a small-to-big template as for example in 'assassin' leading to 'assassination'. In contrast, backformation goes big-to-small – for example, the verb 'burgle' comes from the noun 'burglar' in a process by which the noun was separated from its suffix following the pattern of 'scholar', 'beggar' and 'liar'. A similar evolution can be seen in 'electrocute' from 'electrocution', 'swindle' from 'swindler', 'abled' from 'disabled', and 'babysit' from 'babysitter'. These developments can take a while to catch on – consider the currently and variously contentious status of 'enthuse' (enthusiasm), 'accrete' (accretion), 'butle' (butler) and 'ush' (usher). In fifty years' time, these might well have become mainstreamed. Meet me here, same place, same time, and we can compare notes.

Purists don't warm to backformations. They deem them illegitimate, the outcome of faulty design. They also usually argue that the newfangled word is redundant. What's wrong with 'be an usher'? Why do we need 'to ush'? The logic here (if we may call it logic) is that a form already exists, so therefore it must be superior. They forget that that esteemed word was itself once the young upstart. It's pretty safe to say that the true objection here is not the actual newfangled word but the fact that it is newfangled.

Fortunately a book published by Oxford called *Ologies and Isms*, about word beginnings and endings, does not adopt this prescriptivism.

If the '-aholic' suffix is now a bit dated, a recent arrival currently promenading around town is the borrowed Spanish suffix '-ista', for a fan or supporter. The suffix came to prominence in 'Sandinista', a member of a political group following the thoughts of Augusto César Sandino. Since then, it has morphed into 'Blairista' (a supporter of Tony Blair) and 'Guardianista' (a reader of the *Guardian*). Somewhere in the processes of bringing '-ista' across the English Channel, it acquired a derogatory overtone, absent in the original form (for example, in 'Fidelista' or 'Peronista').

Another foreign borrowing, this time from Italian, is the suffix '-erati', denoting groups of like-minded people, as in 'literati' (educated people interested in literature) and, historically, 'castrati' (male singers castrated in boyhood). Playfully, if also pejoratively, English has added 'glitterati' (celebrities who like to party), 'chatterati' (the discussion-loving educated), 'belligerati' (pro-war public commentators) and, one of the newest, 'cliterati' (post-femocrat feminists).

On the model of 'aristocrat', 'bureaucrat', 'autocrat' and 'democrat', we acquired 'technocrat' and the above-mentioned 'femocrat'. And for a slightly down-market version of the same, we have the relatively recent 'blabocrat'.

'To self-destruct' was backformed from 'self-destruction', following the pattern of 'abduct/ion' and 'construct/ion'. The pre-existing verb 'destroy' behaved beautifully on the day, moving over on the park bench, letting the new 'destruct' sit alongside and have its own restricted meaning – each word carving out its own spot. Ironically, no destruction involved, no one threatened, and everyone the richer.

Mixed metaphors

I do so love a juicy mixed metaphor. On a recent morning walk with the dog I was delighted to find an old neighbourhood cottage sporting a brand-new sign out front: 'Original Blank Canvas Awaiting Your Midas Touch.' Artist-with-easel meets Greek myth. Anyone looking for property will know it's dilapidated, ripe for capital investment. Buy, renovate, sell, make a killing.

I date my fondness for the mixed metaphor back to my schooldays. An English teacher returned a marked assignment to me. In the margin – where teachers mostly write their 'not happy, Jan' remarks, interspersed, on a good day, with a sprinkling of ticks – he had written 'mixed metaphor' and in the text he had drawn a squiggly line under some of my writing. Of course, the thing about marginalia – that lovely umbrella word for stuff that goes in margins – is that they lack intonation. Well, they don't lack it when said out loud, but being written, you usually have to invest the words with an intonation. In my case of the 'mixed metaphor' + squiggly line, I had no trouble – I could discern the disapproval back then, and still can.

Somewhere, sometime, someone decided that mixed metaphors were a big no-no and with one imperious sweep of the 'not happy, Jan' pen, the rejected items were relegated to the bad list. Thus classified, they take centuries to resuscitate, if indeed they ever do. Meanwhile, ordinary folk are wont to think that there's logic in the ruling but in fact it's merely whim, capricious whim. (A comparable caprice surrounds the ruling against double negatives. There's nothing inherently bad about them; they work beautifully in Spanish, for example, causing ne'er a hiccup.) The thing is that Mr Whim is also Mr Power, so such rulings have accrued remarkable stamina.

Metaphors are so integrated into our language that, beyond the four walls of an English class, one pays them little heed. This is a good thing. In fact, being paid little heed is the very best thing that can happen to a metaphor. A good metaphor lurks about subliminally, affecting you without your knowing it. Indeed it's an irony that the pinnacle of metaphor ambition, to which every fledgeling metaphor aspires, is to become so naturalised as to be unnoticed. Rather sadly, at this point they're called 'dead metaphors', though personally, I'd much prefer to think of them as 'sleeping'.

Sometimes a metaphor is so spot-on that it can't help escaping our attention. When this happens, an interesting process ensues. We are touched by how perfectly and unexpectedly – the surprise element is important – a metaphor captures a particular circumstance, and henceforth you tend to link the two indivisibly. This happened to me recently when I read Peter Gay's memoir (*My German Question*) of growing up Jewish in Nazi Berlin, before he and his family escaped to Cuba and then to the USA. Gay's childhood overlapped with Germany stripping Jews of their human rights and their protection under law. He calls what he experienced 'a poisoning'. Later, trying to understand how these early experiences impacted on his life, he describes them as fragmented shards of glass that he would pick out of his skin for many years to come. Incidentally, poisoning and shattered glass are two entirely different images, but neither demeans or compromises the other.

I am prepared to concede that mixed metaphors can be risky. If they are too incongruent or jarring, they protrude and call undue attention to themselves, where, really, they ought to be snoozing, undisturbed and undisturbing. A former Queensland premier, cited by Pam Peters in *The Cambridge Australian English Style Guide*, notoriously mixed his metaphors when he said that someone 'had his head so deep in the sand that he didn't know which side of the fence he was on'. This premier did at least furnish us with a lovely exemplum. And not just one, either.

Bear in mind that risk also hovers around the extended metaphor. Again, the danger is that an image is flogged so relentlessly that instead of lying subtly beneath the surface, it jumps out and yells at you. Nonetheless, inexplicably, some extended metaphors become celebrated, protected, achieving a status that has them, as it were, metaphorically laminated. Consider Cassius's words as he urges Brutus towards action (in IV:3 of Shakespeare's *Julius Caesar*):

> There is a tide in the affairs of men,
> Which taken at the flood, leads on to fortune;
> Omitted, all the voyage of their life
> Is bound in shallows and in miseries.
> On such a full sea are we now afloat,
> And we must take the current when it serves,
> Or lose our ventures.

If you wrote that in a school essay, you'd likely get a squiggly line plus some scribbled disparagement in the margin. Sigh.

Adjectives on the loose

Language teachers have been known to sit around at morning tea howling with laughter at the bloopers their learners come up with. Sometimes they compile them and post them on staff noticeboards. This might sound cruel but in fact it's less in malice than wonderment at the flexibility of language and the complexity of the learning process. The student who thought a person from Nepal was a 'Napoleon' brought the house down.

Well, can you blame him? We have 'Chile/Chilean', 'Norway/Norwegian', 'Iran/Iranian'. What is intelligence if not the ability to construct generalisations from similarities in sets of data? By this measure, Napoleon would have it wrapped up as a citizen of Nepal.

Alas, while 'Napoleon' is logical, even cutely risible, it's wrong. In fact, the rules driving the formation and use of adjectives have exceptions as numerous as examples. What sense can you make of a rule that draws 'Frenchman' from 'France', 'Dane' from 'Denmark', and 'Vietnamese' from 'Vietnam'? Why not a 'Frane', a 'Danish' and a 'Vietman'?

Complicated? I'll show you complicated! Just to be able to show national connections, you need to know three bits of information. First, you need the adjective that is used to refer to things that come from that country: Danish design, for example. Second, you need to know the word for a person who comes from that country: a Dane, for example. And third, you need to know what word is used (along with 'the') to refer to the whole nation: the Danes, for example.

Usually the 'a' word and the 'the' word are the same: a Dane / the Danes. But not always: we have a Frenchman / the French, a Briton / the British. A sub-rule says that nationality words ending in 's', 'ese' and 'ch' have the same form for singular and plural. Thus one Swiss, two Swiss; one Japanese, three Japanese. But again, not always: we have one Czech, but for the plural it's as many Czechs as you fancy.

Another sub-rule says the adjectival form ('Polish', say) doubles as the name of the language ('Polish'). So do 'Greek', 'Thai', 'Indonesian', 'Dutch', 'Russian', 'Maltese' and 'Norwegian'. But Arabs speak Arabic (not Arab), Australians speak English (not Australian), and Israelis speak Hebrew (not Israeli), though the Israeli linguist Ghil'ad Zuckermann controversially argues that the Hebrew spoken by Israelis is so far removed from the classic language that it ought to have its own name. He suggests 'Israeli'.

It's not just nationality adjectives that are problematic. What's wrong with this phrase: 'a leather black shiny small handbag'? And what about this one: 'a glass Venetian triangular green ashtray'? If you reshuffled the adjectival order to 'a small black shiny leather handbag' and 'a triangular green Venetian glass ashtray', pat yourself on the back.

Yes, there's a rule about the order of adjectives before a noun. This time, when you do the reshuffling for the following phrase, try also to extrapolate the underlying rule: 'a Swedish lightweight tennis nylon and steel grey expensive racquet'.

More backpats if you produced 'an expensive, lightweight, grey, Swedish, nylon and steel tennis racquet'. As for the rule, below is a summary of what my trusty dog-eared grammar proffers, before finally capsizing with 'the exact order is too complicated to give practical rules'. From right to left (that is, from the position closest to the noun, 'racquet', to that which is furthest away), we have adjectives indicating purpose (tennis). Then, what the thing is made of (nylon/steel). Then any adjective indicating origin (Swedish). Then comes colour (grey) and then anything to do with age, shape, size or temperature (lightweight). And then any other descriptive adjective (expensive). Seen from left to right, the formula is: descriptive + size + colour + origins + made of + purpose of + noun. Disturb that order and you'll sound foreign. But try teaching it to a foreign learner and you can cause mental paralysis or stuttering.

My Polish-speaking father did dreadful things to English adjectives. He was forever railing against the restrictions that the adjectival rules of English imposed upon him. It would seem that the Polish language has much greater adjectival freedom than English, and he would fight against what he saw as an adjectival straitjacket. No surprise that he was particularly fond of Polish-style compound adjective clusters. His favourite was: 'The just-got-pregnant woman got onto the just-about-to-move bus.' He thought it a masterpiece of syntactic precision. I said, 'Yeah maybe, but it's not English.'

I recall thinking at the time that maybe too much freedom was a bad thing.

Singular pants

A reader wrote to me about something that got on his goat [sic]. Describing it, he seemed to be goading his goat onwards, almost to the point of frenzy. Not a nice image.

He wrote:

Take 'pants'. What is the intent of advertisers in turning the normally plural item of clothing into the singular: pants/pant, trousers/trouser? It strikes me as pretentious, probably because you see/hear it more up the snooty end of the market. But recently I've seen it happening in the no-frills, value-for-money sector. They've now joined the bandwagon and it's 'pant' here, and 'pant' there. Everywhere you look now, someone's on about 'a pant'. Why do they do it? Is it pretentious or is it just me? Why does it not work for 'sock' or 'slack'?

He was wholly put off by the singular pant. He perceived it as a cheap device to add an unwarranted exclusivity. Like the embedded location in 'Hugo's on the Bay'. He'd say all Hugo needs is 'Hugo's'.

The goat must have been contagious, for soon afterwards I started noticing that pant of his everywhere. And like him, I began to wonder about it, a state of mind that sent me poking around in the matter of grammatical plurality. This may seem relatively straight-forward (one dog, two dogs, add an 's', easy-peasy) but poke a bit further and you discover that dog/dogs is just a facile surface pat-tern masking an amazing complexity. Such complexity might drive you to have only one of everything (*a la* Noah, but half) but, of course, that wouldn't really solve the problem, because plurality is everywhere, and sooner or later we have to bite the bullet. Ah, make that 'bullets'.

Languages have their own internally logical rules for mark-ing plurality. French (*bateau/bateaux*) does it differently from Japanese (*kimono/kimono*), which does it differently from Hebrew (*kibbutz/kibbutzim*). This is fine so long as languages operate inside their own little picket fences. Enter war, invasion, conquest, empire and arranged royal marriages – and down go those picket fences, up go the borrowings, and suddenly (in glacial terms), there's a mass of plural patterning that seems chaotic, but mostly isn't.

Words that are ancestral borrowings maintain their original end-ings ('alumna/ae', 'crisis/es') but can be so 'un-English' that the pres-sure is on to change (for instance it's years since I heard a politi-cian say 'criterion'). Words that came to us from Italian or Spanish maintain their original plurals ('canto/cantos', 'piano/pianos'). Ger-man not only gave us 'ox/oxen', but also 'shoe/shoon', which we ditched. With 'brother' and 'brethren', we reserve the old plural for certain limited circumstances, and prefer 'brothers' for the ordinary plural. A rule of thumb in this Amazonian thicket of complexity is: the more exotic the word, the faster it anglicises – think 'kayaks', 'canoes' and 'igloos'. Perhaps the singular form is so un-English-seeming that the conventional English plural ('-s') is an attempt to rein in the foreign factor and hasten the local grounding. Just a thought.

Though we tend to think singular and add the '-s' suffix as a plural marker, sometimes we're forced to start at the other end. For example, some foreign words are most familiar as plurals – 'candelabra', 'data', 'graffiti', 'algae', 'opera'. The pedant will insist on 'correct' singulars: 'candelabrum', 'datum', 'graffito', 'alga', 'opus'. Over time, we make the plural work harder ('operas', 'candelabras'); or we turn the word into a mass noun, which means it won't unitise ('some graffiti'); or we bifurcate (compare the librarian's and the doctor's 'appendix').

Language changes organically, constantly, expeditiously, and sometimes capriciously. Disney's dwarfs became Tolkien's dwarves. Still, scissors and trousers are inherently plural, their grammaticality echoing their reality. Scissors need two blades to work; pants need two legs (amputees fold over one trouser leg, perhaps 'a pant'?)

And why 'a pant'? Maybe to be brief (a pant / a pair of pants). Maybe to be friendly. Maybe to preen an insider status. Maybe to appear to be inclusive. Maybe to seem cool. Maybe to appeal to connoisseurs, they who really understand clothing, appreciate quality, spare no expense. You can get a good pant at Country Road, a good coffee at Bar Coluzzi, a good tan at Bondi.

Listen to the pants around you. Pretty soon, a pattern will emerge.

Osama

'Get Osama', screamed the front-page headline of a tabloid on the day Kabul fell to the Northern Alliance. The hunt for the ever-elusive bin Laden was seriously happening.

Suddenly, as the noose tightens, we're on a first-name basis. This is surely a departure from the conventional manner of referring to political leaders – by surname (Chirac), or surname with title (Mr Arafat). Despite the facetious 'Dubya', Bush is mostly called (Mr) Bush, as Clinton was called (Mr) Clinton. Across the Atlantic, Blair is (Mr) Blair, though with his man-of-the-people yearnings, one almost expects him to say, any time now, 'just call me Tony'.

Of course, names attract jokes and jokes propagate, and, like mud, they tend to stick. 'Tricky Dicky' did Nixon not one bit of good. Carter's 'Jimmy' only worsened his limp, ineffectual image. 'Billary' gave credence to the twin Clinton occupation of the White House, and perhaps paved the way metaphorically for a Hillary bid for the Oval office. But for the tall, be-robed, be-bearded, be-head-garmented terrorist son of a Saudi millionaire, it has become 'Osama'.

This is not without precedent. A decade ago, Saddam Hussein became and remained 'Saddam' to the West, perhaps to distinguish him from other Middle Eastern Husseins, notably the then Jordanian King. Or perhaps it worked well in English, being phonetically and serendipitously aligned with 'sadist', rendering an easy intertwining of name and notion. This would have aided the process of demonisation – a necessary step in the build-up to war. Not that Saddam needed much outside help in this department.

This, however, doesn't explain 'Osama'. Let's think back to some historical baddies. In newsreels from before World War II, terms of address featured Mr Hitler, Mr Mussolini, and Mr Stalin, alongside Mr Chamberlain. Perhaps the circumstances of appeasement encouraged a titular politeness. Presumably, Stalin's wartime status as ally meant he retained his 'Mr' for the duration. Come the Cold War, he promptly lost it. That tells us something, though it still doesn't explain 'Osama'.

Back then first names were a no-no – even with your friends' parents. It would have been outrageous to call anyone in public office 'Neville' or 'Winston'. (Bar royalty of course – they'd long ago traded their surnames in for dynasties.) Certainly, those newsreels made no reference to an 'Adolf' or a 'Benito'. Unknown it

wasn't – in the six years Hitler took to arrive at the point of invad-
ing Poland, 'Adolf' was the most popular boy's name in Germany
(but in 1946, it was as rare as hens' teeth).

When I was growing up, and the Chinese Cultural Revolution was
in full swing, it was 'Mao' to one and all – most of us, ignorant of
Chinese conventions of name order, thought this was a tongue-
in-cheek friendly reference to a faraway tyrant. So, too, there's
something about the 'Osama' that denies the man the same status accorded to the big-time nasties, just as using 'Adolf' today to
refer to Hitler would infantilise him and threaten to mock the suffering of his victims. Idi Amin of Ugandan notoriety mostly retained
both names, allowing him not quite full status as a historical baddie (perhaps because his monstrous acts took place in Africa?), but
avoiding the ridicule of 'Idi'.

There are parallels in other areas of life. Successful and up-and-
coming film directors, writers, scientists, actors are usually referred
to by first and last name – Mel Gibson, Peter Carey, Germaine Greer.
The greats, on the other hand, are known by surname alone –
Darwin, Freud, Hitchcock, Shakespeare. (In academe, this honour
is furthered in the present tense convention – 'Shakespeare wants
his audience to ...' – signifying timelessness, perhaps.) The greats in
art (Monet, Picasso), literature (Molière, Proust, Heine, Sartre) and
music (Mozart, Beethoven, Verdi) are, again, all surnames. Maybe
it's simply a matter of how long you've been dead. The longer the
better – O'Neill and White have some way to go before they drop
their 'Eugene' and 'Patrick'.

Names are not without their superstitions. Every culture has
a folklore that includes stories about breaking the power of the
evildoer through naming. Think of Rumpelstiltskin. Once named,
he was just an angry little man. But naming conventions are also
bound up with how status is conferred, recognised and withdrawn.
There's a tribe in Madagascar who so revere their royalty that when
their new Queen's name happened to overlap with a word in the
language, that word was dropped. Closer to home, think of the status difference in referring to Lady Thatcher, Margaret Thatcher, Mrs
Thatcher, or Maggie Thatcher.

It may be that 'Osama' allows us to keep at bay the fear of what he represents. And as that fear remains substantial, it's not yet in the West's interests to iconise him, even as a baddie. Certainly, were he brought before a Nuremberg-style court, he'd lose the 'Osama' quick smart. By then, though, we'd likely have less reason to fear him.

The shelf life of a euphemism

When 'old' goes with wine, we think of good vintage. When it goes with furniture, we think of antiques and while doing so we might even smell the polish. When it goes with painting, we think of the Great Masters. When old goes with money, we think upper-crust establishment. My general practitioner father had a few 'old money' patients out in the country – twentieth-century descendants of a one-time squattocracy. I remember they didn't pay their bills.

But when 'old' goes with person, we're in altogether different terrain. We've arrived in the use-by-date domain. Just as the 'young' and the 'new' are valued for having spent less time on the planet, so the 'not young' and the 'not new' are devalued for having spent too much time. The problem is it's a short step from 'devalued' to 'demeaned'. Meanwhile, on a parallel planet, the caption alongside a new beauty product – 'Age Less' – feels less like a noun or adjective than an imperative verb.

Stigmas boost word numbers, even though this is not their intention. Around the 'old' stigma emerges a host of euphemisms. These new words hover over the core notion while painstakingly avoiding saying the bad word itself. People reach for less confronting alternatives, such as 'mature', 'senior', 'Third Age' or even 'seasoned'. They add bits ('older', 'older person'), perhaps to alleviate the baldness of the stark monosyllable. At other times they invent new bits as substitutes ('the golden years'). The shelf life of a euphemism is short, as Kate Burridge's *Blooming English* points out. Pretty soon, the stigma catches up with the label, at which time the infection spreads and the euphemism begins to break down. 'New American' became 'migrant', which morphed into 'ethnic', and then into the quasi-hyphenates ('Asian Americans', 'Muslim Americans'). Similarly, 'crippled' changed to 'handicapped' to 'disabled', and then to concept plus past participle ('developmentally delayed', 'hearing impaired', 'vision challenged').

The adjective 'geriatric' arrived in 1909. It was a respectful term back then, as was 'senile', hard though it may be to believe from the present perspective. In 1938, 'senior citizen' was introduced for a post-retirement person, but it wasn't long before it too began to display the signs of general community uneasiness. 'Elderly' arrived in the 1960s and, predictably, the stigma quickly reattached. Recently, 'senior' has re-emerged, along with special cards, discounts and a monthly newspaper. The annual Seniors' Week (advertised as 'the best time for ages') is replete with activity: ballroom dancing, computers, information on arthritis, pain relief, bridge climbing and political speech-giving. The grey vote is growing too fast for politicians to ignore.

Then 1998 was the Year of the Older Person, which, like the 'fuller figure', hedges the cold impact of the simple adjective (old) by adding '-er'. It comes at the cost of imprecision. Older than whom? Well, older than they used to be. As old as even you will be one day. Tick-tock, tick-tock.

The thing about stigmas, too, is how they interconnect in the underbelly of society. Ageism is an offshoot of the quest for perpetual youth and cutting-edge newness, from technology to kitchens to style of jeans. Our discomfort with disability is an offshoot of the demand for physical and intellectual perfection. I wonder if there is a society somewhere that treats its disabled citizens admirably – with no disdain, contempt, condescension or neglect. Were this to be so, I bet their word for 'disabled' would be stable, attracting neither stigma nor euphemism.

And there in the underbelly, stigmas and taboos snuggle up close. Age links neatly with our taboo on death. After all, the old are closer to the end point. Closer to death's door. English is replete with euphemism: we insure against death but call it 'life insurance'; we 'pass away'; we're processed by 'morticians' and 'undertakers'. We dread the suggestion to 'get your affairs in order'. Shakespeare's King Lear said it best when the Earl of Gloucester pleaded to kiss his hand: 'Let me wipe it first; it smells of mortality' (IV: 6).

Still, while it's grim, it's not all bad news. Agatha Christie once said she loved being married to an archaeologist: the older she got, the more he appreciated her.

Fading into eternal peace

We humans celebrate birth, we mark rites of passage and we mourn death. We might do these differently, according to the culture that we were born into or adopted. But underpinning these surface differences lies an all-pervasive universality.

In our experiences of life's vicissitudes, we sometimes take comfort in these beautiful lines from Ecclesiastes 3:1, 'To everything there is a season, and a time to every purpose under the heaven.'

But when words pass out of common currency and eventually out of the dictionary, they do so with little fanfare. Beyond the team of earnest lexicographers who collectively reached the decision, no one knows what's excluded from a new edition of a dictionary. It's hard to read absence.

Yet words do die: as surely as new ones are coined (think, 'AIDS', 'chatroom', 'smart card'), old ones languish and finally drop out of usage. It's gradual and almost imperceptible. The fading can take hundreds of years. The word might be tagged 'archaic' (like 'alas'), meaning 'no longer in common current usage', although it may still be found in literary works or used for historical flavour in contemporary writing. (I have heard archaic forms like 'prithee' spoken rather bizarrely by the young Argentine man I mentioned earlier who'd most unwisely taught himself English from Shakespearean texts.)

Or the tag might say 'old-fashioned', as it does next to 'cad' in the *Collins Dictionary*. Or 'obsolete' which is a bit further along the road to the lexical cemetery. But rubbery indeed are the boundaries between 'old-fashioned', 'archaic' and 'obsolete'.

According to linguist David Crystal, in *The Cambridge Encyclopedia of Language*, a number of different processes cause words to die. The first is obsolescence. Just as technology ages, words too can cease to serve. Sometimes this is simply because the word is no longer part of a people's reality. Clothing, for example, has changed: when did you last give any thought to or utter 'smock', 'corset', 'bodice' or 'top hat'? Shifts in thinking and attitude connected to social change affect words in use. Think of the traditional English vocabulary of sin and virtue and how dated words like 'sloth', 'verity', 'temperance', 'avarice' and 'gluttony' have become. That, of course, is not to say that none of us are lazy liars who eat too much; simply that the lexicon of sin has faded somewhat.

Another factor with a major influence on the patterns of word loss and formation is the notion of taboo. Because of our difficulty in talking directly about sex, body parts and functions, we invent euphemisms. But over time the euphemism gets contaminated by the original taboo. Often the euphemism takes refuge in a general word and, as the contamination of the taboo reaches the euphemism, the general meaning narrows to its sexual sense alone. Words like 'copulation', 'orgasm', 'ejaculation', 'erection' and 'intercourse' were once all general words until reduced to their sexual meaning. The word 'liaison' was originally a seventeenth-century cooking term for thickening sauces. Then it came to mean an illicit sexual relationship, and later industry, commerce, government, the military and even schools all adopted liaison officers of one sort or another. So now people have 'affairs', or 'flings' or 'a bit on the side'. The net effect is that we develop an ever-changing chain of vocabulary that is linked to taboo and euphemism. English apparently has a staggering 2,500 expressions for male and female genitalia.

Euphemisms also apply to food – 'lamb's fry' for sheep's liver, and 'lemon fish' for shark in New Zealand. Given BSE, we may soon begin to hear soft alternatives for 'beef'.

Words can also vanish for no discernible reason. Who knows why we stopped using our handy little word 'gry' for the dirt under fingernails? We used to have simple verbs for buttoning and unbuttoning ('fibulate'), basking in the sun ('apricate') and lying face down on the floor ('groof').

And to the lasting chagrin of those who check homework and share housework, there was once a mightily useful noun ('velleity') to name a mild desire too slight to motivate any action.

Whistling cads

In Victorian England, the upper classes used to enjoy believing that it was only the great unwashed who used foul language. Meanwhile, they had their upper-stratum lexicon, which amply served their own swearing needs. Back then, you were using fighting words if you called a man 'an insufferable young puppy' or 'an unmitigated cad' or, for a slightly less awful cad, just drop the unmitigated. But never anything remotely stronger or cruder. 'Bastard', for instance, simply wouldn't do, as it rang uncomfortably literal for too many wannabe blue bloods.

Words like 'cad' and 'cur' are no longer in common parlance. I've known many but never called them that. Such words are flagged as 'archaic' in today's dictionaries. But they don't want your pity for they live there quite happily. While their productive use is way down, we still encounter them – in old books, timepiece films and plays. In a TV show, *Confessions of a Cad*, the word 'cad' was liberally applied.

I confess that I am sad at times to see words relegated to 'archaic' and would happily mandate their resurrection if I thought an instruction of mine would have any sway. But language doesn't operate like that. It's far too unruly and headstrong.

Still, it's worth a try, I trow, don't you? 'Trow' is an intransitive verb that means 'believe, think, suppose or trust'. It is derived from an old Indo-European root (*deru*), meaning 'to be firm', and also serves as the source for words like 'truth', 'trust' and 'betroth'. Next time you want to muse in public, share your thoughts, consider your beliefs, try a 'trow' for a change. Your meaning should be clear from your context and your interlocutors may well be impressed.

Another one that is sorely missed is 'verily'. From Latin (*verax*, truthful), it moved to Old French (*verai*, true) and then Middle English (*verraily*, very). Yes, I hear you protesting, we have good old 'very'; what need is there for something more? However, 'verily' is not identical to 'very'. It's both an adverb ('and verily did the chains fall from his hands') and a sentence adverb ('verily, I say to you'). Further, I suspect that to use 'verily' effectively you have to be dressed for the part. 'Very', on the other hand, would go fine with denim.

There's another adverb that has a bygone ring and yet is close enough to Modern English to be readily understood. I refer to very old-fashioned-sounding 'mayhap'. Historically, it is a reduction of the phrase 'it may hap', from Middle English's *happ*, derived from the Old Norse word that means 'luck' or 'chance'. I rather like 'mayhap' – it borrows from 'may' in its sense of probability and from 'happenstance' in its wistful nostalgia.

Then there's the trio of 'howbeit' (however it may be), 'sobeit' (provided that) and 'albeit' (although it be). Only 'albeit' has escaped the lexical dust heap. It is still used, albeit in rather restricted registers. I can well imagine a small cluster of barristers walking into court uttering or muttering their fair share of 'howbeits', 'sobeits' and 'albeits'. I did once know a builder who barely let an utterance pass without an 'albeit'. I suspect he thought it elevated his language and perhaps it did; that is, if you could abide the mental distraction of a conversation so riddled with concessions.

A lovely book called *The Word Museum* is subtitled *The most Remarkable English Words ever Forgotten*. Its author, Jeffrey Kacirk, has no qualms about expressing his lament – namely, regarding the sacrifice of the archaic to make way for the neologistic. While I dispute the suggested causal link between the concept of archaic usage and the healthy production of neologisms, I find his collection a pleasurable window on things that used to matter.

Like 'glad-warbling', a word for singing or walking joyfully. The glad-warble would seem to have already gone the way that 'whistle' is destined to go. These days we have whistleblowers and umpires' whistles, but rarely do you hear a carefree whistle, which better than anything else signals a satisfaction in the moment and nothing more. Perhaps we're all waiting for permission, apropos of which I noticed recently a small bright yellow notice on a university noticeboard. It said, rather MontyPythonesquely, 'Cheerful whistling permitted.' I wonder if there were many takers.

BETWEEN THE LINES

Language is commonly and comfortably seen everywhere as a tool or vehicle for communication. We use it to get things done, to establish and maintain relationships, to conduct our daily business as much as to talk about the past and speculate about the future. Language brokers an infinite number of speech events, both commonplace and complex, through our lives. It allows us to be precise and technical as well as romantic and quixotic, if not all at the same time. What is less commonly realised is that language also affords us the possibility of being, if we so choose, vague, approximate, ambivalent, evasive and equivocal. Indeed, given that our major task in life is to coexist with others – from the household to the neighbourhood to the institution to the nation and beyond – arguably the most important function of language is to help us be social beings. To achieve this, language enables us to say what we need to say without necessarily saying what we mean while our meaning can be understood between the lines, as it were, of what we say.

Not inclined to say 'no'

Question: What do Nancy Reagan, Moses and any 18-month-old toddler have in common? Answer: None of them has trouble with the negative.

Let's start with Mrs Reagan and her advice to young people faced with the 'should I or shouldn't I?' dilemma of drugs. Easy-peasy, says Nancy: 'Just say "no".'

How does this miss the mark? Let me count the ways. There's the majestic naivety with which turning to drugs is constructed – as if it were on a par with, say, reaching for a chocolate bar or picking which movie to go to. The underlying conditions – including, more often than not, the hopelessness and helplessness – are swept under the carpet. Then there's the assumption that anyone of the age at which Nancy is pitching her slogan might be deterred by her injunction. Picture it if you will. The skateboard kid is reaching for the cocaine, he recalls Nancy's slogan, he pauses, having second thoughts, then he shakes his head and just says 'No'. Now that wasn't so hard, was it? And there's the inane, insane 'just', as if anything about the drug culture were facile enough to warrant a 'just'.

But mostly there's the obtuseness of suggesting that saying 'no', in any context, is easy. Because mostly it isn't. Think teenage girl in car with overheated boyfriend. Think Weight Watchers patron on empty stomach, confronted by cheesecake. Think oncologist faced with plea for hope. Think request from the boss to work late, yet again. Think a feed-the-homeless charity collector approaching you on the street. In its bare, bald, glorious just-ness, 'no' is rarely easy.

Like Nancy, Moses had little difficulty with the negative. Thou shalt not kill. Thou shalt not steal. Thou shalt not covet thy neighbour's wife. These direct negative commands are a far cry from their less in-your-face equivalents: killing people is quite unacceptable; society is not positively disposed towards acts of theft; monogamy is generally considered preferable. Maybe mountain-tops afford safety from the social consequences of directness. Might be worth the investment in hiking boots.

As for the toddler, what parent hasn't marvelled at the ease with which children acquire 'no' in contrast to 'yes'? They're programmed to leap on the word as their first major act of rebellion. Eat your veggies. No. Come and have a bath. No. Turn the telly off. No. It's bedtime. No. Is there any other word? No.

Languages vary in how far they favour the bald over the oblique. The variations are many and subtle, contributing regularly to the quagmire of cross-cultural hiccups. The perception of 'direct' is often as 'rude', though you'd never guess it from Nancy. English, on the whole, favours the less-than-totally bald. (An exception is the New York City parking sign: 'Don't even think about it.')

For most situations outside New York, we have what British professor Walter Nash calls the 'middling negative'. This involves a 'not' plus a negative adjective; for example, 'not unkind', for the middling position between uncomplicated 'kind' and uncomplicated 'unkind'. It's rife in diplomatic-speak. For example, after a summit meeting, a press release announces that the parties are 'not displeased' or 'not unoptimistic' about outcomes. A lawyer might warn: 'It's not unthinkable that you'll be found guilty.' A mediator could say to the principals: 'It's not unreasonable to expect both sides to compromise.' Academic writing attracts its own hedging phraseology to maintain neutrality: 'Not unlike Napoleon, Hitler's push eastwards was to prove his undoing.'

The beauty of the middling option is that it affords retreatability in the event that a denial is needed, which is far more often than you'd think. ('Do you know where that chocolate is that I left in the fridge to have later?') Plain-faced 'no' is awfully unambiguous. It leaves you stranded, egg on face, unable to backtrack graciously or credibly. Impaled, as it were, on your own words.

Because I'm personally not very inclined towards the oblique, or, more baldly put, I tend to speak my mind, a fridge magnet keeps me centred. It's a picture of a gorilla, hand across its mouth. The caption reads: 'Better to keep your mouth shut and appear stupid than open it and remove all doubt.'

Vague approximations

When is a dog not a dog?

It's a good question. Let me explain. On a morning walk, my labradoodle and I encountered another labradoodle, just a pup, and her owner. It's always a treat when one breed member meets another. Great excitement. Some cautious circling and sniffing. Soon we were all safely vetted and firmly acquainted. The other owner launched into a paean of praise for the breed, most especially for the fact that 'they don't moult or flea.'

Yes, that was the first time I had heard 'flea' used as a verb. It took me a moment to grasp her meaning. Besides, not-flea-ing is not a universal labradoodle trait as my Honey might not moult (the Lord giveth) but she does flea (and the Lord taketh away).

So within minutes I too had started. That is, started using 'flea' as a verb. When I told the other owner that my dog doesn't moult but does flea, she confirmed that the non-flea trait was a very recent genetic innovation.

Genetically modified dog. You could argue that any deliberate mating involves some degree of genetic modification, but that's a far cry from breeding out the moulting and the flea-ing.

Apart from noting the introduction of the verb 'to flea', does all this have anything to do with language? Well, it does insofar as it links in with 'fuzzy concept theory'. I'm seduced by the above incident to venture the question: 'When is a dog not a dog?' If the dog doesn't moult and doesn't flea, is it still a dog? In terms of doggy characteristics, what has to go and what has to stay for the dog to remain a dog?

Analogically, does a bird have to fly to be a bird? No, witness the emu and the penguin, neither of which fly and both of which are classified as birds. My neighbour has a couple of birds who are house-tamed to the point of being unable to fend for themselves. So she has clipped their wings so they won't fly away, because, were they to do so, they'd surely fail to survive. In light of the fact that they can't fly, are they still 'birds'?

The notion of 'fuzzy concepts' applies to language too. A noun is a noun and a verb is a verb but a gerund is a bit of each – a verby-looking, verby-feeling word ('smoking') that grammatically behaves like a noun ('smoking is forbidden'). Gerund is to noun or verb what penguin is to sparrow, perhaps.

As we move from the core essential (dog that moults and fleas) to the periphery (dog that does not moult/flea), we get fuzzier and vaguer. And as we get fuzzier and vaguer, we get more informal.

There is a correlation between formality (seriousness of register/context) and degree of precision (tolerance of vagueness). An art critic writing on why s/he liked a particular artwork would be expected to articulate with a high degree of precision and specificity. Clearly, 'I kinda liked it' would be inadequate, although it would serve well as the answer to a question you asked casually of a friend who'd been to see a film you were intending to see.

Casual and laid-back in fact go nicely with vague. And the language has furnished us with a subset of expressions to help us out. Like 'whosywhatsit', 'whatchamacallit', 'thingamajig'. Placenames that have slipped the tongue are easily substituted by 'Blogsville' (an imaginary remote place), 'back of beyond', 'the Boonies' and 'outer Mongolia' (remote, isolated, with the implication of cultural backwardness).

I was in the queue at my local fish and chip shop. The woman in front of me said rather indolently, 'I'll have a thing of chips.' When her chips arrived they were housed in the 'thing', which had been expertly understood by the man behind the counter. It would be preposterous for him to have asked, 'What do you mean by "a thing"?' He knew that she meant a unit of, whether it comes by weight, or cup, or price. Just one unit.

Granted, it's a long stretch from dogs-and-their-fleas to a-thing-of-chips, but can you kinda see what I'm getting at?

Clarity

I used to think that meaning was contained in words, that mostly people meant what they said, that clarity of communication was the default position. It seemed a logical assumption to make, like assuming everyone else is as sane, honest and benign as you believe yourself to be. Yeah, I know, it was a tooth-fairy kind of innocence that eventually, sigh, came to an end.

With my gradual advent of wisdom came the peculiar discovery that meaning is a whole lot more rubbery than a naive or folk view would have us believe. Indeed, the field of Pragmatics, an area of Linguistics, is dedicated to the notion of inferable meaning, or how we arrive at the between-the-line meanings that are so essential to the lubrication of social interaction.

When I say to my daughter, 'The dog hasn't had her evening walk yet', she knows this is not a simple observation about daily doggy routines, but a request for action. How does she know this? How does anyone, for that matter, pick up on any implicit meaning? How, for example, do you know that 'the jug's over there' means 'help yourself to coffee', possibly with the sub-text of 'don't expect me to wait on you'? Or how do you know that 'the milk's off' just means 'the milk's off'? How do you know that it isn't a request that you run up the road and get some fresh milk? Or, for that matter, that it isn't a thinly veiled disparagement about your nasty habit (how many times have you been told?) of putting off milk back in the fridge?

We mostly make the right inferences and this is not accidental. If we didn't, life would grind to a slow, intolerable, laborious halt. We'd be spending all day in linguistic repair mode, and we wouldn't be getting anything done. The fact is that we infer correctly most of the time because we know the pragmatic rules. And we know these much as we know the grammatical rules by which we make our verb agree with our subject, or our tense align with our time sense. Generally, we don't know the rules explicitly, in the sense of being able to recite them like maths tables. Rather, it's a Rumsfeld way of knowing: we know but we don't know what we know or even that we know. It's a very low-maintenance kind of knowing that serves us when we need it but otherwise doesn't take up much cognitive space.

So the pragmatic rules are mostly invisible. They become visible when you encounter a situation that capsizes precisely because it can't build on implicit knowledge. Take this perfectly feasible example: a Japanese student learning English at a Cambridge language school is asked a question – 'what's it like?' – by someone she just met. To this she answers 'chocolate'.

Now, various interpretations may apply. One is that Mikio is a hardcore chocoholic, living daily in the clouds of her addiction, to the point that the word 'chocolate' spontaneously and randomly forms on her lips. This is possible – sounds mighty familiar, actually – but, in truth, not very likely.

More likely, Mikio's response is an appropriate rejoinder to what she thought she heard. It's possible that hearing 'like' alongside the question marker 'what' cued her to 'what do you like?' to which her Mars Bar kind of answer works. Operating solely at the level of uttered text, Mikio didn't invoke pragmatic knowledge – such as, what can one reasonably expect to be asked in this situation? – and therefore got it all wrong. She's probably been taught the rules of grammar until they're coming out of her ears, and equally well she's probably not been taught the relevant pragmatic knowledge, such as what kinds of questions you might be expected to answer in various kinds of situations. This omission leaves her ill equipped to respond to meanings that are shaped by factors beyond the literal level of the language. It's not Mikio's fault – it's a clear case not of what she's been taught to do but of what she's been taught *not* to do.

Text-level, word-embedded meaning is only part of the puzzle of communication. Perhaps it's an idealised form – in the sense of 'unreal', not in the sense of 'utopian'. And perhaps we orientate towards this level, while being aware that mostly we don't arrive there.

Mostly, too, it's a good thing that some things aren't spelled out. This is especially the case if we have tracks to hide – as faking it, in all its shapes and forms and colours, is a very large part of our world.

Oops

'Oops', said the email to Ian Thorpe after his disqualifying false start during the Australian swimming team's trials for the Athens

Olympics in 2004. And the word 'oops', Thorpe later said, best summed it up.

Australians love to talk sport. If you could count up all the words used on the topic of sport on one nominated day, across all media, across all conversations, across Australia, then put a tax on it, you'd raise enough money to pay off the foreign debt of one small, war-torn, famine-ridden, landlocked African country. Yes, Australians love to talk sport. Or maybe it's a boy thing.

But of all the talk in all the fall-out from Thorpe's fall-in, I liked 'oops' best. Simply for its pithiness, unbeatable.

A person prone to pithiness is said to be laconic. This word has a telling story in its backpack. It's a toponym – a word derived from a place name – from the ancient Greek state of Laconia in the Peloponnese, best known for its capital Sparta (from which, incidentally, we derive 'spartan'). Laconians had a reputation for being minimalist and terse in their language, as well as all else. When Philip of Macedon sent the threat 'If I invade Laconia I shall turn you out', the Laconian magistrates replied in one word: 'If'. Now that's pithy.

Pithiness has been defined as 'terseness and economy in language use achieved by expressing a great deal in just a few words'. The fact that this definition itself is quite unpithy seems to have escaped the notice of the team of lexicographers assigned to 'p' words. I would have thought it would be nice to define 'pithy' pithily, if only for the quiet satisfaction of a smug moment as you enjoy its pointed reflexivity – the way one can with 'spellczech' and 'typo'.

What's missing from this long-winded dictionary definition is pithy's positive connotation. The fact is we tend to like the pithy, and dislike the long-winded. Perhaps we flatter ourselves through the association with slim-of-body and lithe-of-limb – beats long-winded, so distracted by weighty layers of verbal excess.

So if a piece of language were terse and economical but the meaning that it was packing so neatly into a small space were essentially negative – like the notorious adolescent 'whatever' – I wouldn't call it pithy. I'd call it rude.

We live in an age of information overload, where the news is the sum total of so many discrete soundbites. Fast, furious and finished. We read the reviews but not the books, skim the headlines but not the article, watch lifestyle programmes rather than have a lifestyle, see the holiday on the TV programme *Holiday* rather than take it ourselves, eat the allegedly home-cooked meal that's a takeaway. Not surprising, then, that the short-and-sweet appeals more than the long-and-tedious.

Consider the cluster of words that congregates around 'concise' in the thesaurus – 'crisp', 'succinct', 'to the point'. Then consider what congregates around 'long-winded' – 'wordy', 'garrulous', 'pretentious'. As a culture, we clearly award the brownie points to concise. Putting it pithily, less is more.

But it's not merely brevity that accounts for pithy's appeal. Built into the pithy remark is a wealth of assumed knowledge that the speaker willingly shares with the listener, or, in the case of Thorpe's 'oops', the email sender with the receiver. Packed tight into 'oops' was compassion (I feel for you), commiseration (I'm sorry this happened to you), alleviation (could happen to anyone), consolation (look ahead). In addition was a gentle admonishment – 'Thorpie, it's only a race. No one died.' If you doubt this, consider how inappropriate 'oops' would be after a fatal motorway head-on crash.

I recall an instance of pithiness that was attributed to H. F. Wolcott, a respected qualitative researcher who probably got sick of having to justify his position – namely, that words provide meaningful data – to 'quant jocks' who find meaning only in numbers. When asked what you can learn from one case study, he replied, 'All you can.'

The loaded request

The elongated preface is no stranger to me. For years I was on the receiving end of students using one of multiple variations on the original theme of: 'Hi, um, I was wondering, um, if you, I mean, d'you think, if I came by your office, only, um, if it's OK with you, of course, I mean, um, is it possible you might look over, um, my thesis, or just a bit of it, and sort of, maybe, tell me what you think of, um, where I'm up to, do you think?' (Marked rising tone is helpful here.)

It's a jerky, fumbling, even bumbling, apparently inarticulate, HughGrantesque style of putting a request. But it works. I mean Hugh Grant got his girl by the end of *Four Weddings and a Funeral*, even while starting off as a total verbal ditherer.

Once you understand what fuels the elongated preface, it loses its capacity to vex and irritate. For this to happen, we need to recognise that it's an instance of 'negative politeness' which is a rather opaque term for beating-about-the-bush. This usually happens in what's called 'asymmetrical power exchanges', which translates as when one of the participants has more push-and-shove than the other.

As a speech act, the elongated preface is a cousin of the 'whimperative' that happens when your boss tells you to do something but does it nicely.

My students' negative politeness achieves three ends. First, it cues me to their overtly deferential behaviour. While I know that this is mere lip service to the status and power differential, I also know that it's pragmatic that the hat be tipped. Doing so, of course, is a strategic choice on the student's part, deriving from their knowledge that they don't actually have to have/feel respect; they merely have to display it. Face, after all, is all/only about appearance; very little to do with substance, even less with reality. Play the game, social lubrication (and much else) is yours; ignore the rules, and welcome to Planet Abrasion. Close the door behind you.

In other cultures and eras, petitioners might throw themselves prostrate on the floor before the one of whom the request is to be made. A kind of powerfully symbolic (albeit less bloody) form of we-who-are-about-to-die-salute-you.

Second, the elongated preface – the shortened form is known as the 'but preface' ('Sorry to bother you, but'...) – cues me to the fact that a request is coming. I may not yet know the substance of the request; it's enough that I know it's imminent. You know it's coming, and you intuit it's going to be a biggie – in fact, the more the dithering goes on, the bigger the biggie.

Third, and most importantly, it affords the receiver sufficient time to devise a response, perhaps an acceptable refusal-to-comply. You may want to say 'no', and your position may allow you to do so, but you still have to exit nicely. A myriad social constraints urge you to find a way that attends kindly to the face of the petitioner, who, despite being lower down the silly pecking order, is nonetheless entitled to escape with their face intact.

And you do this, not because you particularly care about their face, but rather because living as a social being means that your face depends, to a large extent, on the preservation of their face. At the end of the day, it's this very pain-in-the-arse mutual vulnerability that maintains social equilibrium.

A similar game-like tussle happens within the home. When my teenage daughter begins a favour-asking request with an 'are you able...?' – for example, 'are you able to drive me to the party tonight (*pause*), other side of town it's (*pause*), over the bridge' – the cues start coming. I know there's a request on its way, that it's a biggie (measured in terms of my inconvenience) and that she invests it with serious importance. This last variable is designed ultimately to give me fewer reply options and altogether less wriggle room.

'Are you able?' has been chosen over 'can you?' It's less usual, more formal, and more visibly reeking of emotional investment. 'Can' is what we use when we're not treading on verbal eggshells; 'are you able' is the strategic choice when we have a goal in mind. Its generous portion of processing time – *are* + *you* + *ay* + *bull* – totals the space of four normally stressed syllables. This is much more than the very minimal, single, unstressed syllable ('can') which attaches so swiftly to the next sound that it's barely a fleeting alveolar flutter prior to the main event.

Denial

Imagine that you ask someone the time, and they respond with '3.15'. You'd assume it is and you proceed accordingly. Or imagine you invite friends round for dinner; they say 'Love to'; you assume that they are pleased and will be coming as arranged. Or imagine you ring your doctor about the results of some recent blood test, and you're told 'all clear' – you assume they are cooperating with your wish to know the truth.

Human communication proceeds from two fundamental assumptions – that the people you interact with are both cooperative and truthful in intent. That's not to say they necessarily are (or even always should be); only that the way we interpret their utterances assumes that they are.

Imagine that instead of 'all clear', the doctor says, 'Um, actually, I'll put you through to my receptionist and I'd ask you please to make an appointment to come in and see me so that we can talk about these results.' You continue to operate under the twin assumptions (cooperation, truth) and interpret the request in a particular way (bad news).

The language philosopher H. P. Grice proposed that on the basis of the twin assumptions, we operate by four maxims – called Relation, Manner, Quantity and Quality – which we routinely deploy to read meanings. If an utterance abides by the four maxims, then it can be interpreted at face value. Specifically, if it is relevant, it abides by Relation; if it is unconvoluted, it abides by Manner; if it says as much as is needed but no more than is needed, it abides by Quantity; if it is truthful, then it abides by Quality.

Accordingly, the doctor's 'all clear' is relevant, straightforward, appropriately concise, based on facts believed to be true, and therefore means what it says literally – 'all clear'. Everything's OK. Nothing to worry about. Put it behind you.

Not so the doctor's alternative remark – 'Um, actually, I'll put you through to my receptionist and I'd ask you please to make an appointment to come in and see me so that we can talk about these results.' This is vague, wordy, evasive and begs to be interpreted at a non-literal level. Its meaning therefore resides between the lines, as it were, in the 'implicature', which is a fancy word for a kind of pragmatic grey space where inferences go to be unravelled. Like a holding bay.

Politicians go to Implicature School before they get elected and only the top graduates get called. Consider the following para-phrased statements of denial issued by politicians Bill Clinton, Tony Abbott, Mark Latham and Bob Carr respectively, all in relation to their earlier experiments with marijuana:

I did, but I didn't inhale.

It was a long time ago and it never happened.

Yes, I did, and I have got to own up, I did inhale.

I refer you to my previous answer: I haven't smoked it and when I didn't smoke it, I didn't inhale.

Yes, all men, all politicians, all on the past, all playing with denial in some way, even when, in Latham's case, by owning up, he's denying the need for a denial.

Take each and prise it open. We see how Clinton flouts the maxim of Manner, adding a qualification to his 'I did' that is meant to ameliorate its effect, but in fact backfires.

Abbott also flouts Manner: he offers two remarks, each referring to an 'it'. The problem is, their propositional content makes them mutually exclusive. If it never happened, it wasn't a long time ago. If it was a long time ago, then it did happen.

Latham overconfesses, so violating the maxim of Quantity. He does it in triplicate: yes + I did + I inhale[d]. He violates Manner by his convolutions: the confessional preface ('I have got to own up') and the emphatic 'did', both of which contribute to the very denial quality of a supposed non-denial. Put differently, he doth protest too much, methinks.

As for Carr (2004 Prizewinner in the Most Convoluted category), he wittingly flouts all four maxims and gets away with it because the humour grants its own licence, radically shifting the conversational rules.

It would seem, then, that there is a logic in the courtroom formula: 'How do you plead, guilty or not guilty?' You're forcibly constrained to the exact minimalist text of one out of two mutually exclusive options. Good strategy for avoiding foot-in-mouth.

Gradability

I was driving along thinking about nothing in particular – a mode that feels empty but is actually highly receptive – when my eye caught a FOR SALE sign at the front of a Bondi block. It said: 'Funky one-bedder. High ceilings, polished fls, ocean aspect'.

It was the phrase 'ocean aspect' that set me off. What exactly does that mean? Not as viewsy as 'ocean views', nor even 'ocean glimpses'. On a gradient from 'uninterrupted panorama' right down to 'touches of hinterland', I'd place 'ocean aspect' after 'glimpses' but before 'coastal living'. In fact, on a continent the size of Australia, 'coastal living' might even apply to a home a few hundred kilometres inland from the shoreline.

But real estate has an elastic approach to the truth, notwithstanding the truth-in-advertising principle, which in any case doesn't extend to the names of buildings. I've seen 'Miramar' (meaning 'seaview' in Spanish) on the façade of houses miles inland (maybe the Spanish because, opaque to most, it creates leeway for nostalgia).

Not surprisingly, gradability is an important notion in linguistics. Language is a window on life and last time I looked, there was nothing black-and-white about that. We need to be able to express degrees – of certainty, likelihood, bounty, scarcity, blueness ... and oceanic proximity.

Consider all the ways we have for describing how we might know a person – despite lacking the Romance languages' distinction between knowing something (*savoir*) and knowing a person (*connaître*). We say 'know of' when we don't actually know, but know about, even if just the name. We might know someone in the sense of recognising a face in the crowd, or of making someone's acquaintance, or of becoming mates or friends (although this may be a process-of-time more than a point-in-time). Then 'being friends', and from there, the intimacy grows.

A rule of thumb – the more a concept has its own word (a process called 'lexicalisation'), the more central its importance to speakers of that language. We all know about Eskimos and their words for snow, and Arabic speakers and their words for sand. Yiddish and Hebrew have a very useful word (*machutonim*) for the swathe of in-laws that marriage brings into the family. While *machutonim* sets up a differentiation between kin-by-blood and kin-by-marriage, by anyone's barometer, it's more welcoming by far of the newcomers than 'in-laws'.

English can describe different types of snow (tight-packed snow, loose surface snow) but we haven't lexicalised the terms. Clearly, neither snow nor in-laws are that important to us. If global warming continues, words for 'hot' might multiply.

It's fuzzy concepts applied to language again. Take the concept of bird. Is a sparrow more or less birdy than a penguin? Place them both on a gradient called 'birdiness', then add other bird-like creatures – owl, bat, albatross, pigeon, finch, lorikeet. Good luck.

Gradability is built into the grammatical system. We have pretty, prettier and prettiest, but to grasp the nuance we need the context. My father was setting up as a country general practitioner at the same time as he was learning English. From books he learned that 'better' is better than 'good', and 'best' is better than 'better'. But when a patient said, 'Better', in response to, 'How are you today?', it didn't mean better than good. It meant less than good but better than, or not as bad as, before.

Nothing's simple. Most adjectives are gradable ('big', 'dirty', 'green'). Some are non-gradable ('alphabetical', 'pregnant', 'federal'). Some can be gradable or not depending on the intended meaning ('a public highway'/'a very public quarrel'; 'a British passport'/'a very British accent'; 'an open door'/'a very open attitude'). Some adjectives are conventionally considered absolute and therefore non-gradable ('complete', 'ideal', 'unique', 'impossible', 'eternal', 'equal'). In practice, however, we have shades of grey. As George Orwell said, 'All animals are born equal but some are more equal than others.'

I've travelled far since 'ocean aspect'. As a pragmaticist at heart I have to say: to truly know (and yes, I know I'm splitting my infinitive) what this 'ocean aspect' is, you have to be there. It's nearly all the way down Bondi Road, going east, inspections on Thursdays at 12 noon. Be quick. Offer won't last.

Linguist presents as virus

Some time ago, a friend of mine, also a linguist, was incapacitated with a certain malady that he felt was more serious than 'a cold', yet not grave enough to qualify as 'the flu'. So he went to his doctor to inquire whether English had another word to describe his particular affliction which, while entirely incapacitating in the short term, certainly in regard to work, nonetheless wasn't, well, truly nasty.

Strange, perhaps, to go to the doctor in search of a word, rather than a treatment, for his ailment. But single-minded of purpose, he knew that he wanted a vicious-seeming, diseasey-sounding thing that would engender the same degree of sympathy and comfort that descends when one is struck down with something deemed serious. Minus the long-term debilitation or disadvantage, of course.

The doctor quickly divined his reason for being there. After all, they had an established doctor–patient relationship and she was aware of the forces that drive him. She showed sympathy for the problem and went on to explain that unfortunately, no, this was another example of the impoverishment of English.

The doctor was ready-and-willing to launch forth on this topic. (You'd be surprised at the number of doctors who fancy themselves as lay experts on language.) And she was chuffed, too, to have an attentive audience. In this instance, she declared, one has recourse to two quite disparate words.

One, of course, is a 'cold' – a word that is what it means. Comfortless cold. The kind of cold with which you have to turn up for work. This is zero-sympathy cold. It's get-on-with-it cold. Not much leeway there.

The other word lies at the end of a long continuum of suffering, and this, of course, is the 'flu'. Now 'flu' connotes an intense, bed-ridden, Anadin-filled condition. Large doses of dour-faced sympathy. Multiple, exciting, hang-the-expense medications with which one can try to slow the flow from various leaking orifices. We're wont to use 'soldier on', suggesting the suffering and stoicism of the trenches.

It's worth noting that the pejorative 'cold' is further denigrated by its oft-accompanying adjectival consort, 'common'. Indeed, so common is 'cold' that my friend reported feeling quite queasy about suggesting it was this that brought him to the doctor's door. To pile on the insults, while 'cold' takes the nondescript 'a' (as in 'anyone can have a cold'), 'flu' is graced by the stately 'the', as in:

Did you know that so-and-so is ill?
Yes, I'd heard (pause). The flu, isn't it?

Once these difficulties had been resolved, the doctor proceeded to the physical examination. Prodding softnesses and probing orifices, she sought evidence for that which she had already quietly decided was a cold. But to make him feel better (he suspects), she started at that very point to slip in the word 'virus'.

One of the nice things about 'virus' is that it *sounds* nasty. They say a virus can lie dormant at the base of the spine for years only to emerge, ravenous, when the host system (dinner party metaphor intrudes here) is stressed and off-guard.

Then there are the connotations of plague. Ebola. Something out of control. Jet-in-jet-out epidemiologists. Brightly coloured, uniformed State Emergency Services personnel, strategically positioned with ropes and things. Hysteria only just kept at bay.

This is nice, my friend thought. Disease couched in predator language. Darth Virus. Projected as enemy. Easily demonised. Potential candidate for attack during a State of the Union address. It offered mileage, social capital, a slippery pathway from incredibly ill (now) to fully recovered (later). With loads of sympathy along the way.

The doctor was keen to point out that in being a virus, it was therefore not a 'bacterial infection'. This gave 'virus' the added bonus of being untreatable. Now, with an untreatable virus on board, and a certificate to support said fact, my friend began to feel decidedly better. He'd made clear, descriptive progress. Something terminal, but without the end. Paradoxical. Useful. Time to go.

'Yes', murmured the doctor, with an understanding smile, as she walked my friend to the door, 'I think we can safely say that today you present as a virus.'

Dopey, hairy-backed sheilas

The hairy-nosed wombat is a burrowing marsupial, heavily built, with short powerful legs and long claws well adapted for digging. It lives in a burrow, emerging at night to feed on grasses. The name derives from its distinctive muzzle covered with short brown hairs.

The term 'hairy-nosed wombat' is both descriptive and classificatory. For wombatologists, it qualitatively marks out a kind of wombat, without fear or favour or offence.

I can imagine having the following conversation with the RSPCA:

Me: Help! There's a wombat in my backyard!
RSPCA: What kind of wombat is it?
Me: Hey, what do I know about wombats?
RSPCA: Is it the hairy-nosed kind or the common wombat?
Me: Hello! To see its nose means to come up close.
RSPCA: We're on our way. Meanwhile, don't approach or
    antagonise it.
Me: No worries there.

The term 'dopey, hairy-backed sheila', on the other hand, is the designated term for a particular woman – to wit, a 45-year-old South African mother of three, who made specific allegations about having been verbally abused by Australian cricketer Shane Warne.

'Dopey, hairy-backed sheila' is a term used by the then cricket coach David Hookes who came out in a Warnian defence. Hookes defended his language, claiming that 'hairy-backed' is 'a commonly used' term to describe South Africans and that its use, in his sentence, was therefore descriptive, not derogatory.

Of course, descriptive adjectives don't have much meaning on their own, out of context. They live their real life in actual utterances, surrounded by other words, preceded and followed by co-text (the surrounding text). Meanings are attributed to them within certain contexts by members of specific discourse communities who, by virtue of their membership of such communities, have agreed that these meanings are part of their shared understandings. Hookes's comment about the 'dopey, hairy-backed sheila' was uttered in Australia for an Australian audience and whether or not he was using another dialect's slang, he had to know that the uptake of his words would happen in Australia.

Let's carve up this adjective + adjective + noun compound and see what we find.

'Dopey' is slang for silly: not completely there, something missing, not altogether. In other words, says the thesaurus, dimwitted, slow on the uptake, thick, dull, stupid or simple. It can be a fixed state (a sandwich short of a picnic) or a transitory phase (a temporarily lower level of awareness). In the latter sense, the implication can be that the dopey person is in a semiconscious state, as would be the case when one is under the influence of drugs (dope). We say 'don't be a dope' to someone behaving foolishly. Certainly it's not as strong as 'idiotic' or 'moronic', and there are contexts where it might even be quite friendly.

Not, however, I would suggest, when it's placed alongside 'hairy-backed'. Now it's not untrue that 'hairy-backed' is commonly used in South Africa. The *Collins Dictionary* includes 'hairyback' (noun) as an offensive slang term, in the South African context, for an Afrikaner. So, even in its original context, 'hairyback' is offensive. Transported to Australia, and deployed as it was by Hookes, the word loses its Afrikaner associations, though not its offensiveness. There's no need to trawl back through former Australian Prime Minister Paul Keating's speeches (a rich source of invective) to sense that phrase types involving hyphenated body features ('hairy-backed', 'big-arsed', 'fuck-witted', 'small-minded') serve nicely as abusive epithets.

Hookes's 'hairy-backed' is attached to 'sheila', which is an informal (if now rather dated) term for a young woman, derived from the common nineteenth-century Irish girl's name. You still see it on some doors in Australian pubs, adjacent to one that says 'blokes'. Still, I imagine the only creature in the Australian context – male, female or metrosexual – that wouldn't take offence at 'hairy-backed' is the wombat (or related furry bush counterparts). After all, if it's OK to have hair on your nose, what's a patch on your back? But let's face it, in the city at least, the epilating industry does a good trade on the perceived ugliness of back hair, no matter whose back we're talking about, or behind.

In terms of the elements, we have dopey + hairy-backed + sheila. Our context is Australia and our speech community Australians. Is this merely descriptive or verbally abusive? You be the umpire.

Gerunds

Smoking is forbidden. Being lucky is an advantage. Playing for Australia is an honour. These 'ing' words, or gerunds, look verby but act nouny.

They are nouns in the grammatical sense of ostensibly doing what nouns are supposed to do: name things and act as subjects or objects of verbs. But they're certainly not nouns in the way dog or love are nouns. Their verby quality derives from the sense that the action implied (to smoke, to be, to play) is so frequent, repetitive, habitual perhaps, that it's taken on the character of an event or state.

Gerunds are halfway between a noun and a verb, with a sense of both. They're a Janus doll, facing two ways, dressed in different clothes. The nounier the action becomes, the more the verbal sense (of performance) is detached, allowing the appearance of a proposition to emerge. Clearly, gerunds are weird-but-wonderful creatures that reside in a magical part of Grammardom, achieving that larger semantic force for being more than the sum of their parts.

Time magazine once put Tom Cruise's exquisite face on the cover under the headline 'Being Tom'. The cover story amply delineated what 'being Tom' meant: the sum of an infinite number of thoughts and acts that might be collectively summed up as 'typically Tom'. What better way is there to express this? It could have been: 'Tom Cruise, The Life of'. Or 'A Day in the Life of Tom Cruise?' Or 'What it's like to be Tom Cruise'? Or 'Tom minus Nic'. Or simply 'Tom Cruise'. You can see, can't you, that 'Being Tom' was tailor-made for the gerund.

Consider processes that happen slowly, invisibly perhaps, but inexorably. Philosophically, is 'global warming' a verb or a noun? It's things that we do (verbs) that contribute to the state (nouns). Again, this is a perfect call for the gerund. Interestingly, a new coinage is 'global dimming', which, no, isn't the effect on the world's population of years of dumbing down (some might cite the contribution of MTV, but I'll desist). Rather, 'global dimming' is a term for a progressive reduction (about 3 per cent per decade by some estimates) in the amount of light and sunshine reaching the Earth's surface. (I must confess to being unable to reconcile 'global warming' with 'global dimming' as surely the sun is a source of heat as well as of light, but as I dropped Science the first chance school gave me, I'm well outside my comfort zone. Science aside, the terms serve us well as examples of the gerund.)

If it's not yet apparent, I confess to being a gerundophile. If grammar is a microcosmic representation of something larger, then gerunds bespeak a very attractive universe. One that acknowledges that shades of grey are the norm, not the nuisance. And I know I'm not alone. Every time I speak in public about the attractiveness of the gerund, there are people in the audience whose body movements indicate that they resonate with my pronouncement. I also get the impression that many closet gerundophiles are loath to speak about their predilection not from shame but because they're likely not to be understood. If I had time, I'd start a support group.

What gerundophiles share is their respect for the complex role that gerunds perform. We know that they fill a tall order, satisfactorily marrying noun and verb which, while they're careful to maintain a diplomatic cordiality (like the subject–verb concord rule), aren't, um, natural bedmates.

If nouns and verbs were created first in the Garden of Eden, things got tricky when gerunds arrived. They refused to conform to the template. They made it clear they were happier living on the margins. With time their peripheral stance became a protest against Life's binariness. You're black or white. Pro-Bush-and-Blair or pro-Saddam. A suburban mortgage-slave or a DINK (Double Income, No Kids). Male or Female.

Interestingly, sexuality provides a nice metaphor in the war against the binary. Think of bisexuality, or even the new 'bi-curiosity', as a brick hurled through the window of the Binary headquarters. Our gerunds, then, are bisexual. They want their world to straddle both camps (or their camp to straddle both worlds). They want to be limited to neither, be more than each. They've taken on more than they had to. Good luck to them, I say.

POLITICAL

All the sections in this chapter share an abiding theme. In various ways each engages with language associated with the political. In the broad sense, this means any domain of life where power inequities exist (which, let's face it, is everywhere). In the narrow sense, 'political' means the arena in which politics happens. It is not surprising that language features prominently here because perhaps no other domain of public life requires language to work so hard. Who else (other than perhaps royalty and celebrities) employs speechwriters, minders, spin doctors and press officers? So much of public life is shaped by perception which itself is mediated and therefore shaped by reporting agencies, like the media. In a democratic society, elections are run on the fuel of public perception; wars are allegedly fought for reasons that are deemed acceptable to the electorate; policy is debated and sold to the nation for reasons that are acceptable in the public domain. People in power want to stay in power and they too use language to serve their vested interests, as do those who seek to wrest power from incumbents. In all such cases, constructing this acceptability is largely a linguistic matter.

Where the truth lies

Truth is the most fragile of concepts. Nowadays, you can say almost anything. A school up the road with a pretty dismal record and reputation recently had a nice coat of paint. A new sign's been erected proclaiming the new school name and its new slogan/motto/logo. Something along the lines of 'leading the field in quality education'.

A coat of paint. New words. The eternal question re-emerges: is there less 'fat' in KFC than there used to be in Kentucky FRIED Chicken?

A while ago, I read, in a Ph.D. thesis, a quote from something I'd written. Flattering, but worrying too. The quote was accurate, as was the referencing, but the meaning imputed to be mine wasn't. (*I* should know.)

So what happened to truth here? Someone else's opinion had been overlaid on my opinion and presented as mine. Might've been a deliberate contortion to further an argument. Might've been an honest misinterpretation. Who's to say? We're wading in murky waters – that pragmatic wet space that opens up between YES and NO and provides us with retractability when it's needed.

Being elastic with the truth is not the exclusive province of any one group. Adolescents have a particular talent for this. Regard the following authentic exchange between parent and adolescent son:

> Did you take the car out last night?
> *I didn't go by bus.*
> But did you take the car?
> *Um, the car was used during the evening, y-e-e-s.*

They're not alone. These days you can do wonderful things with a CV, the readers of which may even collude in the conspiracy. Real estate agents have long been masters of truth-stretching to the extent that everyone automatically decodes, so minimising false expectations – cosy = cramped; waterside = glimpse of blue; leafy = not-entirely-concrete.

Former Serbian President Slobodan Milošović, on trial for war crimes, could poke his chin in the air and say, 'Atrocity? What atrocity?' Hitler's former secretary can say he was a lovely man who, in private, never said un-nice things about Jews, only showing some phobic symptoms in those last dreary days in the bunker.

So when is a lie a lie? Look up 'lie' in the *Oxford English Dictionary* and you get 'a false statement made with intent to deceive'. Here what is primary is the intention of the information-giver. So, lying when you think it's the truth and have no intention to deceive is not lying. It's 'unwittingly spreading incorrect information'.

Yet it's a slippery slope. What if you fail the *cui bono* test (to whose advantage)? The US/UK Coalition wants to topple the Iraqi regime, and cites intelligence reports of weapons of mass destruction. No such weapons are subsequently found and controversy continues to this day.

Is it a lie when you fail to check the veracity of information that you then indiscriminately disseminate? Who knew what, when, and how did they convey it? At what precise moment does a rumour become a falsehood? Is it when it is uttered by one who knows it to be false? Or is it when one hears it and fails to check its authenticity? The US writer Henry David Thoreau said: 'It takes two to speak the truth – one to speak and another to hear.' I wonder what *Yes Minister*'s Sir Humphrey Appleby would say.

Perhaps rather than a slip of the tongue, it could be a slip of the ear – a selective and collective hearing impediment that allows politicians to hear some things, miss others, make assumptions, fail to check facts, and generally blunder onwards. Aurally challenged, rather than politically expedient. A disability is so much more forgivable than a moral lapse.

Bomblet

'Attention, people of Afghanistan', says the US broadcaster, 'our yellow, can-shaped cluster bombs are not to be mistaken for our yellow, square-shaped food parcels. Bomblets that fail to explode on impact may lodge in the soil and explode if disturbed. Please be careful.'

Life, never simple, got worse in Afghanistan during the US attack after September 11. Any number of complications conspired to this end. Imagine an Afghan child seeking to determine the shape of a yellow-object-fallen-from-sky. She pokes it about in the dirt. Or she runs up to it, tripping over a partly concealed explosive. Or extremes of hunger and despair make her ignore safety precautions.

Or, because the local translation of 'bomblet' maintains the same cutesy-pie connotation of the original broadcast, her very last thought is of food, not danger.

'Bomblets'. The diminutive affix '-let' turns your regular-size bomb into something smaller. But we're not only talking size here. In fact, a 'bomb' (nasty) is altogether different from a 'bomblet' (cute). No doubt, bomblets have changed daily life for Afghanis. They've also changed the way I feel about diminutives.

Adding '-let' is a linguistic device that allows us to achieve a number of commonly allied functions in one breath. The most apparent is the diminishing function, by which something is reduced in size. We've long had 'droplet', 'piglet', 'couplet', 'booklet', 'pamphlet', 'leaflet', 'bracelet' and 'platelet'. Pharmaceuticals gave us 'caplet', and now, thanks to the military, we have 'bomblet'.

Along with the size-reducing function, '-let' can also express affection, familiarity and triviality. Indeed, the multiple functions cleave together rather like the strands of a rope. Expressing smallness inevitably carries one or more other functions. In Spanish, for example, lovability can be conveyed by adding a diminutive (such as when Pablo becomes 'Pablito'). A Spanish-speaking mother might say to her child (in translation): 'Oh poor little elbow! You gave it a little knock. Mama give it a little kiss and it'll be better in a little minute.' Here, everything goes small – the elbow, the knock, the kiss and the recuperation. Only Mama's size stays the same. Bound up with this affectionate littling process (as distinct from not-so-affectionate 'belittling') is a familiarity, and, in this case, a nuance that the elbow injury is no mortal blow. There's a generalised, economical diminishing – the physical size of the people, the seriousness of the event, and the social distance between participants.

In Spanish, too, you can add the diminutive ending to a word in order to minimise the imposition conveyed: 'Can you give me a little lift?' English achieves this through 'just': 'I wonder if you'd just help me write my Ph.D./sort out my tax/help me understand superannuation.' The 'just' doesn't make the imposition smaller, any more than the 'little' reduces the lift's mileage. What it does do is signal that the asker is uncomfortable about asking, and that's called politeness.

Italian uses its intricate system of diminutives to highlight and signal multiple nuances, levels and differences. Take *vento* (wind). Diminutives allow Italians to have *venticello* (a light gentle breeze), as well as a *ventaccio* (a most unpleasant, blustery wind). Or take *donna* (woman). There's *donnina* (little woman), *donnona* (big woman) and the pejorative *donnaccia* (slut). Endings can also be markers of social status – if the wife of a government minister addresses the wife of a shopkeeper as 'Mariuccia' rather than 'Maria', the guise of the diminutive may convey (albeit crassly) her sense of superior class status. On the other hand, it may not – and the difference is in the contextual circumstances. There's nothing rigidly absolute here: slippery rules afford wriggle room, which provides inbuilt retreatability, should it be needed.

By contrast, Australians largely use the diminutive as a political marker. It enables them to reduce everything to a bland egalitarianism where everyone's equally laid-back and there are no experts or other uncomfortable social asymmetries: 'Forget about prezzies this Chrissie – let's just have a barbie with the rellies' (Forget about presents this Christmas – let's just have a bbq with the relatives). It's the great unsubtle leveller, like childbirth and cancer, minus the pain.

But 'bomblet' is a different kind of leveller. It comes from the same place as 'friendly fire', 'clean hit' and 'collateral damage'. No mention of the woundlet, painlet and deathlet that go with the territory.

Sport as war, war as sport

On the fields of combat, it's all the same game.

Sport and war: the spectacles coalesce. The line is blurred. Both are made-for-television events; both draw from the same cultural pool of language and imagery. Which are you watching? Does it even matter? War and sport. Brought to you by the team you can trust.

Remember *Saving Private Ryan*? Well, during the Second Iraq War we had 'Saving Private Lynch'. There are people who wander the globe and trawl the dailies searching out opportunities to buy up film rights for human-interest survivor stories. They locked onto Iraq and were on the scene, hovering vulture-like, over a kill in the making. The clock was ticking, mobile phones were ringing, emails were unloading – TV show by September? Once the Coalition of the Willing's body count began, Private Lynch was just the thing. She was uplifting, heroic, action-packed, all rolled into one, and blonde and female to boot. What more could you ask for? If she hadn't actually happened, she would have had to be invented.

Now the casting is going to be fun. The feelers would be out already. Demi Moore proved she had good khaki connections in *GI Jane*. Meg Ryan's got the hair, but she is perhaps a bit long in the tooth. Either way, they're women dressed up and speaking like men. And who will they choose for the role of the American assault leader? Maybe dirty-singleted Bruce Willis or Tom (missile-matching name) Cruise? Or will a smooth new hunk self-launch on the event? Either way, they'll first have to check the on-location chemistry with Demi-*cum*-Meg. Fast-forward to a moment's solemnity (fallen comrades) on award and accolade evening.

The history of baseball is steeped in the sentiment of combat, dating back to the US Civil War when it was a popular diversion – for both soldiers and officers, and on both sides of the combat. During the fiftieth anniversary of the Korean War, a blurring of images and icons unfolded – the Pentagon, baseball and the Tomb of the Unknown Soldier, all melanged together. Again, war, sport and spectacle intertextualise seamlessly.

A sweet-faced marine on a tank headed for Baghdad is interviewed for television. He says how he's looking forward to getting there – there, where the bombs fall. Seeing artillery fire from a distance is a let-down, he says. Sparks, yes – the night sky lights up – but Baghdad is the mosh pit. Bring it on.

For years now, we've constructed sport as war. After all, the original Olympics were formal postwar tributes to fallen relatives. A ritualised mock battle, with adrenaline-driven opponents, whose purpose is to beat down or take out the enemy and claim victory. Players are lethal, they stage showdowns, suffer setbacks. Athletes take to the field of battle, they charge at each other; they have defence and attack positions. Sides withdraw or surrender. Sportspeople are warriors (usually 'true', often 'heroic'). A war cry rallies teams, which might be well drilled with solid rearguards. Advances may cause havoc. Fans can be hordes that run riot. Team captains marshal their troops. Coaches and managers bunker down in war rooms, where they talk tactics and rough out strategies. It's blood, sweat and tears all round.

Combative images are reinforced by the mechanistic. Words such as demolish and dismantle alongside cogs, blowtorch and engine room. Further down the dehumanised pathway, we have robotic imagery: injuries are referred to as 'damage', healing as 'repair', weaknesses or flaws as 'faults' or 'defects'. What's left over is only faintly human.

It's a man's domain, like the locker-room and the battlefield. Couch-potato spectators are rewarded with testosterone surges. Behaviours, like language, assume a woman's absence. After all, she can't share those inflated, rock-hard, can-do feelings, where fatigue, pain and grit (read 'soldiering on') push over into euphoria. Self submerges, loyalty sublimates, rationality is sacrificed at the altar of the greater good. Or maybe women's roar-and-surge moments are quieter, cleaner, more personal, less televisable.

It's tempting to think these two constructions – sport-as-war, war-as-sport – are accidental, even idiosyncratic. But if we were less conditioned, through spectator sport, to the adversarial images of aggression and antagonism, wouldn't we be more horrified at the real thing – at war constructed as sport? At misplaced humanity? Where barracking for your team or your country becomes one. Where exploding buildings and a home run are indistinguishable.

Truth as a house

We've long known that truth is the first casualty of war. It's also the first casualty of pre-election public debate. During the 2004 Australian federal election campaign, John Howard accused Mark Latham of being 'sloppy with the truth'. I wasn't sure about Latham then – he'd had fewer opportunities to lie, but he was young and we were approaching election-promise land, so the harvest was looking good.

Truth is a rubbery notion to get your paws around. Mahatma Gandhi gave it a capital 'T' and had no doubts at all about what it meant. Maybe the view was clearer in those pre-post-colonial days, with the battle still ahead and the eye on the goal. Or maybe the ascetic lifestyle bestows unparalleled vision. Few others have grasped the notion so unambiguously, although perhaps Arnold Schwarzenegger, dubbed 'the Governator' of California, showed an inkling of its complexity in the apparent oxymoron of the film *True Lies*. Then again, this may have been unwitting serendipity or simply someone else's decision.

What would truth look like if it were a house? There'd be a number of rooms – one for faithfulness, another for accuracy, a third for authenticity. The house wouldn't have been entirely built in the same era: the 'faithful' room would have been part of the original design while 'accuracy' was added later, perhaps with new owners.

More illuminating than the semantics is the grammatical configuration. What does it reveal, I wonder, that we have a verb 'to lie' but no equivalent verb, such as 'to true'? Truth clearly prefers to operate as a noun. As such it's out there, substantive, verifiable. As things stand, to go verbal the noun 'truth' needs a verb, turning the combination into a verb phrase – to 'speak the truth', to 'tell the truth', to 'proclaim' or 'declare the truth'. It's as if truth needs acting on in some way in order to be operationalised.

Lying, on the other hand, is a primary verb (to lie), as well as a verb phrase (to tell a lie). Perhaps this is to be expected. We know that speaking with forked tongue has always been more slippery than its opposite. Is it going too far to speculate that keeping truth as a nominal rather than a verbal construct is a protective act, based on an awareness of how fragile it is, how easily unravelled, dismantled, diffused?

Given the stubbornly nominal quality of truth, it is significant that it is defined by the verbal – by our actions, both by what we do and by what we don't do. When we swear to 'tell the truth, the whole truth, and nothing but the truth', we are promising not to leave anything truthful out, as well as not to speak untruths. Acts of omission, then, are evaluated as equal to acts of commission. And that is surely as it should be, because acts of omission are both easier for the teller (how easy is it after all to say less than the full truth?) and less risky (it's far more difficult to audit an omission because, at the very least, it means recognising an absence). Occasionally, though, such behaviour is challenged, as in the Australian 'Spycatcher' trial in 1986, when the UK Cabinet Secretary, Sir Robert Armstrong, famously used the phrase 'being economical with the truth'.

We talk about a person being careless or sloppy with the truth, or flexible or elastic or rubbery. We speak of wriggle room, which is a kind of buffer zone that affords retreatability and deniability. 'Spin doctoring', sometimes called Spinnish, is a cynical term for an accepted practice, in public life especially. At my fruit and vegetable market, some veggies are pre-selected, wrapped and placed under a sign that reads 'reduced for quick sale'. Much nicer than 'cheap rotting food here'.

What does it say about truth that it can be masked, cloaked, too close for comfort, or that it can be flushed out? Or that we talk about opening someone's eyes, or that someone reveals their true colours? What does it say about us that we might read between the lines or swallow the line or take something as gospel or that we might bury our head in the sand?

In 'Ode on a Grecian Urn', John Keats said all we need to know is that Truth and Beauty were one. But can you trust the word of a Romantic?

War words

Wars spawn words. In 1991 Saddam Hussein promised that the Gulf War would be 'the mother of all battles', and for the next decade 'mother of all' was everywhere. As the preferred superlative descriptor, it was the new flavour of the month-*cum*-decade. With its limitless applications and its quirky foreign nuance, it became the mother of all recent word adoptions: for the baby (mother of all tantrums), for the new car (mother of all 4WDs), for the Caribbean trip (mother of all holidays), for the new boyfriend (a mother of all...well, no, maybe not).

It means biggest, best, most powerful and all-consuming. Perhaps its power lies in its return to the source – mother as progenitor. Certainly, 'mother of all' has served us well over the past decade, notwithstanding its birth in international conflict. While we would all gladly undo that chapter of history in terms of death toll, civilian suffering and environmental damage, we'd like to hang onto the mother of all word compounds, please.

A decade later, the Second Iraq War, still not over, has given us a few beauties. First cab off the rank was 'the Axis of Evil', which was immediately applied to umpteen contexts. Around the same time, 'weapons of mass destruction' hit the airwaves. It soon abbreviated to WMDs and was applied successfully to a diverse range of phenomena, from new cars (the 4WD in particular) to the weather (cyclones, especially). A companion term to the axis of evil and the WMDs was 'the Coalition of the Willing', which started life as USA plus its allies and then morphed to less belligerent contexts, such as when the boss says at about 5.0 p.m., looking around the office with a try-hard attempt at a benevolent expression: 'I'm looking for a coalition of the willing.' In other words, unpaid overtime.

Yes, wars spawn words. In this, the two Iraqi wars have been no different from other conflagrations. Let's trawl backwards and see what remains of the lexical outgrowths of some of last century's battlegrounds. A superb resource for this purpose is John Ayto's

20th Century Words, which comprises a decade-by-decade account of new English words and their contexts of origin.

Winding the clock backwards, the Kurds' war with Saddam gave us 'safe haven', though, sadly, it gave them neither safety nor a haven. From the break-up of the former Yugoslavia there arose 'ethnic cleansing', a grim new label for an ancient pastime. England's war with Argentina over the Falklands (Las Malvinas) yielded 'the Falklands effect', a term for how war can revitalise domestic polls (please direct any questions to Maggie Thatcher). In the 1970s, the Argentine military gave us 'disappeared' as a transitive verb (as in, 'the military disappeared thousands of allegedly left-wing students') and 'dirty war' (one is tempted to ask, is *any* war not dirty?), perhaps so named for being a civil war.

The Vietnam War yielded 'body count', 'frag', 'defoliation', 'Agent Orange', 'cluster bomb' and 'boat people'. The last year of that war saw the first use of the term 'collateral damage'. Post-Vietnam, the term lay low for a few decades, to be revived (sorry) in the Gulf (or First Iraq) War, which also resulted in 'bomblets' (see page 000) and 'smart bombs'. Apropos the latter, the Second Iraq War has added the comparative 'smarter bombs'. Supposedly the 'smart' factor resides in the precision, but if this were totally the case, 'collateral damage' would not have made a comeback.

Cambodia gave us 'killing fields' and Pol Pot's 'year Zero' recharged an older term, 'ground zero', which has re-emerged since 11 September 2001. The Korean War gave us 'napalm' while other communist conflicts in Asia turned out 'running dog' and 'bamboo curtain'. The Second World War produced 'blitzkrieg', 'final solution' and 'kamikaze'. Another Second World War outgrowth was 'genocide', which even rated its own United Nations definition. This proved theoretically useful in Rwanda and Bosnia, and currently in Sudan. The First World War left us with 'D-day' and 'trench warfare'. 'Concentration camp' – an English invention, as apologists for Nazism delight in reminding us – came out of the Boer War.

Prior to the invasion of Iraq in 2003, there was a lot of huff and puff, otherwise known as diplomacy or a talking war. Even as that was happening, the body bags were no doubt already being stacked in a Middle East warehouse. It didn't take the mother of all geniuses to predict that the mother of all restraint was needed to avoid war. Did anyone think those body bags would remain unpacked to gather dust?

War words II

Conflict and warfare leave bodies on the battle-scape, words on the language-scape.

The Greeks gave us 'Pyrrhic victory'. It's certainly not their fault that we've failed to learn the lesson, again and again and again. Napoleon met his Waterloo in 1815 in Belgium and, since then, anyone can meet theirs at any place. The so-called 'war to end all wars' gave us 'in the trenches' for getting down and dirty, and 'over the top' for mindless slaughter. The 'fifth column' came out of the Spanish Civil War. The 'Blitz' immortalised the destruction of Coventry and East London. The Nazis gave us 'the Holocaust', thanks very much. Northern Ireland gave us 'The Troubles', a spooky understatement for three decades of rampant sectarian violence.

Sometimes war is given a different name. A flashpoint. A breakdown in diplomacy. Sometimes the distinctions make sense only to those who devise them. In 1956, Anthony Eden told the English House of Commons: 'We are in an armed conflict [with Egypt] . . . There has been no declaration of war.' You have to wonder who stood to gain from the nitpicky name-game.

Vietnam-the-war gave us Vietnam-the-concept. Now we have Iraq, which, Bush insists, is not Vietnam. It's not, it's not, no, it's not. We may not believe or trust him. But when he says that Iraq isn't Vietnam, we know what he means.

'Vietnam' is the elemental modern symbol of bloody, protracted conflict. It's the scar across the heart of a generation, the thorn in the Pentagon's side. It's the quicksand that sucks you down, the quagmire with no honourable exit. The told-you-so mantra that American presidents dread hearing – echoes from Somalia, Grenada, Bosnia, Afghanistan, Iraq. One of the tragedies of the US involvement in Vietnam was that it gave us 'Vietnam' as a generic term for unwinnable war – a reminder, if we would only heed it, that carnage and honour should not appear in the same sentence.

The parallel between Vietnam and other wars is not a facile equation. To work, a number of correspondences need to be in place. The combat is on foreign soil. The invading/liberating force massively outnumbers the opponent in firepower and resources. The opponent is demonised, if altogether unclearly differentiated. Labels for 'other' shift about loosely – insurgents, rebels, terrorists, guerrillas, factions, loyalists, militias. Civilian and military targets blur until they each bleed into 'enemy'. Shoot first, ask questions later – hesitation is an unaffordable luxury.

Some Vietnams begin with involvement, which becomes engagement, and then escalates, and protracts, and finally stalemates – a grotesque parody of the 'no one's going anywhere' of trench warfare. Mostly, they start out with the apparent intention of a short, sharp, swift action. Almost invariably, the conflict reaches the point of bogged-down-edness where no amount of superior firepower or excess reinforcements changes anything but the quantum of suffering.

Television means that at one level Vietnams get fought out in lounge rooms. After all, 'body bag' was a product of that time, the imagery saturating the evening news. If one lesson was learned, it was the strategy of 'embedding' journalists. The words of US presidential statements – addresses to the nation, assessments, promises, conditions – all ring increasingly hollow while, as Barbara Tuchman puts it in *The March of Folly*, their governments pursue policies 'contrary to the nation's self-interest'. It's the quintessential conundrum – the resolution depends on an exit strategy which remains elusive. Meanwhile, the body count rises.

'All wars', said Grantland Rice, a famous US sportswriter, 'are planned by old men'. Said Carl Sandburg, American poet, wistfully: 'Sometime they'll give a war and nobody will come.'

France's Vietnam was in Algeria, Russia's in Afghanistan, Israel's in Lebanon, England's in Northern Ireland. The scarred are drawn from both sides of the combat, and from both fronts, military and civilian. Contemporary historians perceive, interpret and label; the next generation's historians will revisit, reinterpret and re-label. Minor distractions in the onward march of folly.

They said the First World War was the war to end all wars. British Prime Minister David Lloyd George agreed, but added that the next one was too. Years earlier, far-sighted German Chancellor Otto von Bismarck had said that any new war would be likely to 'come out of some damned silly thing in the Balkans'. A powder keg is a powder keg.

Iraq is not Vietnam, Bush insists. Yeah, right, and denial is a river in Egypt.

The Governator

The Californians voted. Arnold Schwarzenegger morphed yet again. From small-town Austrian to champion bodybuilder to actor to real estate developer to Governor of California.

But despite these metamorphoses there's no doubt about the consistency of this man's core persona. And given that the 'Vote Arnold' campaign was predicated on the promise of certainty in uncertain times, Arnold's resolute, unchanging persona no doubt serves him well.

Whether speaking as immigrant-made-good, billionaire actor, aspiring politician or Governor-elect, Arnold speaks his own kind of English. Made familiar through his string of action movies, his German-accented Arnold-speak has taken on a kind of cult status.

Arnold-speak has some defining features. First is the tendency to use simple syntax – subject + verb + object – in one-clause sentences: 'I love America.' This is well suited to electioneering because it facilitates the key message and minimises the chance both of interference and of faulty inference.

Second, there's the absence of modality – those devices in language that carry tentativeness or caution. Everything is an assertion. After all, this is Arnold of 'I'll-be-back' fame. In *The Terminator*, he didn't say he might be back, or he was thinking about being back, or it was possible he'd be back. No. It was total certainty, knowledge and commitment. Again, such language is well suited to the discourse of political promise. It's a style for which Arnold needs no coaching.

Third is a landscape devoid of questions – the kind that might suggest humility, openness or just curiosity. Not only has Arnold no questions, he seems to believe he has all the answers. One of the resources available on his website is: 'What is best in Life? Arnold has the answer. Ask Arnold.' In fact, the whole of www.schwarzenegger.com is a monument to Arnold's no-shades-of-grey universe. Whether you click on 'Actor', 'Athlete' or 'Activist', or something disingenuously called 'Life' (where Arnold's biography blurs into the capital-L abstraction), you are confronted by a stunning consistency of language and image.

In 'Life', you're invited to bone up on Arnold-trivia to impress your friends. In 'In His Own Words', reminiscent of something being heralded from the Good News Bible, we have 'Arnold speaks! This is the place to hear it straight from the Oak himself. Hear what he has to say.' His personally endorsed nickname, the Oak, suggests unambiguously strong-and-sturdy-as.

You can read quotes from Arnie on anything from bodybuilding to fiscal reform. Under 'Retro-clip', you're invited to visit his former lives with the encouraging header 'We can't live in the past. But we can visit', alongside the offer of regular video clips from 'the Arnold archives'.

You can also read the 450 endorsements from Californian organisations. Hear wife Maria Shriver's ten reasons to vote for Arnold: he's clever, compassionate, motivated, keeps his promises, loves California, is a can-do kinda fella, etc., etc.

Listen to the lyrics of his rousing campaign anthem:

We're not gonna take it,
No we ain't gonna take it,
We're not gonna take it anymore,
We've got the right to choose,
And there ain't no way we'll lose it,
This is our life,
This is our song.
We'll fight the powers that be.

Clearly 'we' and 'our' refer to people-who-vote(d)-for-Arnold, while 'the powers that be' refers to those who don't/didn't. Now that Arnold's removalists have moved him into the Governor's residence, he might give some thought to changing his anthem, or maybe just the pronouns.

There's nothing on the website about groping or spanking. The last frenzied days of campaigning saw pro-Arnold women coming out everywhere. One placard proclaiming 'Arnold can grope me any time' both misses the point about non-consensual sex and puts women back half a century. Predictably, Arnold sailed above it all, responsive only to adulation.

Underpinning Arnold-speak is the unabashed mantra: 'Look at me. I'm fantastic. Be like me. Be fantastic.' Cleverly, Arnold invited his viewer to coalesce into his voter. Positioned in this way, the actor and the politician blend and before you know it, they've become the one Arnold. Neat.

Then they voted. And he won. An outcome that perhaps reveals more about the constituency than the candidate.

Doing tolerance

The term that made multiculturalism happen, that built a nation, is the verb 'to tolerate'. An article by Andrew Stevenson (*Sydney Morning Herald* 11 January 2003) unpacks the ugly underbelly of 'tolerate' – the sense that it's a withdrawable privilege, that it has a certain one-wayness. Stevenson argues that it's time to move on. Yes!

Let's track the verbs strewn along the path of Australia's brave immigration experiment. We had (1) 'assimilate' (become a true-blue Aussie); then (2) 'integrate' (maintain your discrete identity within the jigsaw puzzle); then (3) 'tolerate' (extend human rights to other people); and now (4) 'accept' (acknowledge that difference, not sameness, is the norm).

Verbs 1 and 2 refer to what newcomers had to do in relation to whom they found here, while verbs 3 and 4 relate to what oldcomers have to do about new arrivals. The spotlight shifts: it was on newies, now it's on oldies. Notice, too, that verbs 1 and 2 are about the expectation of action, while verbs 3 and 4 are about the expectation of attitude. Further, while it was once expected that newies act in certain ways, for the oldies it's a matter of how to react.

Of course, the new/old categorisation is simplistic. A generation passes, newies become oldies. Or do they? Are they the 'middlies'? If we measure success by how quickly newies become oldies, what of our acceptance of difference? What of the phenomenon that some of the staunchest door-closers have been of migrant origin? Is this shut-the-door-behind-me a function of local conditions, or a larger universal?

I have a problem with passivity. When I 'tolerate', I put my xenophobic tendency on hold. I refrain from doing, rather than actively do. So, too, with 'accept'. It's a soft word that camouflages the hard work beneath the surface. 'Accept' is the last phase in the journey of facing death. No one could suggest that this leap is anything other than hard work. And you can't arrive until you've been through what comes before, none of it easy. Accepting otherness requires work from the acceptor. This work is the willingness to change – like reconciliation, which requires that White Australia make an active shift in its consciousness of Black history.

Some examples of the internal-shift kind of work: teaching basic functional Greek to the radiographers (rather than basic survival

English to the patients) in a Melbourne hospital whose patients are largely ageing, terminally ill, non-English-speaking Greek migrants. Or training customer service representatives on the police assistance phone line to understand accented telephone English and to speak more effectively to a stressed limited-English person, at the other end of the line. Or enabling people in gatekeeping positions to understand their own reactions to the different ways English is spoken.

Worldwide, more people speak non-native, rather than native, varieties of English. Global English, as a lingua franca, requires its speakers to have a more elastic definition of what English is. It's not that we can't make the shift to understand different accents (we do for Nelson Mandela and Nicole Kidman). It's only attitude that makes it harder with less prestigious varieties of accents.

In other words, the onus is on the listener, as well as the speaker. The light bulb has to *want* to change. This means oldies, too, have some learning to do. Mostly about themselves.

As a little girl, I stood with my mother in a shop queue. Two women in front of us were complaining about the uncharacteristically cold winter. One suggested, in all earnestness, that this came from allowing in people from 'northern' climates. My mother reached across and tapped the shoulder of one, and said softly in Polish-accented English: 'Look, I've got some leftover snow right here in my pocket.'

As a child-of-migrants, I cringed at my mother's audacity. As a newie-now-become-oldie, I'm proud of her own small efforts in the education of a nation.

Rainbow colours on the political spectrum

Colour has long been linked to politics. Think only of the white flag of surrender. But the political dimension of colour just intensified. On the eve of recent German elections, public talk was all about the likely composition of a coalition government. As different parties are associated with different colours, the talk was of various shades of a 'traffic light coalition'.

Then a television anchorman stole the show by referring to a possible 'Jamaican coalition'. A late-coming set of contenders comprised the Christian Democrats, led by Angela Merkel (identified by the colour black); the Free Democratic Party, led by then Chancellor Schroeder (yellow); and the environmental greens. This colour combination just happens to make up the Jamaican flag.

Colours, of course, are nothing new on the political stage. The French tricolour was born in the exhilaration of post-Bastille storming. The Italian tricolour was established during the Napoleonic Wars by French republics in northern Italy, who styled it after the French model.

If anyone doubts that symbolic power is jam-packed into colour, or that colour speaks a language without words, take a moment to think about red. The red–left link dates back to the 1848 liberalist revolutions across Europe. The culmination was the Russian Revolution, and, though Lenin, Stalin and Mao are long dead, it will take a bit longer for 'red' to shed them.

But red is not unilaterally left. For Garibaldi's Risorgimento movement, 'redshirts' were nationalist. Red has moved across the political spectrum to rightwing militarism, as in the Japanese Red Army. In the USA, the conservative Republicans are denoted in red on political maps, Democrats in blue.

Red infuses the culture and hence the language. It's linked with love, both romantic love (Valentine heart) and its carnal cousin ('redlight district'). It's the symbol of blood, hence the heart (red tick on heart-friendly foods), lineage ('blood') and bonds ('blood brothers'). It suggests strong emotion – 'seeing red' for provoked anger, 'redfaced' for embarrassment or shame, 'red-blooded' for vigour.

Red suggests heat (the colour on the hot tap). Red signals stop (traffic light) or warning ('code red'). In Christianity, red symbolises the presence of God and the blood of martyrs. Red is associated in mythology with war, the reddish planet Mars being named after the Roman god of war.

Given the power of colour as metaphor and given the catchy–quirky factor of the recently coined 'Jamaican coalition', some predictions are in order. More Jamaican-style coalitions are likely to be spawned, just as 'Watergate' led to 'Irangate' and later to 'nipplegate'.

Apparently, German media were quite carried away with the Caribbean connection, perhaps because its associated culture offers a respite from notorious Teutonic angst. Cartoonists went to town, drawing Ms Merkel with dreadlocks, and alluding expansively to reggae and marijuana. The Jamaican embassy issued a cautionary note to the German press to desist from trivialising the overt symbols of Jamaican culture, but back home in Jamaica the tourist industry saw only benefits flowing from their heightened public profile.

You can please some of the people some of the time.

INSPIRED BY BOOKS, FILMS AND MEDIA

Language is everywhere – so pervasive and ubiquitous that paradoxically it largely travels below the radar. And everywhere it achieves outcomes, some of which are contrived and planned, many of which are unplanned. Language comes out of our mouths, our pens and computers and phones. It also comes into our world via sound and written text. One step removed, perhaps, from our own immediate productive and receptive needs, is language that we're exposed to in textual representations. I'm thinking here primarily of the language we encounter in books, films and various forms of media. This chapter contains a collection of observations made about instances of particular language use as encountered in texts that are intended for the public domain, including films, book titles, television, advertisements, dictionaries, speeches and newspapers.

Judgements on a book's cover

My local second-hand bookstore, Books On Bronte (referring to the Sydney suburb not the writers), takes full advantage of its large front window. A rapid turnaround of titles makes for pleasant gazing on my morning or evening walks with the dog. Indeed, she has learned to stop and sit patiently while I peer at the display.

A recent example – there one morning, gone that evening – was *How to Succeed in Business Without a Penis*. The owner of the bookstore told me later that it was in the window barely a nanosecond before it was spied and snapped up.

Title-gazing certainly reinforces the power of a book's title. I'm not discounting the other para-texts – messages transmitted via colour, texture, size, smell, typographical choices, back blurb, etc. – all collaborators in the process of impression-management. But titles do it for me.

The truth is my own shelves are lined with books acquired for their titular allure alone. The day I bought the expensive hardback *Khrushchev's Shoe*, I wasn't looking for something on public speaking. But it resonated with my inner Baby Boomer – so clearly do I recall the shocked world on that day when, in the United Nations, Mr K took his shoe off and delivered his prediction (erroneous, as it turned out) that communism would bury capitalism (though, I've since been told by a Russian speaker, the text was poorly translated). No doubt, if not for that shoe, his rant would have disappeared down the drain of the forgettably ordinary.

Then there's *How to Visit America and Enjoy It*. I'm struck by the power of the 'and' – the implication is that visiting and not-enjoying America is the default position, but it's not obligatory. Subtext: buy me and find out how! A sobering lesson for a writer – never take an 'and' for granted. Published in 1964, this book emits a gravitational pull of nostalgia for a bygone world.

A title can teach you something you didn't know you didn't know; then make you want to know more. Such is Edmund White's *The Flâneur: A Stroll through the Paradoxes of Paris*. The back blurb tells me a *flâneur* is one who strolls about aimlessly, a lounger or a loafer (hence the type of shoe?). I tumble in love with the subtitle, partly for its alliterative 'p's, partly for the dissonance of warm-and-fuzzy (stroll) alongside hard-and-sharp (paradox). I've strolled in Paris but not contemplated the paradoxes. This book urges me to buy it, hop on a plane, and go stroll in said paradoxes – altogether well in excess of the price of the book. More reason, then, to buy it and live vicariously.

Some titles trick you by hopping inside your head, seeing the world momentarily through your eyes, and representing this emblematically in the title. This lends legitimacy to your ignorance while rewarding your curiosity, as with *Why a Painting is Like a Pizza* – a guide to modern art that allows you to find something ugly before you find it meaningful and that actively encourages you to interrogate the nature of art.

Others offer immediate comfort. I saw Bruno Bettelheim's *A Good Enough Parent* when in the throes of baby-raising and in that instant of 'phew!', gave myself permission not to be perfect. Amazing what a load is lifted when the expectations are lowered.

I'm convinced that Stanley Coren's *How to Talk Dog* was titled with me in mind (linguist with new puppy). It made me pick it up and then it walked me briskly to the cashier. It's an intelligent phrasebook – of Doggish, as distinct from doggerel – translating canine language into human terms. For example, a slow tail wag with tail at a moderate to low position means 'don't quite understand what's happening but I am trying hard to get the message'.

I'm so thingy about titles that I derive great pleasure simply from browsing through them in publisher's catalogues. I noticed one in the relatively new genre of poop-fiction: *So Grotty!* by J. A. Mawter, promising more than enough toilet humour to satisfy the apparently insatiable demand for same. At the other end of the seriousness continuum is the recent *Learning to Speak Alzheimer's* – a title more than replete with meaning and sadness.

Certainly mystery is a factor in making a browser pick up one book and not another. Consider: *The Unbearable Lightness of Being, Reading Lolita in Teheran, Miss Smilla's Feeling for Snow, In Cuba I was a German Shepherd, Fierce Invalids from Hot Climates* and *Leaning Towards Infinity*. The last, a friend tells me, apparently has nothing to do with leaning or infinity but has an entrancing nipple on the cover.

An irony about titular allure is that it too, like parenting, can be good enough. You can flâneur through a bookshop, bypass the book-as-text, and browse those titles unfettered by material constraints.

Disarticulate

It's not often that an evening at the movies sends me rushing home to consult a dictionary. *In the Cut* did just that. In this latter-day sisters' take on *Looking for Mr Goodbar*, Meg Ryan plays Frannie, a solitary and slightly loopy English teacher who goes around collecting words.

She gets dreamy-eyed at odd bits of poetry encountered on the insides of trains. She hoards random verbal droppings which end up Blu-Tacked onto the walls of her apartment. As wallpaper, these seem to offer a protective layer between her rather vulnerable self and the seedy, menacing world she inhabits. This world – more like an underbelly really – both attracts and repels our Frannie for reasons that are rooted deep within her biography and that remain ominously vague and shifty. All the better to scare you with, my child.

The central event is the brutal murder of a young woman whom we find out was 'disarticulated'. Now there's a word you don't often run into. Rendered mute (was my first thought) by the removal (I assumed, calling on my memories of phonology lectures) of the sound-producing mechanisms in the mouth and throat – vocal cords, larynx, tongue, hard and soft palate, lips. Rather nasty and rather over the top. I mean, the easiest way to render someone inarticulate is simply to kill them. Disarticulation seems like a perverse optional extra.

But I was wrong. As the story unfolds, I discover that disarticulation means a kind of dismemberment. Bits of the victim were found in the grassy area under Frannie's window. Strange, I thought, sitting there in the dark, suppressing the urge to rush home to my dictionary.

A few hours later, the urge was discharged. 'Articulation' has two senses. With one, there's a distinct language connection. This emerges in meanings like expressing oneself fluently (an articulate document), or speaking in a clear, distinct, well-enunciated way (an articulate voice).

A second, entirely different (and, as it happens, earlier) sense comes from zoology. As an intransitive verb (having no object after the verb) 'to articulate' means 'to be jointed', clearly derived from Latin *articulus*, a small joint. The transitive form (taking an object), 'to articulate something', where the said something is the thing being articulated, has the meaning of 'to separate into jointed segments'. This was thought-provoking. It's OK for chicken pieces intended for the evening curry (unless you happen to be the chicken, or a vegetarian). Less OK for randomly dispersed victim-bits.

It's at first glance unclear how the language meanings of 'articulate' relate to its Latin root *articulus*. As is often the way, the connection is a metaphoric leap away: the sense of dividing up vocal sounds into distinct and significant parts. It seems too that this enunciating sense of 'articulate' (1594) predates by about a century the later expressive meaning.

In the Cut is a clever psychological thriller that plays with the tension between attraction and repulsion. One side of Frannie's world, the lighter or upside, is the language sense of 'articulate'. It's Frannie's word-person side. Words are central to her identity: they fuel, nurture, identify and protect her. But the other side, the dark side, the downside, has the second meaning of 'articulate', the dismembering sense.

Frannie walks a risky path between the seedy and the noble. 'Articulate' becomes a metaphor for the tension between the delicate, ethereal world of her poetic imagination and the savagery of her actual life. (Things might improve if she'd just stop walking down dark alleys late at night.) The two sides of her world collide in the bar where she meets with her student to collect his new batch of words, and where she witnesses the first phase of the murder, and so becomes embroiled in the investigation. Frannie's world then begins to disarticulate, complicated by the red herrings that, of course, this genre dictates.

A strange thing about disarticulated is the prefix 'dis'. If 'articulated', in the transitive form, means 'separated into jointed segments' then we actually don't need the 'dis'. There's a small cluster of words like this, that duplicate unnecessarily. One rather reflexive example is the term 'reduplicative' for words like fuddy-duddy, hanky-panky, heebie-jeebies and mumbo jumbo. As 'duplicate' means to repeat the form, the prefix 're' is unnecessary. I've searched but haven't yet unearthed an explanation. Sometimes, illogically, we just repeat ourselves. Repeat ourselves.

Legal and orderly comfort

Docket No...The state versus...
   ...for the defendant.
   How do you plead?
   Not guilty, Your Honour.
   We apply for bail. The defendant has strong ties to the community.
   The People object, Your Honour. The defendant has committed a heinous crime. The man is a vicious predator and he poses a serious flight risk. The People oppose bail.
   Your Honour, the defendant has lived in the city for three years; he has a job to go back to after he's acquitted.
   Bail is set at...The defendant is released on his own recognisance. (Bang!) Next case.

In a world of chaos and uncertainty, few things offer more comfort than the arraignment text of Channel 10's courtroom drama *Law and Order*. The defendant always pleads 'not guilty'. The Defence always asks for bail. The grounds always cite 'strong ties to the community'. The Prosecutor always refers to the crime as 'heinous' – sometimes 'especially heinous' – and cites the defendant as 'a flight risk'. The tone of the Defence is always righteous indignation; that of the Prosecutor feigned shock, diluted by weary exasperation. The Judge, having heard it all before, is minimal, bored and itching for a recess.

The arraignment's appeal is its ultra-bald language. Step inside the courtroom and the rules that govern ordinary social intercourse have changed completely. Gone are all the niceties with which we typically adorn our words. Gone are the constraints that compel us to mitigate and hedge, defer and allay.

No one pleads 'kind of guilty'. The Prosecution has no qualms about denigrating the defendant. The Judge sets bail without apology or explanation, banging down that gavel with a frenzied force that in another place and time might be a guillotine.

Gone, too, is the imperative to orient towards harmony. New rules apply here. Perhaps because of the inherently adversarial structure of the court system, the issue of face – protecting one's own and that of others – is irrelevant. The Judge is the only exception, and even here it's not personal but rather a compulsory ritualised respect for the notion of Justice. It's not for nothing that His Honour wears robes and sits elevated above his fiefdom.

Disobey these rules at your peril. People are routinely threatened that they risk being charged with 'contempt' which at the very minimum includes temporary incarceration. But isn't 'contempt' a delightful term? Wouldn't you just love, in a regular domestic dispute, to cry out 'Contempt!' and call for the bailiff to escort the perpetrator-of-contempt out of your sight?

As well as 'contempt' and 'heinous', my other favourites are 'depraved indifference' and 'reckless disregard'. The first of these is where you fail your duty-of-care obligations and the second is where you choose to overlook the consequences of your actions. Or maybe it's vice versa. Not sure. Doesn't matter. These noun phrases roll off the Assistant District Attorney's tongue with studied, disdainful agility.

The defendant, apart from being allowed to voice the plea, is spoken of as if he were absent (forgive the male pronoun, but it rather goes with 'heinous crime'). Call him 'a vile predator' or 'a mass murderer'. No one flinches. Pussyfooting is out. Direct is in. 'Did you kill your wife? Yes or no?' Not 'Do you feel in some way that your actions might have led to the ultimate demise of your wife?'

The closest we get to indirectness, our conventional means of politeness, is, 'Are you aware of the penalty for perjury?' – itself barely a nano-step less direct than 'Are you lying?' No witness has ever replied, 'No I'm not. What is it?'

All of this contributes to the courtroom's quality of black-and-white, no-shades-of-grey. All told, it's a comforting cosmos – apart from the central heinous crime. Yet, heinous as it is, we know it's merely a vehicle for reinforcing a reassuring ideology – the things we want so much to believe in. That crime (mostly) doesn't pay. That the police (usually) get their wo/man. That baddies are distinguishable from goodies. That cops are (mostly) not on the take. That lawyers (well, at least those acting for the People) are driven by a core view of a moral society. That law offers justice and that justice is blind and fair. That the courts are efficient and effective. That the system works.

From crime scene to Rikers Prison in fifty-nine minutes, including ads. Seamless. Deluded, but comforting nonetheless. And so neat. You put the criminal behind bars. You put the plot to rest. And you put yourself to bed.

Outlander

Car advertisements. They're in a class of their own. Recently, thank goodness, we've moved beyond the genre of scantily clad females draped over bonnets in a crude equation of horsepower and lust. And onto something more, well, subtle.

Take the television advertisement for the Outlander. In an evocative tone, part nostalgic, part aspirational, the voice-over accompanies steel-grey scenes of a four-wheel drive in a solitary landscape:

To the outdated, the outmoded, to the out of touch, the out of step, the out of sorts, it's time to break out, to strike out, to go out on a limb, to get out of the rut and get outside, to the out of reach, and the out of sight, to outdo, to outmanoeuvre, to out-turn, outgun, outrun, outplay, outlast, to out now, outclass, to get out of the ordinary and into ... (*strategic pause*) ... the Outlander.

For a few reasons, this sentence is unconventional in the formal sense. There are the long strings of infinitive verb phrases, meant to be evocative and resonant. There's the way it starts out – directing itself to the addressee, as if attracting the attention of this specific consumer demographic – a poke in the ribs, a slight insult (who wants to be told they're outdated, outmoded, out of touch, out of step, out of sorts?), and then an invocation. It's time.

In the Australian context, there's not a Baby Boomer around who would miss that allusion to a mid-seventies' election slogan, even if it slips in subliminally. Even if you were/are not a Labor voter or a Gough Whitlam fan, 'it's time' will take you back to your younger self – when the future was where you faced, the past irrelevant, the stomach muscles firmer, the hair thicker. Those years that everyone tells you are the best in your life but you don't get it until they've passed.

And there are the bits that are missing, but implied and understood. Like the 'you' subsumed by the addressee: 'It's time (for you) to break out'...and get (yourself) into an Outlander.

While there's only one finite verb (the contracted 'is' of 'it's'), do notice the veritable oversupply of non-finites in the form of the infinitive – 'to break out, to strike out,...to get out'...I counted sixteen in total. Now the interesting thing about infinitives – philosophically speaking, grammar being but the face of philosophy – is that they are outside of conventional finite time. They're out there, up there, doing their own thing, unrestrained by the specific demands of a particular tense or moment or period in time, unsullied by the constraints of an earthly subject or object. Nothing muddy like the tyre of a 4WD.

Janis Joplin got it wrong. Freedom's not another word for nothing left to lose. It's another word for the infinitive. The plethora of infinitives is what gives the Outlander text its particularly aspirational timbre of...I don't wanna be here...I wanna be out there...free as a bird...free to be me...

Notice how first we're insulted (*to the outdated, outmoded*) and then we're tempted (*outdo, outrun, outclass*). But there's no gain without pain and the pain is the risk (*break out, strike out, go out on a limb*).

It's simple: this is who you are; that is who you could be; here's how.

Clearly the central motif is the notion of 'out' in the adverbial sense of a where-ness, a not-here-ness, an unknown terrain. 'Out' means a point beyond ('step out', 'reach out', 'out of focus'). It's upwardly mobile – there's a feeling of wanting more ('being out for something'). It's a striving towards a goal, the end point of anticipated action ('check it out', 'work it out'). Built into it is the sense of comparison and relativity ('the best car out').

But 'out' is risky too. There's the 'out' of withdrawal (the jury is out), rejection (that idea is out), malfunction (out of order), prohibition (drinking is out), error (the sum is out by), nerdiness (out of fashion), industrial trouble (out on strike), completion or depletion (run out of), exhaustion (out of it) and termination (over and out).

In summary, this sentence is less a sentence than a set of strung-together, bead-like syntactic fragments that simulate, *à la* stream of consciousness, a linear flow (a smooth-driving car?) of meaning particles. It's a mistake to look for organised precise meanings because the text defies the attempt. The bits elude you, leap out of your grasp, and all you're left with, at the end, is an emotion, a yearning…which doubtless is no accident, and which doubtless would be sublimely relieved by, you guessed it…owning an Outlander.

Unless

It's publishing's squillion-dollar question. What makes a book-browser become a book-buyer? What propels potential into actual?

Try watching browsers from afar. There's a pattern. The head tilts (so as better to read the spine). The hand reaches out (so as to dislodge the book from its snug shelf). The hand opens the book, flips through it, lingers here and there, turns it over.

Somewhere, the senses engage, taken in by colours, texture or smell (yes, smell). Or a mélange of these. The back blurb is often the clincher. Browser moves to cashier who assists in the act of parting with money.

Typically and paradoxically, but not accidentally, the back blurb both satisfies and seduces. You see, titles of fiction are designed to entrap. Unlike non-fiction (*The No-Garden Gardener*; *How to Make the World a Better Place*; *How to get a Ph.D.*; *Life in the Moslem East*), where titles are intentionally transparent. With fiction, the book-shop becomes a site of contestation – between the desire to walk away *with* the book, and the common-sense-trying-to-prevail desire of trying to walk away *from* the book. Oh what a difference a preposition makes!

In my case, as I've said earlier, it's the title. Therein lies my undoing. A recent purchase was *Missing*. Drops of moisture on the brow. I de-shelf and seek to know if this be the present participle acting as adjective with the noun understood and omitted – for example, missing (person). Or whether it's the present continuous tense of an understood verb, as in the soldier was missing (in action). And which meaning of the polysemous verb 'miss' is intended? Is it miss as in 'homesick'? Or as in 'unable to find'? Or as in 'take aim but not be on target'? Or as in 'be late for the train'?

Sales are surely boosted by the fact that titles are bound neither by copyright nor the usual constraints of sentence mechanics. 'Missing', for instance, can occur all alone in a discourse fragment:

Q: Where's the file for the last tax year?
A: Missing.

My most recent battle lost was *Unless*, by Carol Shields. Again, conquest by title. You don't have to be a linguist to know that 'unless' hardly ever occurs all on its ownsome. Being a conjunction (literally, join with), its mission in life is to connect one part of a sentence with another: Unless it's fine, I won't go to Opera in the Park. Unless you're a twin, you can't understand what it's like. Unless you're sure he's the one, don't marry him. Unless I get a raise, I can't afford this place.

In each case, we have 'unless' introducing a conditional clause that only makes sense when attached to the main clause. 'Unless' means something like '*if…not*'. In the above examples: If it's not fine, I won't go to Opera in the Park. If you're not a twin, you can't understand what it's like. If you're not sure he's the one, don't marry him. If I don't get a raise, I can't afford this place.

A solitary 'unless' is a rare thing. Its conjunctive role binds it, you might say commits it, to sentential relationships. Being a grammar word (like 'the', 'although', 'when'), its function is to help the sentence happen. By contrast, information words (like 'dog kennel') only need to be semantic.

'Unless', all alone, raises questions. We know there's a situation and an interconnected problematic condition. But apart from the relationship between these two, brokered by 'unless', we're in the dark.

Intriguing. Provocative. Seductive.

Duly captivated, I bought and read Shields's book. It led me to discover that its title is a perfect entrée into a delicate mental space, inside the narrator's head, which is the book's setting. Our narrator's sanity, equilibrium and well-being are, as it were, pitched on the edge of a cliff, at the mercy of random malevolent forces. I'm reminded of something I heard from my mother – parenthood is the willing taking on of a lifetime of vulnerability. Well, she didn't actually say that. She said that once you're a parent, you never stop worrying. A Swedish friend of mine puts it differently. When you give birth, you get a lump in your throat, and it never goes away.

Life, then, is rather like language. It's replete with isolated events that seem unconnected and sense-defying. For them to come together, to cohere sensibly, little chips of grammar are needed. Then the fragments relinquish their flotsam-and-jetsam quality and, at least temporarily, make some sense.

But what's it about? I hear you ask, irritated. What happens? How does it all end?

Unless you read it, you'll never know.

Expert language

Danny Katz, a.k.a The Modern Guru (advice columnist in the *Good Weekend* magazine), was asked if décolletage was appropriate at a funeral. He responded: 'I don't see how the public display of female cleavage could be inappropriate anywhere or any time or in any way. As far as I am concerned, cleavage is a fundamental aspect of life, so it should be a fundamental aspect of death, too.'

Granted, Katz prefaces his remarks with 'maybe it's just because I'm a man' and, clearly, his advice is a case of expertise being sacrificed on the altar of testosterone. His style cues the reader to his easygoing tongue-in-cheekery.

Katz has been set up as an expert in modern manners. His readers address letters to 'Dear Guru'. It raises the question of what we mean by expert. How, I wonder, did Katz acquire this expertise? Is he extraordinarily well mannered? Does he have a Master's degree in Etiquette?

Beyond the Katz question, what makes one an expert? Who decides? How are experts invested with authority? Can they be divested? How and by whom? What about those JIJOEs – the jet-in-jet-out experts, who, like rock stars, fly into town with prestigious imported know-how but precious little local (dare I say embedded?) knowledge. Where in the constellation of variables do the words 'lay' ('a lay opinion') or 'folk' ('a folk theory') fit in, and what about 'dilettante'?

The designation 'expert' contains something fascistically non-negotiable. Years ago, I left my car double-parked in an underground facility in a corporate building. I intended to be gone barely a minute (as you do). In my absence, a courier crashed into my car. Once he found me in the building, he proceeded to hold me legally responsible. My natural sense of guilt rose to the fore and agreed with him. A moment of serendipity had it that a lawyer happened to overhear and he intervened on my behalf. 'Shoosh!' he said to me, and turned to the courier: 'Her being illegally parked, if indeed she was, does not give you the right to crash into her car.' I was confused (the state of the non-expert) and said, unwisely: 'But surely it *is* my fault. I *was* double-parked.' To which the lawyer, frustrated, responded with a line that ended the discussion and has stayed with me ever since: 'I'm not going to argue the law with you, Ruth.'

It took a few years for the penny to drop. Expanded, his response might read: 'I know the law. You don't know the law. If you're asking me a question as a lawyer, then the answer I give you is not open to debate.' The tone had the surety of: 'Birds fly, fish swim.'

I'm not like that. When asked a question that calls on my expertise, I immediately move into teacher mode. I endeavour to contextualise, exemplify, clarify, apply all investments in my listener's comprehension. And while I'm thus launching forth, I'm reading the other's non-verbal cues, and adjusting my language accordingly, seeking a congruent fit.

While shopping one weekend, I ran into an old friend. He said: 'About that column you wrote, the one where you mention that your daughter was having lunch with an old friend. You mean "longstanding", don't you? After all, your daughter's too young to have an "old" friend, surely.' This was accompanied by a modicum of wink-and-nudge.

A number of thoughts went through my head. (1) 'Old' can mean grey and wrinkly, or not new, depending on context. (2) Meanings don't fall off the backs of trucks – they're embedded in the context of utterance. (3) Friendships between the young and the grey-and-wrinkly are not unthinkable nor out of the question.

But I didn't go into any of this. It was a hot day. I was in a hurry (yes, car double-parked again) and said: 'Look, John, I'm not going to argue linguistics with you.' It fell out of my mouth, a gem, a reformulation of that line from the lawyer years earlier. I figure the line must have been sitting there, just waiting for an opportunity to launch out into the world.

My friend, expecting a long-winded argument, seemed shocked at the brevity of my response. Deferring to my expertise, he pulled in the claws and invited me to lunch. Not a bad result, I thought. Must be something you learn at law school.

Speaker roles

I have a book on my shelves called *How to be a Better Speaker and Listener of English.* I forget where it came from. Maybe a *Reader's Digest* special offer, or a second-hand bookshop. Maybe it's a long-time loan from I-forget-whom. Its hyper-transparent title is as what-you-see-is-what-you-get as you could ever hope for. Half the book is cleanly devoted to speaking better; the other half, just as cleanly, to listening better. There are no hidden extras and no nasty surprises.

You might be forgiven for thinking that the roles of speaker and listener are distinct, discrete and separate. That rules and maxims separate and divide the two. That when you're a speaker, you're not a listener and when you're a listener, you're not a speaker.

But just think of any ordinary casual conversation, and the rapidity with which speaker and listener roles are taken on and given up. Such an instance of authentic interactive discourse reveals in a tick that speaking and listening are joined at the hip. It would seem, then, that to understand them, uncoupling them is the very worst thing you can do.

In any case, the unhelpfulness of separated roles is not the only hassle. In his seminal *Forms of Talk*, the sociolinguist Erring Goffman calls such classifications 'global folk categories'. This is a relatively polite way of saying ordinary intuition is sometimes misleading. Goffman posits that accepting the roles at superficial face value is unhelpful. Far better, he thinks, is decomposing them into smaller, analytically coherent elements.

Let's try doing that with the speaker's role. Take a regular, quite unremarkable, even platitudinous short conversation. Say two women, who are neighbours, encounter each other over full trolleys at the local supermarket. They stop briefly to chat. Here we might well say that the choice of words, their delivery and the responsibility for them are bundled together into, for each participant, the one speaking role.

Fair enough. Let's move to another speech event – this time a long way from the supermarket aisle. The US presidential spokesman is addressing a news conference at the White House, following rumours that war with Iraq is imminent. This is a simple enough scene, in terms of props, scripts and expectations, but when analysed through a Goffmanian frame of reference, the status of elements in the 'speaker bundle' unwinds into separate strands. This itself is a telling move.

The presidential spokesman is speaking to the press in a planned, non-spontaneous address. He stands at the lectern and reads a prepared statement. Out of his mouth, in his voice, come words that serve *qua* presidential message. It's the town crier writ modern. Into the spokesman-as-speaker, three sub-roles are collapsed. Of these, the spokesman himself is only, in Goffmanian terms, the 'animator' – that is, the conduit, the means of delivery, the vehicle by which the message is conveyed. Not unlike the evening television newsreader.

Most likely, President Bush himself did not write the statement. Presumably, he cast his eyes over it, but he's not its 'author'. It would have been drafted, redrafted, cut-and-pasted, conferenced, minder-ed and focus-group-tested by an intrepid team of speechwriters whose task is to find the right language to express the perceived-as-right sentiments for the attainment of maximum political advantage for the particular moment. In other words, spin. Margaret Thatcher is said to have found *Yes, Minister* amazingly realistic.

The presidential role, apropos the words spoken by the spokesman in Bush's name, is that of 'principal' – the third of Goffman's terms for the sub-roles of speaker. The principal is the one to whom the responsibility for the words falls – because that's where the buck supposedly stops. Of course, knowing what we do about the manufacture of evasion in high places, we can imagine that when the buck actually does come to a stop, it won't be a smooth, gentle halt, but rather a massive screeching of brakes, a mighty swerving around obstacles, and no short supply of smokescreening. Power of this magnitude seeks mostly to preserve itself.

Arguably, the charisma of a John Fitzgerald Kennedy inaugural speech, or a Robert Kennedy eulogy, derives from the seamlessness with which the three sub-roles of speaker blend and blur – the sense that animator, author and principal are one – even if, or especially if, they're not.

Dictionaries

I'm drowning in dictionaries. They line my walls, balance precariously on my desk, and stand in jagged, jutting piles.

Sometimes I sense them calling out to me in hushed tones. My back is turned, my hands are poised over the keyboard. Self-consciously they whisper among themselves, pointing at me, casting aspersions on my choices. Arrogantly, they are convinced that better ones, mine for the asking, lie within their covers.

Australians all once had a compact, dog-eared *Oxford English Dictionary* on the desk, a steadfast companion towards which we'd reach to check which 'stationery/ary' we wanted. Many of us grew up equating *Oxford* with truth. Now, in the marketplace of lexicography, such remarkable abundance prevails as would give Messrs Webster and Roget and company much cause to salivate.

There is a range of sizes from the hernia-producing tome to the concise, the compact, the gem and the pocket. I breathlessly await the 'thimble'. Where once the road bifurcated into British or American, Australians have their own *Macquarie Dictionary*, which gave unprecedented legitimacy to the Australian dialect. It was the *Macquarie* that moved my compact *Oxford* from its pedestalled position on my desk. (Love it though I do, I've never fully recovered from the experience of finding Tom Cruise in it.)

A newish subspecies is the 'school' or 'student' dictionary, designed to bring the average weight of a school bag to just under a tonne. The *Macquarie* has the *Australian Learners Dictionary*, its beauty lying in definitions pitched below the level of the keyword. This is no mean feat, but, for the learner, absolutely essential – what's the point of an explanation if it's too difficult to decipher? The illustrations, too, are helpful, though I wonder why, in the diagram of male and female bodies on page 83, the man is awarded a 'nipple' label but the woman is not.

There's even a sub-subspecies of learners' dictionaries, such as the *Longman Activator*, billed as 'the world's first production dictionary'. The speciality here is the focus on language we use when we want to express ourselves (in speaking or writing), as contrasted with language we use (in listening and reading) when we need to understand the texts produced by someone else.

Specialisations proliferate. Phonological dictionaries tell you about the sound side of language, probably far more than the average person ever needs or wants to know. Most standard dictionaries provide enough phonological information in their minimal coded guide to how the words are said, using the International Phonetic Alphabet, which is easier to apply than it seems. When my daughter recently laughed at my pronunciation of nauseous, I rushed to the dictionary to show her that both her version ('nor' as in Norway + 'shes' as in the second syllable of 'anxious') and my version ('norz' as in gnaws + 'ee-ous' as in the final two syllables of 'delirious') were acceptable. Her 'whatever' rejoinder was a good indicator of her interest level.

Perhaps the long-time favourite among word buffs is the etymological dictionary which provides the genetic lineage of a word; if you like, its DNA. More innovative and recent is the combinatory dictionary which tells you what goes with what. Does 'different' take 'from', 'to' or 'than'? Does one protest 'about' or 'over' or 'at' or none of the above? Given the unstable state of rogue prepositions, I predict combinatory guidance to be a niche market for the future.

There are dictionaries devoted to cliché, idiom, metaphor, phrasal verbs, foreign expressions, slang, colloquialisms, Biblical allusion, mythological references, symbols, eponyms, classical roots – just for starters. One, *Ologies and Isms*, goes even smaller than the word – focusing on the level of the morpheme, the smallest unit of word meaning – specifically, in this case, dedicated to beginning and end bits.

There are reverse dictionaries (work these do how?) and dictionaries for crossword and scrabble aficionados. One of these is *Word Menu*, whose words are organised according to subject matter. So under 'love and romance' are 'liaison', 'liberties', 'necking', 'ogling', 'one-night stand' and 'osculation', listed alphabetically, with a somewhat refreshingly absent comment on appropriateness.

Word Finder was written by a man who grew sick of his kids saying: 'How can I look it up if I can't spell it?' The *Describer's Dictionary* is designed for people looking for the precise term for, say, living along a river, for which no standard dictionary or thesaurus is helpful.

Dictionaries ignite extreme passions. The granddaddy of English dictionary-makers, Samuel Johnson, pronounced rather unhappily on the lexicographer's task in his own *Dictionary*, suspecting his endeavours were under-appreciated: '*Lexicographer*. A writer of dictionaries, a harmless drudge'. Ambrose Bierce, the writer of *The Devil's Dictionary*, famously said a dictionary was 'a malevolent device for cramping the growth of the language'.

Eric Partridge in *The Gentle Art of Lexicography* quotes an elderly lady who returned a borrowed dictionary to the library with the comment: 'A very unusual book indeed, but the stories are extremely short, aren't they?'

The new slow

Last year I bought a book because of its cover. It was *How To Be Idle*, by Tom Hodgkinson. The front has an old-fashioned drawing of a man lounging under a tree, head on pillow, legs on tree trunk, book open in lap. The inside front cover blurb says: 'The key to a life of pleasure, freedom and guilt-free lounging around is in your hands.'

I remember thinking that 'in your hands' was a nice symmetry of the literal and metaphorical.

The inside front cover was as far as I got. No time. Ironic, really. I need to read *How To Be Idle* in order to be idle enough to read *How To Be Idle*.

I was reminded of all this recently when someone asked me, apropos of something entirely different, whether I thought the 'idle' in 'idle chat' had any purpose or whether purpose was automatically excluded by the notion contained in 'idle'.

Interesting thought. Not surprisingly, in a work-obsessed world, idle comes up negative nearly every time. Its closest companions are 'lazy' and 'shiftless'. It's mostly frowned on, like poor hygiene, nose-picking or lateness. 'The two carpenters idled the afternoon away.' Or proverbially, 'The devil finds work for idle hands.' An engine that idles is out of gear, going nowhere. I've heard of teachers saying their students are 'idling'.

Mostly, idle implies the idler should be working. But there's another idle that's an alternative to fast and frenetic. 'Slow' is having a renaissance. It's the new, eco-gastronomic way to eat, as well as to travel, live, love and learn. It's process over product, journey over destination, less over more, small over big, present over future. One day it might even constitute praise on a report card. Finally, a small subset of pulsating humanity is realising that life is not a race. First one to get to the end is – well, dead.

Hodgkinson's book isn't alone. There's *In Praise of Slow* by Carl Honore, who realised he had a problem when he found himself attracted to buying a book called *The One-Minute Bedtime Story*. And another title is *Slow Living* by two members of the global Slow Food society, Wendy Parkins and Geoffrey Craig.

These aren't how-to manuals for the speed-obsessed, but rather contemplations of the life we lead, the decisions we make and the options we have. Hurry up and have a look, before it's too late.

GENDER

The sections in this chapter share a preoccupation with matters of gender. By gender I don't mean the grammatical device by which the notions of masculine, feminine, impersonal or neuter are realised and conveyed linguistically, though this of itself is fascinating. Nor am I concerned with the biological notion of gender which differentiates living organisms on the basis of their reproductive roles. Rather, the notion of gender underpinning the pieces in this chapter has to do with the social construction of masculine and feminine identities. Given the importance of language in society, it is hardly surprising that socially constructed gender will have linguistic accompaniments. Granted, gender and language bring us to a rather murky place, where the tensions and contestations that accompany much of what is called 'gender politics' jostle and compete, and will probably continue to, so long as the ranks of the powerful are bastions of male privilege. As things stand, both historically and presently, one side writes the rules in its own image, and as long as this is so, language both reflects the effort and shapes the reality.

Lazy poet

An advertisement for a tiny mobile phone on the back of taxis. Full groinal frontal. Be-tighted male ballet dancer, crown jewels compactly grouped into an explicit, eye-catching bulge. Accompanying message – 'a helluva lot in a very small space' – applies to both commodities: tiny phone/groinal bulk. OK. Sex sells. We knew that.

Perversity aside, there's the sheer economy of words. One phrase fits two unconnected phenomena. Groins and mobile phones had little in common before this. Poetry's like that too. Amazing condensation of meaning into minimum space. Saying little, meaning much.

Another genre with a deft, tense interplay of precision and inference is the personal advertisement. Columns perimetered by various sexual orientations, but linguistically alike. Little verbal gems offering the thrill of inferencing.

Here's a man-seeking-woman example:

Lazy poet, 50 and handsome. Smiling blue eyes. The heart of a child. Passionate, earthy, Jewish, Scorpio, intellectual. Smokes, drinks. Loves food, arthouse movies and Bridge. Offering and seeking love and commitment and fidelity. Age and nationality open.

Clearly, the meaning of words resides only partly in dictionaries. Their richness is in the pragmatic space between what is said and what is meant. In this space, loose and unanchored, float notions like shared experience of the word/world, cultural understandings, connotations and associations – a well of possibilities from which one draws to infer and construct meaning.

So what can we know of this lazy poet? Certainly, that nothing here is accidental. The hours spent on his thirty-eight words was an investment in impression management. Ironically, the degree of angst is likely inversely related to the surface quality of laid-backness.

Choices galore! Which words, which order? Which to exclude. It's the fish John West rejects that makes John West the best. If 'handsome' is the winner, who were the contenders? – 'attractive'? 'spunky'? Why were they rejected? If 'handsome' is to fifty what 'spunky' is to twenty-five, then we have more than two bits of information; we have consonance, which is itself a message.

This 'lazy poet, 50' can afford to write poetry. No sign of mortgage woes. How many poets are on a living wage? Our man wants us to infer an independent means. Comfort that allows him to be a poet.

Not just a poet. A *lazy* poet. And not really a poet – a dilettante – because he needs to name himself thus.

He seems comfortably upfront with his age – until we reach 'the heart of a child'. No doubt this is to suggest the magical (that is, impossible) combination of maturity and innocence. So far, I see a self-conscious bohemian type masking emotional neediness under a cool, layabout façade. But hey, I could be wrong.

Nothing's accidental. Note the 'and handsome'. Prominence goes to his indolent wealth while his appearance is an afterthought, thrown in carelessly. A sweater flung belatedly over the shoulders. Here's a man who needs to tell us that he's handsome but wants us to believe his looks don't matter. The casual, natural wet look he spent hours creating.

Moving along, we drift from an adjectival heaviness – lazy, handsome, smiling, blue, passionate, earthy, Jewish – to a brief central verbiness, where acts of consumption are clothed as verbs (smokes, drinks); and then ease out with the concrete nouniness of 'loves food, arthouse movies and Bridge'.

Verbs are more honest than adjectives, which may or may not be verifiable (more on that later), while nouns are the least honourable grammatical class of all. But even our honest verbs are over quickly and then buried. No accident that we exit with warm, gooey. masterstroke abstract nouns – love, commitment. By the time we reach 'fidelity', he wants us to have forgotten that he smells like an ashtray and is home for lunch.

Choice of adjective corroborates the hint of deception. There are few descriptive adjectives where meanings are objectively verifiable (tall is not short; a Sydney man is not from Newcastle). So our poet has verifiably blue eyes and is verifiably Scorpian. But what motive 'Jewish'? To appear upfront? To pre-empt nasty surprises down the track? To indirectly seek a Jewish mate? What then of the open membership categories ('age and nationality open')? Anyway, what does 'open' mean?

'*Smiling* blue eyes' – now that's another story. A pre-ponderance of evaluative adjectives – passionate, earthy, intellectual – tells us

non-verifiable facts about the world, but also what people feel/
think – largely, here, what he wants a female reader to feel/think.
So 'smiling' tells us more than 'blue'.

At last, there's 'offering and seeking'. A consummate choice. The
offer comes before the seek, suggesting a wanting-to-give before a
desire-to-take. An endearing, developed feminine side, oh-so-rare.
The two acts (offer/seek), joined by 'and' suggest... an equality, balance, reciprocity, mutuality, even the ebb and flow of the ocean, if
that's what you fancy.

If I hadn't been warned off by those giveaway abstract nouns (love,
commitment, fidelity), I'd surely have been snared.

Boobs

'My husband shot me but my size 38D-cup boob saved me.'

I'm not sure whether it was the intriguing notion of breast *qua*
saviour that made me buy the magazine. Certainly, that sentence
on the front cover – elliptical, ambiguous and decontextualised –
was a contributing factor. I reluctantly confess to habitual magazine
purchases triggered by front-cover bait, a habit untouched by years
of critical literacy and media savviness.

The cover story was of course a let-down. There was no tragic
incident of domestic violence, as intimated. Rather, an accidental
rifle-shooting, leaving hubby just as contrite as wifey was sore. And
as for the salvational qualities of the breast, it turns out said wife
was shot by said husband in the chest, but the passage of said
bullet was stymied (cushioned?) by the plenitude of fleshy terrain.
Size apparently does matter, at least when your husband's shooting
you.

Notice please the woman refers to the item in question as a 'boob'.
This is consistent with research that indicates that women's preferred term, when in the company of other women, is boobs or tits.
Yet can the front cover of a magazine be interpreted as 'in the company of other women'? I would have thought not. Rather, I'd see it

as hanging it all out there, in the public domain. But there you go – linguistics is not an exact science.

Around the same time, *The Sydney Morning Herald* published a front-page colour picture of an autumn thunderstorm, photographed at sunset. The clouds in the photo resemble a bunch of nude, full-breasted, curvaceous, roly-poly women who many of us wish would rollick back into fashion, and quickly. The caption read: 'Evening glory... weather watchers call these clouds "mammatus" because they resemble breasts.'

The nearest we get to 'mammatus' in the *OED* is *mammato* – in meteorological terms, descriptive of clouds resembling rounded festoons'. This is the first time I was aware that weather people have names for cloud-types. But just as Eskimos have their snows and Bedouins their sands, all that cloud people want is equity. And you can understand why you'd reach for the Latin term (in preference to, say, 'breasty'). After all, the classics are always a noble choice if you're wanting *gravitas* or elevation of any kind.

So two left-field references to breasts in the same week, and both avoid the actual word. I took this as a sign to investigate further. The first snippet of information that came my way was the fact that many languages, and unrelated languages at that, tend to have a word for 'mother' that has a nasal first consonant (*naan, ng, mama, ima, mère, amaa*). Earth-shattering, this isn't – thousands before me have noticed and commented upon the congruence between Mum (the person) and mam (the gland).

A second entirely predictable finding is that appropriate selection of terminology (boob, tit, bosom, bust, hooters) depends on who's speaking to whom and for what purpose. No surprises there. Clearly, the descriptor for the mammogram's flattened fillet of schnitzel will differ widely from the language of the lingerie department, or that of an anatomy lecture, the romantic weekend interlude, the police report and the wet-and-leaky context of lactation. OK, I won't go there.

And, of course, the language that males use is chiefly determined by the composition of the company present. In fact, the range of words available in male-only company bespeaks obsession. Most of their words are very overtly appreciative. Some words reveal (as if it weren't already known) that size and visibility do matter (bazookas, bazoomas, balloons, knockers, melons). But so does functionality (jugs, love pillows, mams), as well as aesthetics and sensual anticipation (amazing, delicious, sensational). A man I know, who calls himself a boob man, exclaims, 'Gosh, if I had boobs, I'd stay home all day and play with them.'

Women, by contrast, seem to have an altogether more pragmatic perspective on their own bullet-stopping appendages.

Mum's the word

Did you wince when Australian cricketer Shane Warne, in trouble yet again for one thing or another, turned around and blamed his mother? Did you get the feeling that this is his knee-jerk reaction – to blame mum? Didn't she, at that moment, become Every Mum?

It's ambivalent, the attitude we have to mothers. We celebrate them on Their Day with perfume, flowers, chocolates and kitchen appliances. If no one buys Mum a new printer, it's because printers contribute little to society's notion of who mothers are.

Look up 'mother' in the dictionary and the complexity of our relationship with our mothers is laid bare.

At the literal level, we have the biological mother or carer. She gives birth, raises, protects, adopts: mother love, motherly, mother's care, birth mother, adoptive mother. This 'mother', the source of all nurture, takes a capital M, if not on the page, then in our heart.

It's old hat but it remains significant to note that 'to mother' means to care for, while its counterpart, 'to father', means to sire or spawn. Test it. Can you 'mother' without being the biological female parent? Certainly. Can you 'father' without being the biological male parent? Not really. You can mother, but not father, someone else's child. The degree to which the language is resistant is a measure of the culture's intransigence.

Then there are the 'mother' words with a metaphorical connection. Here the idea is progenitor, origin or source: 'mother tongue' (first language), 'mother earth' (the soil or nature), 'motherland' (patriotic home), 'motherboard' (from IT-speak), 'mother of pearl' (jewellery), even 'mother of all battles' (thank you, Saddam). 'Mother wit' (common sense) says it all. Add Christian imagery: 'Mother of God', 'Mother Church', 'Mother Superior'. Interestingly, in Aboriginal English, I'm told, 'mother' refers as much to the biological mother's sisters as to the mother herself. A reminder, sorely needed in the West, that it takes a whole village to raise a child.

But there's a semantic underbelly to the word 'mother'. Here we begin to touch on the ambivalence contained in the word and the implied relationship. Take 'stepmother' for instance. This one is so rooted in myth and prejudice (think Hansel and Gretel) that even a Julia Roberts movie (*Step Mom*) couldn't shift it.

Certainly, stepmothers across the world could mount a class action against Hans Christian Andersen, the Brothers Grimm and suchlike, for the deeply entrenched and widespread malignment they have known. Stepmothers in the oral tradition of storytelling are almost without exception evil incarnate – unrelentingly cunning, cruel and known for stepping over bodies, often children's bodies, to get what they want. They are to society what the Jew is to the anti-Semite: a stereotyped one-dimensional caricature, a whipping boy.

Stepmothers are not alone. A different kind of abuse – mockery – is reserved for mothers-in-law. Sitcoms and joke books are replete with the mal-intentioned, interfering, dominating mother-in-law (consider Raymond and Robert's mother in *Everybody Loves Raymond*), a construct that spreads across cultures (Japanese, Italian, Jewish, for example). You wonder why it is that fathers-in-law generally escape the opprobrium meted out to mothers-in-law.

'Escape' may be the key word. What if mothers had an escape? What if there was a shed out back, or a room of one's own, from where the baby's crying could not be heard – would things be different? The kitchen is no shed-equivalent – that's where every-one congregates and anyway, they'll soon want feeding.

'Mother's ruin' means gin. With 'motherfucking' you curse some-one via their mother. A touch of the old Shane Warnes. It's the same logic that fuelled 'son of a bitch': blame the mother.

There's 'mummy's boy' for the overly attached son. Is there an insult for overattachment to daddy? A step away is the enforced rosiness of the infantilised world of Mother Goose and Mother Hubbard – that collectivity of female nursery rhyme characters who remain overweight, overburdened and overjolly.

There's 'mothercraft' – which reduces wisdom to a quantifiable competency, like a vocational diploma. 'Fathercraft' is closer to hov-ercraft than to home and baby. And the phrase 'I'll be mother', spoken by a male leaping up to pour the tea, gently parodies the carer's service role.

A 'motherhood statement' is one unquestionably worthy of sup-port, unarguably meritorious and praiseworthy. But even this deni-grates as it slides towards the platitudinous. Saying, in effect, 'Sure, we know mothers are wonderful. Now let's move on.'

Meanwhile, it takes a lifetime to get over losing your mother. By which time it's another generation's turn to find out.

The gate

The front gate is falling apart. Architect-designed, masterbuilder-built, Japanese-inspired. It's had it. It has dropped, it is rickety, the hinges wobble, random bits are dropping off.

The problem, I've discovered, is in the language.

I was telling a colleague the other day, as I showed him out after a day's hard work together. I said: 'Look at my bloody gate.' He looked and I continued: 'It's only a few years old and it's already on its last legs. I ask you, how this can be? My house is 120 years old and it's fine, still going strong. Why then can't a modern-day gate be built with the wherewithal to endure?'

It was a rhetorical question but he replied: 'You know what the problem is?' matching me with his own rhetorical question. I shook my head as I was meant to do. 'It's the language.' I was mystified – as you probably were a moment ago – and paused for him to continue. He did: 'It's the language of the brief. Your brief. What you told the builder. (*pause*) I can just imagine what you said. This is what you *should* have said:

'Make this gate last one hundred years. I want you to totally over-engineer it. And if it should ever fall apart – I'll hunt you down and kill you like the dog that you are.'

The barefaced extremism of the utterance knocked the wind out of me. Is that how they talk on Mars? Of course, it was nothing like what I'd said to the gate-builder – or any other builder, past or future.

I doubt I'm alone here. Few women have such hyper-transactional language as a default style. It doesn't come with oestrogen, I suspect. Now I'm trying to remember what the words were that I used with the builder. It's three years ago so that's a big stretch. All I can do is imagine the kind of exchange I would typically have in a similar circumstance.

I probably started off by asking him whether he'd like a tea or coffee. And then I would have asked him what kind of gate he himself had in mind. Following more chat about *my* ideal gate, I would have assumed that the picture of my prospective gate that was currently inside my head was visible to him, and that he would have the ability to translate that image into a three-dimensional reality, in a *voilà!* kind of way – and in the end the object he created would be a thing of great beauty and stamina. People walking by in the street would stop and gaze and say, 'Look at the workmanship in that magnificent gate. It will surely last forever.'

The builder, meanwhile, would've taken up the offer of a beverage while thinking to himself: 'Easy-peasy, she's got no idea what she wants, she'll be happy with whatever, coupla days, money in hand, Imoutahere.'

Well, 'not happy, Jan'. Yes, I acknowledge my brief was faulty. But I don't speak hardwarese. I know this because I rarely have an easy time of it in builders' supplies stores. They're ovary-free zones. I always think: 'Have I missed a gents' sign on the entrance?'

Builder Man (BM) is gruffly monosyllabic, with a facial and corporeal stance that says, 'Why-oh-why do they let women in here?' When he sees me, he seems to suppress his inner groan and figures instead that it's time to practise his questions.

RW: Hello, I'd like a – please.

BM: Would you like a – one or a – one?

RW: Gosh, I don't know. Um.

BM: Well, is it for a – or a –?

RW: What's the difference between those two?

BM: Well, a – one has a – while the – one has a –.

RW: Ohhh. Right. So which one do I need?

BM: Well, I can't tell you that until you let on whether it's a – or a –.

RW: But that's at home and I'm here. Can't you give me a bit of a hint.

BM: (*Shrug, slight shake of head, loss of eye contact.*)

RW: (*Travelling in circles. Déjà vu. Sigh. Exit.*)

Recently, I noticed Builder Woman (BW) working there. Smiley face, she looked like she was coping, despite the testosterone-charged milieu. I figured it was a gender thing – she's been hired to attract and attend to female customers.

I fantasise dreamily about future conversations with her:

RW: Hello, I'd like a – please.

BW: Hi there, Ruth. Yes, sure. Here we are. That'll be $ –. On special today. Would you like one of the lads to help you take it to the car?

RW: OK, that'd be great. Thanks. Bye.

La-la land? Probably.

Despondent, I walk home. The gate shudders as I pass through it. I mutter the words: 'I'll hunt you down like the dog that you are.' Somehow they don't have the same timbre.

Clinton at Oxford

It's not easy being the President of the USA. It's even harder being the ex-President. After all, what's an ex-President to do with his time? Apart from memoir-writing and the speakers' circuit, the opportunities for gainful employment are thin on the ground. This may explain, in part, the appeal of the Chancellorship of Oxford College for Bill Clinton.

First though, Clinton has to be offered the job. Not so easy. First hurdle: matters of his reputation for sexual promiscuity will be publicly raked over. This of itself has set off a new spate of Clinton jokes and resurrected a few oldies. (Like the one about Billary on the plane to Geneva. Hills is waxing lyrical about all the great things to do in Switzerland – great mountains, cheese and chocolates. Bill disembarks and asks, 'Where's Heidi?')

So effectively does his reputation for Oval Office Fellatio precede him, that one wonders why Clinton would bother with Oxford. Yet if he's less a predator than an exhibitionist, all the talk about moral depravity might thrill rather than inhibit him.

More interesting is what the public debate enveloping Oxford reveals about attitudes to women. At one end, Dean Cato worries about the safety of women and is, depending on your perspective, protective, pastoral or downright patriarchal. At the other extreme, Phil Hensher, of *The Independent*, is pro-Clinton, if only for the expected flow-on of moneyed panache. He dismisses the danger-to-women argument by claiming that Clinton is not predatory, apparently, because he doesn't need to be ('I bet he turns it down all day long').

But it's Hensher's next remark that warrants even greater analysis. He writes:

Having the most celebrated shagger in the Western world at the head of the university would bring considerable vicarious pleasure to the lives of the university's women, a conspicuously unenjoyed lot.

This is an odd way to describe a group of women. And in linguistic terms, 'odd' is a telltale sign: something is lurking below.

Structurally, a past participle (enjoyed) is reduced from a hypothetical relative clause (who have been enjoyed), converted into a negative verb (unenjoy), reshaped into an adjective (unenjoyed) and transposed to the attributive position (pre-noun), creating 'a[n] ... unenjoyed lot'.

Now the process of transposing a past participle into an attributive adjective is a common one in English:

The boy who got lost – *lost boy*
The sausage that was barbecued – *barbecued sausage*
The dog that was hurt in the accident – *hurt dog*
The exam that was failed – *failed exam*
The snow that was not touched – *untouched snow*
The bra that was unhooked – *unhooked bra*
The women who have not been enjoyed – *unenjoyed women*

Still, 'unenjoyed women' is odd. First, it suggests that not only is it women's role to provide enjoyment to men, but also that their own enjoyment resides in this very provision. Having failed in this task, all that's left to the Oxford women is bottom-of-the-barrel scrapings of vicarious pleasures. They ought to lower their standards. They ought to be grateful for what they can get. Take it away, Bill.

Second, the attributive adjective position is often an indicator of transient states. Once the boy is found, he's a lost boy no longer. The barbecued sausage soon becomes the eaten sausage. Untouched snow won't long remain virginal. But this quality of transience doesn't apply to Oxford women. They're hardly on the cusp of becoming a raunchy lot. The gleeful forecast of rubbing shoulders with the great shagger is at best metaphorical.

Third, the verb 'enjoy' is not conventionally reversed into a negative – you don't, for example, unenjoy a film. The coinage allows Hensher to bury his primary complaint (Oxford women's lack of sexual spark) under the implication that the women themselves failed to derive much enjoyment. I suspect that Hensher himself is not 'turning it down all day long'.

Finally, being 'unenjoyed' alongside the intensifying adjective 'conspicuously' is a heavy-handed hint that the failure to enjoy, as well as be enjoyed, is located in the women's appearance. While the shagger himself is celebrated, the women remaining unshagged are dismissed contemptuously. The implication of non-shagging women is not that this is their choice, but that this is their lot.

The long and the short of it: Heidis of Oxford, look out! You have more to lose than your enjoyment.

Love and text

In the play *Cyrano de Bergerac* (more lately adapted for film as *Roxanne*), the lovesick suitor woos the object of his desires indirectly and from afar. The wooing device is the letter, beautifully crafted to achieve the intended romantic effect. At the centre of this comedy of errors is the written word whose role is to spark sexual chemistry and lubricate the potential in a relationship.

Now fast forward to dating via SMS messaging. Here again we find a central role for language – this time in a play of five acts.

Act 1. Girl meets guy at pub. She's seen him before, on the periphery of acquaintances. It's brief. They chat. Mild flirting. Some chemistry. As she leaves, he hands her his business card. Eye contact sustained a nanosecond beyond comfort. In a low voice, with a slightly upward inflection, he invites her to call him 'some time'. That night, she examines the business card, its size in inverse proportion to the number of communication options displayed. Home phone, fax, work phone (*gen.*), work (*pers.*), email. And of course, the trusty mobile. (Are we so afraid of abandonment that we need umpteen avenues of communication?)

Act 2. Next day, a quick email. Friendly. Not too chatty. 'Hey Joel. How ya doing? Was great to see you. It'd be fun to hang out some time.' Messaging is minimal, spare, cool, promises a lot, says little. She adds her mobile number. No way would she leave her home number. Unstated rule: communication has to be direct. Principals only. No agents. Rule out intermediaries – siblings, flatmates. Definitely no parents.

Act 3. He emails back, confirming first contact. Momentum picks up. 'Great to see you too. Would be awesome to hang out/chill. If you're around the city, let's go for a coffee ...I'll have my fix anyways, but it would be good to catch up...' This is comfortable. There's scope to be friendly, flirtatious, show some personality. But it's still cool (he doesn't need her for his fix).

Then some to-ing and fro-ing. More scope to be funny, clever, laidback. Leaves for dead the nervous 'yeah, awesome' of phone calls. Text, like email, allows rehearsal of spontaneity. Neglectful elegance requires some effort.

Signing off is iconic. First names move to abbreviations – 'Penny' to 'Pen', to 'pen', to 'p'. 'Ciao, Jo' to 'ciao', to 'me'. None of this is accidental. It's metaphoric foreplay. Each step is a strategic, proactive move, lost on no one. The gentle momentum towards informality suggests a closeness which, ironically, is achieved as it is being assumed. Language shapes, not just reflects.

Act 4. She messages him. Now she knows her number's in his phone, and she knows he knows she knows. 'Lattes tmrw sounds good msg me lata.' The reply is fast: 'Make it double caps – spk soon.' The nano-format of SMS means parties feel a closeness that is unsullied by the mundane 'How was your day?' (Who cares about your day?)

Act 5. He messages her: 'Bad day at work ...save me.' At last – she's got topic + opportunity. She calls: 'What's up?' He explains, and asks what's she doing the next day. The ice is broken.

Phone is easy now. There's a pre-existing connection to call on, a history, a veritable bank of text messages, saved in memory. After this, face to face will be easy. Familiarity has promise. Intimacy looms.

Cool is to SMS as floral was to Cyrano. But it's delicate, achieving the requisite coolth (the state of being cool) while also showing you're interested. Not coming on too soon, too fast or too hot, but still coming. You have to know that your advances will be welcomed but until such moment as you do, there's much face to be lost. With each contact you move closer to the brink of that awkward precipitous point of no return. It's a slippery slope, each step offering a decreasing capacity for retreatability. The collision of goals is a constant possibility.

Ironically, the nano-straitjacket of text messages is well suited to the demonstration of coolth (think how nerdy it would look to key in a complete paragraph), and just as Cyrano discovered, words certainly have the power to sway hearts.

All that's missing is the David Attenborough commentary.

Shrew

Imagine that, instead of talking to human celebrities on his *This Is Your Life* TV show, the compere, Ralph Edwards, might one day, just for a change, have spoken to a word instead. Yes, a word.

Imagine him now, holding his red album of clippings across his body, an endearing expression on his smiling face, addressing himself to his celebrity word, as well as to his audience – a deft management of participants that is no easy feat.

Let's imagine the text of the address to the word 'shrew'.

Good evening, Shrew! You begin life as the name for a rodent and later, with the passing of time, you gradually develop monstrous metaphorical extensions, which build on the malignancy associated with rats. Poor hygiene habits among crowded unsanitary living arrangements as well as the odd plague help considerably with these developments. You continue your career by moving into a new area where you develop a satanic sense of evil. At this time you still only apply to males. But as your semantics continue to degenerate, you find, by the early thirteenth century, that you have begun to feminise. The poet Geoffrey Chaucer, for example, mentions you in his *Prologue to the Canterbury Tales*, using you the way we today might say 'bitch' in anger. And then, really before you know it, your use has narrowed quite significantly, so that you start to be applicable only to females. Shrew, congratulations! This is your life!

As we listen to the narrative of shrew's development, we notice the pattern of stigma plus specificity tending to travel together, or at least in neighbouring carriages. Our shrew, for instance, travelled widely through the centuries until eventually it came to be used very negatively and be narrowly applied to women only, and that's when it acquired its stigma. Even being semi-archaic, its meaning is clear. It's an unashamed dysphemism, which as the opposite of a euphemism is an in-your-face kind of word that calls a spade a shovel.

'Shrew' is not alone as a specific stigmatised word for woman, as any dictionary of 'woman words' will immediately attest. A 'hag' was once an evil spirit in female form. A 'harpy' was part-woman, part-bird, filthy and rapacious. A 'siren' was originally an imaginary kind of serpent, which evolved to part-woman, part-bird status – rather mermaid-ish in fact, but with evil, seductive intentions towards men. 'Harridan', derived from a French word for an old horse, developed the English meaning of a haggard, vixen-like woman.

In case you think these old-women words have had their day, consider a line in the strange movie *The Truth About Charlie* – a weird, postmodern hybrid genre of whodunnit meets spy thriller meets romantic comedy. At a pivotal moment, the villain (who earlier was the hero-*cum*-saviour) says to the young woman: 'I was expecting a siren, a harpy, a shrew but you have (*pause*) decency, (*pause*) dignity ...'

The pattern continues. The *Collins Australian Dictionary* lists 'bunny burner', a term for a psychologically unstable woman who stalks her male victim. The term originates with the pet rabbit boiling in the 1987 sexual politics thriller *Fatal Attraction*.

With euphemisms, the same rule applies (see also pages 39–41). Semantic narrowing goes hand in hand with encroaching stigmas. Take the subject of death, which is one of those unpleasant topics we'd notoriously rather avoid than confront. Given such a cultural mindset, when we do have to face it, we're supported by an armoury of words that help us take the edge off all the unpleasantness. But because stigma travels faster than word change, the euphemism sooner or later (usually sooner) runs out of puff. So Stigma's stealth and stamina become Euphemism's limited shelf life.

Soon our pleasant word has become contaminated and has shed its pleasantness. The word 'undertaker' once had a much wider, more generalised meaning – one who undertakes some action – but as it became euphemistically associated with funerals and death, its semantic range narrowed accordingly. Apparently, an 'erection' used to be a word in building construction, while an 'ejaculation' was any surprised spontaneous utterance. But once co-opted, there's no going back.

Gossip

Every picture tells a story. The same could be said about a word.

It helps to think about a word's meaning as something of a career, with the unfolding history being a kind of curriculum vitae. This is an approach I've warmed to since reading Randall Kennedy's book, *Nigger: The Strange Career of a Troublesome Word* (2003).

One way to start, perhaps the most obvious, is back at the beginning. Stripping a word to its origins, we discover how it entered the language, via what routes in other languages and what those sources themselves signified, with what meanings it was initially invested, and then what pathways and trajectories these followed – over centuries, across oceans, through dialects – until we arrive at present-day understandings and misunderstandings.

Take the word 'gossip' and try to ignore for a moment the fact that the academics who study gossip are unable to agree even on a basic definition. The word originated in the Old English 'god sib', which meant something like godparent. Over time, the kin entailed in 'sib' (itself the origin of 'sibling') broadened in meaning and came to embrace any familiar acquaintance. By the sixteenth century, it specialised to denote female friends invited to attend and help at a birth (birthing was an exclusively female domain, male obstetricians having to wait a few more centuries before jumping in).

Over time, 'gossip' moved from a description of people (female attendees at a birth) to the kind of talk associated with such people. The focus then moved to the quality of such talk – it went from 'familiar', moved on to 'idle', from there to 'trifling' and ultimately to the socially unsanctioned spreading of rumour. Associated exclusively with women, because, of course, only women gossip and that's all they do.

Here, laid out baldly, is the misogyny of English. A group of women whose voices are heard from the birthing room could only be getting up to no good. So while it's hard to imagine a more supportive scene than a labouring woman aided by her closest female companions, all pulling (or pushing) together to facilitate a successful outcome, it seems that, from the perspective of the excluded males, those voices must've had the timbre of subversion – perhaps even the beginnings of a (female) plot to overturn (male) hegemony.

What better way to disarm them of their malign intentions, then and henceforth, than to brand their kind of talk ordinary, idle, trifling, spurious and socially damaging.

To lift and separate reveals the naked truth

It's said English has a plethora of synonyms. For instance, for 'fat', we have: 'ample', 'big' , 'chubby', 'corpulent', 'curvy', 'flabby', 'fleshy', 'generously proportioned', 'heavy', 'hefty', 'large', 'matronly', 'obese', 'over-sized', 'overweight', 'plump', 'podgy', 'portly', 'rounded', 'Rubenesque', 'stout', 'strapping', 'thickset', 'tubby', 'weighty', 'well-built', 'well-endowed' – to mention a few. Yet, even amid such plenty, we know that our choice of which fat-word to use is powerfully constrained by factors such as context, audience and intention.

Sometimes gradability helps. For instance, at the other end of the spectrum, for the sake of variety, it's possible to put 'slim', 'lean', 'narrow', 'slender', 'skinny', 'anorexic' on a continuum, and henceforth argue that they carry the same sense, differing only in degree.

The words 'underwear' and 'lingerie' aren't different degrees of the same thing; they're different phenomena. They target different demographics, talk to different audiences, service different clients, display different attitudes. The purpose of underwear is to enhance outerwear. Underwear lifts, separates, shapes, smooths, flattens, supports. Not quite whalebone corsetry, but you get the gist. The objective is svelte, the process engineered, the garment itself best not seen.

On the contrary, far from covering nakedness, lingerie suggests it, promises it, indeed preludes it. Built into the exorbitant price tag is lingerie's pledge: wear me, be sexy. Not for nothing does Elle Macpherson call her range 'intimates'. And women, seduced by the promise, collude in the mystery: they feel sexier in lingerie. Unsupported, more at risk, but sexier.

Nowhere is the tension more evident than in that veritable site of contestation, the G-string. This item of apparel – looks good on very few, feels good on even fewer – pretends to bat for both teams and, in so trying, fails. It winks at underwear's under-outer function by claiming to disappear the otherwise-visible panty line. But it somehow forgets that anything so skimpy, suggestive and uncomfortable has to have lingerie pretensions.

'Underwear' and 'lingerie' reflect and construct opposing world views. If there's a tension between them, it's because, even as they fulfil competing functions, they disingenuously pretend to be cut from the same cloth. Perversely, they each insist on calling the same department home.

TEXT-TYPES

Making meaning in language is a matter of choices. The text of an obituary is radically different from the inscription in a Mother's Day card. A newspaper health report has almost nothing in common with a restaurant menu. And all that the text of an SMS message shares with a bumper sticker or an epitaph is the necessity for brevity. Arguably, a language might be thought of as the sum total of an immense number of text-types, each of which has evolved over time to be appropriate to its situation and to meet the needs of its users. Text-types have two important distinguishing features. First, they are purpose-driven, with the choices being deliberate and strategic – What words are used? What relationship is assumed with the reader/listener? What shape does the text take? Second, text-types are fashioned by culture, as a people's ways of doing and achieving are conventionalised over time; this applies as much to culture in the sense of Spanish or Arabic as it does to subcultural ways – for example, the occupational, linguistic rituals among doctors, carpenters or park rangers – where speaking appropriately to one's identified workplace role is essential to successfully carrying out that role. The sections in this chapter each explore the language choices that characterise ten different text-types.

Menus

Eating is a sensual experience. You go to a fancy restaurant with certain expectations. You know that you're paying for a culinary experience designed in every way to enhance your sensual pleasure.

And you're receptive – all 10,000 taste buds of you – ready for action.

Not much happens outside of words, and certainly the sensuality of eating out begins in the language of the menu. First off, there is the expectation of French as the undisputed language of cuisine. Whatever your view of French politics, from the South Pacific to the Middle East there's no contesting the perfect fit between the French language and food. English, by contrast, doesn't even have a *bon appétit*, a fact that comes as no surprise if you've ever eaten in England.

Let's face it: ordinary mashed potatoes don't stand a chance next to the suave polish of *purée*. I'm not sure who Julienne was, but she's heaps more elegant than 'cut into thin shreds'. Can a muffin even enter the same race as a *friand*? As for meat that's been 'frenched', yes I thought it was rude too, till I checked the glossary.

If the French did a dish like baked beans on toast – it's no accident that they don't even have the words for it – it'd be magnificent. It would arrive as two, maybe three, pouting beans balanced precariously on a thin sliver of something that might in some quarters be deemed a facsimile of something in the toast family, the beans themselves suggestive at once of seduction and disdain.

Presentation is all. Your food will be designed and sculpted, a work of art no less. The menu has foreshadowed it, positioning us vis-à-vis our dish no less than the components of that dish are positioned vis-à-vis each other. Madame's 'pepper-encrusted fillet of Cervena venison' will arrive 'with poached peaches', nestling languidly 'on rocket leaves, topped with shaved Parmesan, fried capers and a delicate lemon and truffle dressing'. Enjoy!

It's crucial that we are made aware of what has been done to our food. Or to put it less delicately, where our food has been before it landed on our plate. The tomatoes have been 'vine-ripened', the goat curd has been 'caramelised', the cumquats have been 'candied', the whipped cream has been 'vanilla-infused'. Meanwhile, the feta has been brought from Persia (hey, isn't that Iran?).

Your waiter is but the last person in a long line of invisible agents devoted to your meal. You won't see the others – the chef or kitchen staff, the delivery person, the market people, the workers at the abattoir, or the farmer who hand-fed the corn to the creature the cut of whose side has ended up on your plate. All that remains of these multiple processes is the tantalising sculpture on your plate. Enjoy!

There are seductive titbits of information about origins and processes (pan-seared Norfolk asparagus spears served with organic Welsh egg-yolk ravioli). These do more than inform (fragrantly steamed Queensland barramundi fillet). By engendering a sense of collaboration (crisp Gungel Farm pork belly glazed with Chinese black vinegar), they lessen your dislocation from the product of other people's labours. You can almost believe, if you want to, that knowing how it happened is akin to participation.

The illusion of intimacy is not accidental. It's fostered by the filo-thin layers of over-information. We're afforded a voyeur's glimpse of backstage. Is there not just the slightest thrill in discovering that the tartare sauce is wasabi-infused? Or that the Sichuan duck is wrapped with shitake mushrooms inside a thin omelette? The négligée is transparent. Enjoy!

Chermoula rubbed Junee lamb rack. Which bit goes with which? Where's the head noun? Are we talking lamb here? Struggling through these long descriptive strings is not helped by the minimalist attitude to punctuation. I recall the time my hungry, French-deprived fourteen-year-old studied the menu in vain, and finally asked: 'Is there a chicken in there?'

But if subtle is the essence of sensual, the menu is wise to work so hard. Contrast our French-laced menu with this less-than-subtle instance of Japlish from a Tokyo restaurant: 'Domestic careful selection of pork with little fat of female liking is used. It has healthy vegetables with salad feeling fully.' Enjoy!

Health reports

'Death', says the dictionary, 'is the cessation of life.' Clear, simple, unambiguous. No further explanation needed. Not so for that peculiar *mélange* of confusion and scariness known as health reports. *Time* magazine devoted a cover story to the 'new killer of women' – heart disease.

So just when we thought it safe to come out – from that frenetic round of mammograms, stress management, genetic counselling and overconsumption of broccoli – we find out that if cancer doesn't get us, heart disease probably will. Something to look forward to.

Let's get things straight. Dissemination of information is one thing. Indiscriminate spreading of bad news, delivered within a discourse of fear and scare tactics, is something else.

If white is the new black, then heart disease is the new cancer. Clots caused by plaque 'travel through the bloodstream, wreaking havoc in the heart or brain', according to *Time*. In women, they lurk about longer, disguised and undetected, but they 'eventually come back to haunt'. There are things out there that will 'get us'. The 'get' decodes as ambush; no warning or provocation.

However, the discourse of fear is largely counter-productive. It raises anxiety, which is one of the risk factors, and encourages the ostrich reaction – how many women eschew breast self-examination, preferring not to know?

Particularly nasty is the hybrid advertisement masquerading as a concerned health report. One in *The Sydney Morning Herald* is launched atop the missile called plaque. 'Plaque can cause heart attacks', it announces. Of course, when you see 'plaque' you think teeth. The moment you do that, you're sucked right in. Then you read: 'If you've already had a heart problem, you should brush up on these facts.'

There's that 'brush' word – so you think you're on the right track – the track you've been led along since your eyes first alighted on the word 'plaque'. And it's no accident.

Three paragraphs down, we find out these plaques are 'obviously not the ones on your teeth'. No, twit, they're the ones in your arteries and, unlike their dental cousins, these ones are lethal.

I like the 'obviously'. This is disingenuous to the max. From the outset, we've been channelled down a pathway where we associate plaque with teeth. And now we're told that 'obviously' here we're talking about something different. This gives meaning to manipulative.

Once you've been positioned into this place called Stupid, you feel the need to support your understanding of the text with a diagram. In the centre of the page you find a cross-section of an artery with a red dot indicating 'ruptured plaque with clot starting to form'. Destinations are offered like holiday options: cardiac arrest or stroke; Paris or New York.

From this point it won't take long before you figure it out. This is no health report. It's a scare advertisement (remember the AIDS campaign for the 1980s, featuring the Grim Reaper at a bowling alley?), brought to us by a pharmaceutical company – 'a leading supporter of heart research . . . around the world' – and no doubt the manufacturer of just the thing you need for those difficult plaque spots you're harbouring in your arteries.

The discourse of fear runs along well-worn tracks. A major weapon is statistics. If you're a woman, according to *Time*, the chance of cancer 'getting' you is one in eight; with heart disease, it's one in three. You're probably already there but don't know it, worn down by the numbers if not the disease.

Case studies drive home the point. Take Kathy. She's forty-three and fit. She cycles, swims, runs, walks, eats well, doesn't smoke. From the list of things she does, it's hard to imagine she can fit in work. End result – a health specimen to be envied. Further from a statistic you can't be. Hell, even Kathy didn't recognise all that chest pain and shortness of breath as the makings of a heart attack.

The boxed section of the ad, listing risk factors with questions to ask yourself, is the clincher. Who has ever done one of these and come out smiling? And next, there's another list of lifestyle factors. Things that you should *stop* doing. Things that you should *start* doing. 'But', you want to scream, 'Kathy lived according to the gospel and she ended up sprawled out on a shopping mall floor.'

The take-home message is: be sensible and, next time, choose your parents better.

Bumper stickers

'Sail!' commanded the blue-and-white bumper sticker on the car in front. 'The wind is free.' Peak hour. I'm on an arterial road surrounded by pre-roadragers. They're people at the simmer stage. Pre-boil. Locked in traffic, I'm as far removed from a sea breeze as is possible – an intended irony, no doubt.

Bumper stickers (BS) are one of those strange phenomena that live in the grey understorey of the everyday. So mundane, their strangeness goes unnoticed. They've naturalised into the landscape. We don't see them any more. Or we see but we don't notice. Or we notice, but we don't heed. Something in the subliminal way.

'Football is Life', said a low-slung model, minutes later. I drift into a speculative trance. Can we flip round the equation and say 'Life is Football'? How depressing! Of course, the rear end of the car in front is the perfect billboard. You're captive, hemmed in, cannot fail to see it. Given the human tendency to search out meaning – and short snappy text especially invites interpretation – you simply cannot disattend.

Like any text, circumstance and purpose dictate its form. BS-text is curt and direct. Space constrains the flowery thought. The command is ubiquitous: 'Plant a Tree'; 'Free East Timor'; 'Ban the Bomb'. (A lot of old cars about.)

Space also favours the minimal factual present: 'I fish and I vote'; 'Vail I like it.' You won't see: 'I tried Whistler. Can't afford Aspen. Thredbo is it. For now, anyway.' You'd run out of bumper. An exception to the minimalist rule was a pre-Olympic one: 'Keep on taking your medication', it said; 'Our Olympic visitors mustn't suspect a thing.' Ironically, this touch of sanity amid madness made me laugh out loud . . . and obey.

If little is said, much is meant. 'My other car is a Rolls-Royce', is a snippet out of a longer, angst-ridden dialogue about class struggle and oppression. The petulant owner of the Mini says, 'I know you're passing judgement about me based on what you imagine my income is. Well, if you knew what my other car was, you wouldn't be quite so sneery.'

BS capture the essence of new-millennium life. There's a peculiar tension between their hardy permanence (ever tried to remove one?) and their transitory uncertainty of post-postmodernity. Now that nothing's absolute and, post-September-11, anything's possible, what's most certain is that your BS will date, even before you do. My son outgrew 'Magic Happens' long before the magic happened. But the sticker lived on, hope springing eternal on the rear of a Ford.

You can be certain, too, that your BS will date you even more than your hair, your music or the cut of your jeans. 'You can't hug a child with nuclear arms' expressed people's worry about uranium export. The threat is still with us, albeit less prominently, but worries, like flavours, are monthly – and this month, it's avian flu.

The BS is a deliberate personal intrusion into a cold, inanimate metal cosmos. Accidental it isn't. It's not unlike the child's 'Mummy! Watch me!' The driver *wants* you to see it. She foists it into the public domain, into your face: 'Keep rainforests in the ground' (a greenie); 'An independent media? Simple as ABC' (an intellectual); 'Mum's taxi' (family values); 'I'd rather be windsurfing' (sporty); 'Addicted to Bass' rock fan 'Global Warming? Good for Golf' (ratbag). What she doesn't want you to know, you won't; not from a bumper anyway. Ever seen 'Premature Ejaculator', 'Repeat Drink-Driving Offender', 'Nose Pickers Are Nice'? No, not likely.

Then again, the message may well be less important than the apparent display of the personal. After all, we're surrounded by the incongruities of mass-produced personalisation. Teenage girls sport brand names to be individual; their older sisters wear designer clothes that are mass-produced. I've almost convinced my teenage daughter that *not* having any body piercing is a statement. We were shopping when I saw a rack of tops that screamed out the text: 'I'm not a bitch. I'm THE bitch!' There's no doubt that whoever buys/wears this will do so believing she's making a 'personal statement'.

Maybe we need a bumper sticker that says, 'I'm a free-thinking conformist.'

Tag-lines

Some types of texts are shaped by the space in which they operate. A classic example is the postcard. Barely room to scribble 'Wish you were here'. I'm not suggesting for a moment that this – the relationship between the space and the text – is accidental. On the contrary – nothing could be more congruent than the confining constraints of a postcard and the sweaty demands of holiday indolence.

The language of greetings-card-ese is similarly constrained. Like the postcard, there's not much room and, like the postcard, the communication is an interpersonal one, not a transactional one. Poetry, bumper stickers, slogans of any kind – all work creatively within confining constraints.

There's another text that is given little conscious attention, but probably substantial amounts of the subliminal kind. This is the tag-line that often accompanies the publicity surrounding a new film.

I read somewhere that the money spent on the publicity that precedes and surrounds a new film's release is not much less than what was spent on the film itself. That's probably an exaggeration but you get the idea. It follows that a great deal of time and bucks will be spent on consulting the right people to advise on what words to use to ensure that the tag-line gets it exactly right. Giving enough of a hint of what you're in for to seduce, but not nearly enough to satiate or demystify. A tag-line that makes you bolt for the box office pleading that they take your money and let you in.

Some tag-lines catapult you straight into the action. It's the 'complication' that conventionally follows the 'orientation' (location of time and space) in a narrative – a format that we all have wired into our motherboards, one that is as much flouted as obeyed, one that we knee-jerk respond to. No surprise that action films favour these tag-lines. Like this one from *The Sum of All Fears* – '27,000 nuclear weapons. One is missing.' Or from *Open Water* – 'Don't be left behind.' Or *The Bourne Identity* – 'He was the perfect weapon until he became the target.' Or *Dog Soldiers* – 'Six Soldiers. Full Moon. No chance'. Or a film with action of a different kind: *In the Bedroom* – 'A young man. An older woman. Her ex-husband. Things are about to explode...' The ellipses leave you suspended, intentionally. Often the tag-line to an action film is so perfect that the circumstances by which the precipitating complication came about are almost irrelevant. You'll forget them within a day of seeing the movie. They don't matter; they never mattered.

Some tag-lines immediately cue you to the genre and that's what you're really going for, not any particular story. For *About a Boy,* it was 'Growing up has nothing to do with age.' Immediately you know Hugh Grant has some lesson to learn, and it's likely to be about how he treats women. With *Bend It Like Beckham* – 'Who wants to cook Aloo Gobi when you can bend a ball like Beckham?' – the illusion of particularity masks a classic ethnic gender-bender. Soppy movies – they typically involve a yearning + major crisis + eleventh-hour re-stabilisation – have tag-lines that hint at the resolution and promise a happy or at least a bittersweet ending. Consider *I Am Sam* – 'Love is all you need.' Or *My Big Fat Greek Wedding* – 'Love is here to stay...so is her family.'

Some tag-lines seem to blur the boundary between participant and spectator. They leap out of the poster or advertisement and collar you; they're addressed directly to you, as if it is you who's about to be launched into the action. Yeah, it's you who'll be making all the important decisions. Like *Minority Report* – 'What would you do if you were accused of a murder you had not committed ...yet?' And *Ocean's Eleven* – 'Are you in or out?' And *The Others* – 'Sooner or later they will find you.' In *Collateral Damage*, it's 'What would you do if you lost everything?' The blurring of second and third person is a clever way to snare you. It borrows from the psychology of spectator horror. Go, watch, be scared, but even while you drip with fear, know that it's not you, it's someone else. That's the 'phew!' factor that turns fear into entertainment.

Tag-lines get away with their economy because of what's not said. They tap into shared understandings. Sometimes these are of life, as in *John Q* – 'Give a father no options and you leave him no choice'. Sometimes they're of pre-existing film knowledge, as in *Men in Black II* – 'Same planet. New scum'. Sometimes there's a play on words that hints seductively at new meanings, as in *Changing Lanes* – 'One wrong turn deserves another.'

Tag-lines are taut, tight and tempting. That's the whole point.

Affirmations

'Affirmation' is a New Age word that crept into the language when our backs were turned. It wasn't alone. Along with it came 'inner child', 'primal therapy' and 'yoga mat'. I recognise its root, of course, and some of its forms, like the response 'affirmative' – that unambiguous, military-sounding, multisyllabic, rather pointlessly effortful alternative to 'yes'.

My thesaurus clusters 'affirm' with like-minded verbs: 'assert', 'insist', 'confirm', 'avow', 'state', 'establish', 'pronounce', 'verify', 'acknowledge'. Get the picture? We're talking nice words.

From a lofty inception, affirmations have been commodified in the tradition of crystals, bath salts and aromatherapy. On my last visit to an 'alternative shop' – where thin, pale organic types (I'm talking people here) stood wanly behind jars of dried, carob-coated banana peel – I noticed a bunch of essences linked to different emotions. I spotted grief, sadness, depression, anxiety – among others that I became too stressed to remember. The range of options is so generous that you're left with the difficulty of classifying your current mood. For the introvert, this is Disasterville. Is sadness a symptom of depression? Is grief a kind of sadness? Can you have anxiety on its own or does it have to bring along some of its mates?

Purchase should be delayed, I suggest, until your mood has firmed up a notch.

Affirmations require less cognitive input than essences. Like horoscopes, they're vague enough to be widely portable. I first encountered them when my daughter was about to go to school camp (read 'boot camp'). First time away from mother bear. Nervous. Worried. Both of us – the daughter (how will I cope without mum?) and the mother (how will she cope on her own?). Bereft of any better idea, I packed into her trunk a bunch of affirmations, one for each day of the ordeal. Take with food, in the morning. A breakfast of spiritual fortitude. Lame, perhaps, but mobiles were forbidden.

These days you'll often find that hospital gift shops carry a line of affirmations. Are they for the visitor, to boost the spirit before seeing the stricken patient? Or perhaps for the patient – a kind of spiritual adjunct to the intravenous drip?

Like Hallmark-card psychology, the affirmation industry has stepped into the spiritual breach of post-postmodernism. Clearly, we all need help shoring ourselves up against external negativity, something more proactive than merely turning off the news. And affirmations seem to offer a low-cost, low-maintenance investment.

After all, what harm can a little sentence do? It's usually a matter of subject and verb, less often an object, which seem to get in the way of wistful yearning: 'Tomorrow may be, today is.' Imperatives are common – 'Live the life you've imagined' – though it's rather odd that New Age types would favour commands. Balanced, parallel clauses are popular too: 'As you think, so you are; as you imagine, so you become.'

Inner resources feature widely – 'Do what you can with what you have where you are' – as does the power of human connection – 'Every blade of grass has its angel that bends over it and whispers, "Grow, grow".' Some are punchy little aphorisms pivoted on wordplay: 'Yesterday is history, tomorrow is a mystery, today is a gift, that's why it's called the present.' Many are *carpe diem*-infused: 'Nothing is worth more than this day.' In fact, arguably the very best thing about the New Age stance is its awareness of life's brevity and frailty.

Regrettably, any significance tends to be bleached out by rampant commercialism. One of my favourites – 'Dance as though no one is watching you, love as though you have never been hurt, sing as though no one can hear you, live as though heaven is on earth' – has started appearing in cards, on mugs, on aprons, even on paperweights. At what point does the affirmation lose its spirit?

Recently at a market, among other treasures, I found a laminated page of one hundred affirmations, called *Life's Little Instructions*. For £2, or 2 Pence per affirmation, it was a good deal by anyone's abacus. Among the profound and the trite was one that tottered on the sublime edge of the ridiculous: 'Live your life as an exclamation, not an explanation.'

If anyone out there is listening, I've been trying, I promise.

SMS text messages

The boy is barely fifteen and he's shy. He's never had a girlfriend. Not a real one. And he likes this girl. A lot.

Finally, they've dodged his friends, her friends, and both sets of parents. They're alone, in the cinema, in the dark, waiting for the movie to start. Side by side, eyes straight ahead, immobile. Seemingly engrossed in the lead-ups to the main feature. Interminable when you're wrapped in a bubble of clammy self-consciousness.

But in an electromagnetic kind of way, they're alive to each other's physical proximity. Suddenly, his mobile phone vibrates, indicating the arrival of an SMS message. The dial lights up so he can read it in the dark. It says, 'You can hold my hand now if you like.' It's from the girl next to him. He reaches out and takes her hand. They smile in the dark. Things are better now. The tension dissipates.

If a frisson of something electric just went down your spine, you're probably around my age. If not, you're likely closer to my teenage daughter, whose response, when I told her of the incident, was a bored, 'Yeah, so?'

Welcome to the world of mediated discourse. Getting messages across without the tacky, risky face-to-face. Very handy for navigating that terrifying terrain where 'nerdy' and 'dorky' vie for first place to best describe how you feel and how you *think* you appear.

With time, these shy forays will turn into such killer lines as: 'What're you doing here?' 'Haven't I seen you somewhere before?' 'Got a light?' 'What're you drinking?' 'Do you come here often?'

But then, having the killer lines may not solve the problem. You can be so alienated from the sound of the words that you're rendered immobile. Could be you're actually over-educated in the strategies. Too much overintellectualising *à la Sex and the City*. You can't play the game without feeling stupid, derivative or nauseous. You watch yourself like a fly on the wall of your own life, and you hate what you see. Too much self-absorption is crippling. Just ask Woody Allen – that's Woody Allen the character, not Woody Allen the director, who's far more urbane than his filmic persona.

We've all been there – foolishness and ineptitude imprinted on the psyche. You think you'll never outgrow it. And then you do, and you realise that goes with age.

It's the need to avoid such pain that spawned the dating agency industry. So, too, the popularity of the personals where you only have to invent the line, not the rejoinder (see pages 108–11).

It's not only in the brokering of relationships that mediated discourse serves us. For the conveyance of bad-news messages, it's second to none. A story in a national daily reported the case of a man who sued his ex-employers for giving him his marching orders via SMS. The message read: 'Its official – u no longer work for [*name of company*] & u have forfided [*sic*] any arrangements made.' Imagine getting that while you're standing on a station platform waiting for your much-delayed train. Don't you wonder whether, a few years hence, we might look back on this employee's reaction of litigious outrage as … well, quaint? And what about other types of unpleasant news – medical test results for one? Will they find their way to you via mediated discourse? It would relieve doctors of perhaps their most unpleasant communication task.

Relationships of the heart are not all hand-holding bliss like our young couple in the dark theatre. They also have their special bad-news moments. Fast forward to the end of a relationship, which in these days of pacey serial monogamy promises to be a frequent occurrence. If mediated discourse proves handy in the icebreaking stage, it really comes into its own for the dump.

Given that dumping and being dumped are major adolescent concerns, SMS texting romps home at this event. I'm told it's far kinder to find out you're dumped from a text message than face-to-face or voice-to-voice. You can see why. Humiliation, like embarrassment, is a very social emotion – it's far less agonising when one's allowed to cool off in private.

I'm told that in New York (where else?) a telephone service allows you to break up with someone with no personal contact – visual, acoustic or tactile. He gets a message asking him to ring a particular number. When he does, he gets another message (not your voice, nor your words) telling him it's over. A Dear John letter, minus the letter.

Well, you can dial a prayer, a recipe, an affirmation. Why not dial a dump? One small step for mankind...

Valentine's Day messages

I've never really come to terms with my visceral distaste for Valentine's Day. I detest the glaringly obvious commercial interests that fuel the occasion. Red roses, chocolates, helium balloons: are they not all supportive accompaniments to pathetically saccharine, excessive protestations of something known as 'love'?

It's a kind of allergy. The more an event meets the criteria of a greetings-card moment, the more it gets my goat. Naturally, Valentine's Day is a prime contender. Has anyone calculated how many trees are sacrificed for the cards people send on Valentine's Day?

That said, I concede that, if the outpouring of written affection confined itself to card-sending and receiving, I could probably cope. Cards, after all, are a direct form of communication between sender and receiver, and they serve both. They can be replete with intimate, romantic sweet nothings, or suggestively raunchy, your-eyes-only propositions. Either way, the mode of communication works, and it does so because it's private.

Out in the public domain, it's a different story entirely. You know how redundant you feel when a romantic couple gazes dreamily into each other's eyes? That feeling turns to squeamishness when the lovebirds start using their pet names for each other – in front of you: 'Hey, boobsie, what time are we going?' 'Oh whenever you feel like, munchkin.' Don't they know no one wants to hear this? You're polite so of course you suppress the groan. Inwardly, though, you're fuming at being rendered into a reluctant voyeur, made privy to what is rightfully a discourse of intimates. One that belongs behind closed doors, if not between sheets.

Worse than the public gazing and verbalised endearments is the Valentine's Day ritual of advertised newspaper space. Here the protestation of love/lust takes the besotted to new dizzy heights. A message to the beloved appears in the full glare of the public domain. This is weird. And it's weird because of the incongruity of a private message being displayed in a public space.

Now if analysing social customs works for anthropologists investigating forgotten tribes, why not here, I thought, deciding to have a close look at the Valentine's Day advertisements.

A few overriding patterns quickly surfaced. The first is the proliferation of pet names. Connie the Cow got a message from Ramming Bull, as did Fatti from Bede, Bella Boo from Shrek, Bub from Baby Boober, Love Bub from Monster, Poopsie from Honky. Some pet names borrow from gastronomy (Pumpkin Pie and Tuna Casserole); or from zoology (Bunny, Duck, Foxy, Baby Panda, Feral, Chicken, Turtle dove; Bears of various persuasions – Gummy, Squishy, Cubby);

or from botany (Frangipani, you still smell sweet after fifteen years; Rose Petal; Like two peas in a pod).

Then there's the less-than-subtle sexual innuendo: Prods and hugs to Belly Dancer whose shimmies shake our world. Or this one from Dusty: I have the leather if you have the handcuffs. Lots of references to hot and ready. Sometimes the names are enough (Muffin, Stud Burger, Baby and Big Banana). Mention of hugs, butts and spanking, of loving heart, soul and 'other good bits' abound.

If raunchiness is alive and well, so too is schmaltz. No prizes for originality. Roses are red, violets blue. Love is total, true and forever. The stars are above and they're for wishing on. Hearts are delicate, they skip beats, and have a generalised fear of being broken. Eyes gaze and brim with joy. There's wondering and dreaming and much looking towards the future. Holding, having and never letting go. There's loyalty and devotion. Coupledom. Togetherness. Fitting and completing. Soulmatedom.

Alliteration abounds – love/laughter, precious/prize, true/together, dream/destiny. As do clichés – love is a many splendoured thing, a dream come true, a chance to be born anew, in the air. The metaphors continue the motifs of courtly love, which elevate and idealise – you're an exotic flower amongst a forest of weeds. And corny finds new definition: Captain Hook. Of all the fish in the sea I'm glad I hooked up with you. Don't rock the boat, baby. Snapper Sue, Fishing with you is so much fun. Catching you is all I dream.

Another characteristic is the comparisons: Until I met you, my life was a desert. And the ultimate declaration: Debbie, I love you more than my car.

Epitaphs

The Queen Mother's epitaph could have been 'Now I can look London's East End in the face.' However, it would have required far too much context to make sense of the text. An epitaph, among other requirements, needs a certain stand-alone quality. It needs to be able to be read and understood in and of itself, now and forever. Well, at least for a few hundred years.

As the text that is written in prose or verse on a tombstone, the epitaph is a most particular genre. More so than most venues of text, the epitaph is quintessentially epitaph-ian because of its location, location, location. Placed elsewhere, it might be a lonely poem, a love letter, a coded message, a school motto, a proverb, a coroner's entry. But not an epitaph.

Historically we associate the lofty, elaborate epitaph with the Graeco-Roman and Christian worlds. These days, in contrast, inscriptions tend to be baldly minimal:

JOE BLOGGS

1923–1989

Loved and missed by Mavis, Beryl

and the children

REST IN PEACE

As an occasional adornment, expect to find a well-known line of Biblical text.

This is definitely a case of function-over-form. Ashes, dust, naked we are born and die, but surely after three score-and-ten we deserve more text than a name, dates of entry and exit, who's going to miss us, and a pointless imperative that the deceased won't hear? An equivalent curriculum vitae would guarantee lifetime unemployment.

A lifespan is enough to produce several verbal titbits to serve as epitaph contenders. Attach these to our will and testament. Leave it to the executor. Or maybe they can be added later, with the hindsight of wisdom. Lawrence Oates's might have been 'I'm just going outside. I may be some time.' Bill Clinton's might be 'I did not have sexual relations with that woman.' Well, perhaps only over Hillary's dead body.

I know a man whose *de facto* moved in a little prematurely and started screwing down the furniture. Asked by a confidant who noticed he was worried, the man shrugged, 'Oh well, you can always unscrew it' – a line, I posit, that would make a great epitaph.

Behind the epitaph, like any genre, lie the forces that shape the conventions of text. An obvious physical constraint is space. Tombstones vary in their dimensions but none can cater for a Bryce Courtenay trilogy. Verse is ideal because it's already spare, compressed, milked of excess. Quoting from *Paradise Lost* has the benefit of having already been copiously edited and refined.

The epitaph is frozen in time and this too is a constraint. Tippex won't help. What's done is done. A mix-up – very high on the oops scale – was the ceremonial unveiling of a plaque to honour the famous actor James Earl Jones on Martin Luther King (MLK) Day. But the plaque mistakenly read 'Thank you James Earl Ray for Keeping the Dream Alive!' Trouble was, Ray was the man who shot Martin Luther King Jr. You can see the slip-up: James Earl x 2; Jones is black; it was MLK day; mention of the dream; Ray shot MLK. I can see one very red-faced stone writer possibly looking for a new job.

Remember, too, the nature of cemeteries and the great outdoors. Our inscription is open to everyone. Wordsworth said that the epitaph 'is concerning all, and for all' – exposed to the elements as well as to the stranger's gaze. Not exactly a niche market. Samuel Johnson was shocked to imagine Erasmus's grave in Rotterdam having a Dutch epitaph. He pressed for an ancient and classical language to be the standard.

Fortunately, epitaphs are unconstrained by truth and are expected to be complimentary. A nasty one was written for Charles II in advance of his death. Premature writing of another's epitaph may be construed as homicidal in motive. By all means do it, but (as with much else) press delete.

Given these constraints, it is perhaps liberating to remember the one saving grace of the epitaph is that the deceased never gets to see it.

Obituaries

Idi Amin is dead. While alive, he didn't do much for the cause of humanity. All that remains, apart from the fractured lives of any living victims and the fractured memories of the descendants of the many dead victims – arguably as high as 500,000 – are the words chosen to characterise his life.

His death certainly furnished opportunities for descriptive language. I refer to his obituaries in the print media.

Conventionally, the genre of the obituary is given over to the celebration of a life. There's a generally agreed-upon, albeit tacit, licence to gloss over the less-than-salutary bits, if any, while highlighting the worthy events of the average three-score-plus-or-minus-whatever. Idi Amin, in death, as in life, broke a lot of rules and certainly his obituaries make no pretence at glossing over, omitting or fibbing.

The language used – in the *Washington Post*, the *Guardian Weekly*, the *Sydney Morning Herald*, among others – to describe the life of Idi Amin might be grouped into four broad categories. In the first category fall words that build a picture of wanton cruelty and contempt for human life. Nouns here are 'bloodthirstiness', 'atrocity', 'violence', 'carnage' and 'lawlessness'. His name is linked 'synonymously with barbarity'. Adjectives are 'brutal', 'despotic', 'ruthless', 'sadistic'. We are told he 'executed' numerous victims, but the euphemism ('murder' or 'slaughter' would be more correct) falsely suggests that such carnage might have had legal authority.

Some descriptions choose to locate Amin's badness wholly within himself. Another way of characterising political evil is to contextualise it, understanding its background, prelude and setting. In Amin's case, this means locating his murderous regime in the context of post-colonial Africa, and placing some of the blame for the violence he unleashed on the particular circumstances of Africa in the 1960s and 1970s. (Just as, similarly, it is wrong to locate the source and responsibility for German Nazism in Adolf Hitler alone.)

The amalgam of heady political power within the mental frame of 'a primitive tribalist' is cast as a formulaic African tragedy.

The post-colonial interpretation does not preclude outrage. Patrick Keatley of the *Guardian* writes: 'Amin brought bloody tragedy and economic ruin to his country during a selfish life that had no redeeming qualities.'

A second category of words implies the various faces of insanity. Amin is described as 'an unbalanced man' with 'animal magnetism', who acted on 'hunches and impulses' and was guided by 'a peasant cunning'. I wonder about the linking of insanity with animals and peasants; I question what these creatures did to deserve such opprobrium. Amin's behaviour is described as erratic manifestations of 'idiocy' or 'madness', like reports that hint at cannibalism or the beheading of prominent opponents – and the storing of these heads in freezers, allowing them to be brought out periodically, to be placed on the dinner table where Amin would have 'conversations' with them. Some stories seem so extreme as to be beyond belief. Then you remember Auschwitz, Cambodia, Rwanda, Kosovo, and you know there is no 'beyond'.

Yet another category is buffoonery. This may be the other side of 'insanity' except that the writer hopes to highlight the comic rather than seek moral outrage in the reader. Among Amin's 'buffoonish antics' are his challenging the President of Tanzania to a boxing match, and his get-well letter to Richard Nixon, wishing him 'a speedy recovery' from Watergate – although seeing Nixon's demise through the metaphor of illness may be less buffoonish than it appears. Amin's over-the-top titles and medals, his ceremonial buffoonery, suggest a deliberately spun confusion, used to entertain as well as intimidate.

The last batch of adjectives describes the other Amin – the one who lived quietly in suburban exile in the Saudi Arabian city of Jiddah – kindly, gentle, sad and pious. Probably just the kind of adjectives used by Adolf Eichmann's neighbours in suburban Buenos Aires. Just goes to show what you don't know about what you think you know.

In times of rapid change, obituaries serve an important slow-down function. *Time* magazine cites the *West Australian* as saying, 'Reading an obituary is a bit like pressing the pause button.' This may well be so. But in Idi Amin's case, fast forward might be the way to go.

Self-help

You don't know how many dog breeds there are until you do. When I was deciding what breed I wanted as my dog-soon-to-be, I visited a website offering to remove the angst. You enter the key features of your personality, lifestyle and circumstances. (Do you stay at home a lot? How big is your yard?) The computer then crunches the information and spits out the name of your ideal dog.

First up, I got a bichon frisé. No way, I said. I want a dog, not an accessory. I returned to the website, changed a bit of my personality, adjusted my lifestyle, and got... a schnauzer. Better, I thought, but not there yet. I then decided to select my preferred breed and reverse the process to find out what kind of personality and lifestyle I ought to be having. Only when I realised I didn't know how to do that did I give up.

Circuitously, but inexorably, this brings me to my topic. Self-help. The website didn't find me my dog, but it did seduce me with its notion of easy personality change. Amend a few details, adjust a few ticked boxes, and bingo.

Those who predicted the death of the book in the Digital Age forgot to factor in the self-help industry. Second only to cookbooks, new self-help titles appear almost daily. Catchy ones, bouncy covers, serene people, Prozac smiles, bowls of fresh fruit, contented children.

Within self-help, there are sub-fads. Like the one that encourages you to embrace your disease. It offers 'metaphysical healing' pitched at the mental causes of physical problems. One volume on self-healing lists alphabetically all afflictions that ever besieged a human. Next to each is a 'probable cause' (a term I'd hitherto known only from *Law and Order*). In an adjacent column, a new thought pattern is suggested and this becomes the 'healing instrument'. One is told, for instance, that an 'anal abscess' comes from 'anger in relation to what you don't want to release'. The new recommended thought pattern, the internal sentence that you're to play over and over again is: 'It's safe to let go now.'

Self-help books are written to a template. Snappy title, verb in the imperative form. Declutter Your Life. Become the Woman You Are. Grow Herbs for a Better Memory. Eat Yourself Thin. You take a complex human situation. Make it a *reductio ad absurdum*. Adopt an unambiguous, overarching metaphor, such as (yawn) gendered planets-of-origin. Throw in a few case studies with ordinary folk paralysed by fear of change before they saw the light. Offer a new way of seeing an old problem. Blend together some scripted scenarios with platitudes that pass as encouragement. Organise a whirlwind, jet-in-jet-out motivational tour. Play the smiling author who tells frenzied crowds they, too, can be great.

Stage photo and merchandising opportunities. Wear the messaged T-shirt you're selling. Keep on smiling.

A runaway bestseller. Best get started on the sequel.

Conversation as expectation

Everyone has an eccentric friend. Sometimes, indeed, a few. One of mine, who is a language lover from way back, emailed me last week with a recent adventure to tell.

Now, this fellow's wont is to refer to himself, as well as to cavort about, as an annoying old fart (AOF). It's a guise that enables (nay, even encourages) him to indulge his love of linguistic play. He writes:

I went into a pie shop yesty and decided I should partake of a steaki'n'kidney pie.

[Note his habit of capturing particular pronunciations through iconoclastic spelling.]

Being an annoying old fart, I ordered a 'snake'n'pygmy pie'. The attendant made no comment and furnished me with a steak 'n' kidney pie.

I ask you: Did she just see that I was an annoying old fart and ignored it; Had she indeed heard that amusing line so many times she couldn't be bothered saying anything; or Did she in fact hear 'steak'n'kidney' even though I'd said 'snake'n'pygmy'?

I assured him that commenting definitively was impossible. You'd have to have been there, to know if (a) she was deliberately ignoring him as an AOF (oh no, not another one this morning); or (b) rather bored, she took it as a standard language play, like asking 'What can I do you for?'; or (c) she had decoded the sound chunk in the usual way, oblivious to the variation on the original. Think nice cream and ice cream.

If I were to take a punt, I'd take the third option. I'd assume she simply heard what she expected to hear. She'd have matched her expectations with the acoustic cues, with today being no different from any other.

After all, expectation is a function of what's usual, commonplace and unremarkable in any particular context. We're awfully good at enabling conjecture to shape our perception. We even have an inner grammatical expectancy that predicts beautifully how any one utterance in any one circumstance is likely to unfold.

And as far as pie-shop scripts go, there aren't a lot of options. There are all your pie fillings, a preference for hot or not, the availability of sauces, plus a cakey assortment of items on display. You're unlikely to hear 'tropical bananas' or 'nuclear war', or even 'global warming'.

All things considered, snakes and pygmies would feel right at home in a pie shop.

Reporting verbs

A reader was 'baffled' by what she called 'the increasing use of "went" for "said"'. Her example: 'I told him to be careful and he went, "Mind your own business."'

She's right that 'went' for 'said' (WFS) seems curious for a reporting verb. But she's probably not right that it's increasing. What's increasing is the written incidence of WFS, giving the impression of an all-round increase.

One explanation is the explosion of new text-types. Email, blogs and SMS lay out in visual, more permanent form what was once aural and ephemeral. So, WFS – and its present-tense equivalents, 'go/es' for 'say/s' – has long characterised informal speech. It's almost mandatory in the historic or dramatic present, common in narrative: 'This bloke walks into a pub and he goes . . .' With such episodes now featuring in informal written communication, 'went'/'go' have travelled far beyond their provenance.

Quoting and reporting aren't easy in English. You need a reporting frame made up of an introducing reporting verb. 'Say' is your easiest, most straightforward example. It can introduce direct text ('He said, "The war will be over soon"'), or indirect/reported text ('He said that the war would be over soon'). On the other hand, 'tell' seems as simple but it isn't, primarily because of its lopsided preference for indirect rather than direct reporting ('He told the nation that the war would be over soon').

Conversely, 'go' and 'went' are not happy reporting anything that isn't absolutely direct. Given their origins in life's spoken hurly-burly, this makes good logical sense. Yet, perhaps the strangest of reporting structures is 'like', as in 'He's, like, mind your own business.' Teenage girls love it but they're not alone.

Anyway, direct and indirect are not different in an apples-and-oranges way. Hybrid forms cleverly mix both, extracting the best of each.

In 'The President was in a bad mood. He shouldn't have promised the troops home by Christmas', it is understood that 'he told himself . . .'. Similarly, actual quoted words can slip in, unheralded by punctuation, in a speaker/writer's own syntax. ('This is life. This is liberty. And by God, this is the pursuit of happiness.')

Bottom line: pure forms, if ever they were, have been replaced by vibrant hybrids. Like, get used to it.

Solving Christmas

My local garden shop publishes a seasonal newsletter. Arriving earlier every year, the November/December issue heralds the coming festive season and contains myriad gardening suggestions. It's a red-and-green, four-sided publication, bigger than a leaflet, smaller than a catalogue. The footer, in big print, reads: 'All the plants and products you need', and then, 'Christmas is solved as well.'

These words gave me pause. 'Christmas is solved as well.' What does this mean? That the shop has everything you need to solve all the problems of having a garden, removing the back-breaking part of garden work, and, while you're at it, you can solve the problem of Christmas?

I appreciate that a nursery might market itself as a problem-solver. After all, tending to a garden is neither intuitive nor self-evident. Different plants require different soils, amounts of sun and shade, quantities of water, types of fertiliser. They're even annoyed by different pests. Constructing a business as a provider of garden solutions makes good sense.

So, by all means, come to the garden shop to find out if blood and bone will help your birds of paradise. But do you also have to 'solve' Christmas? Is Christmas therefore a problem? And if so, of what kind? When did it become problematic? Is finding a solution the answer? Is it a long-term solution or is one condemned to an annual re-enactment of the Sisyphus myth?

But wait – perhaps there's no single problem at Christmas. Perhaps we all make our own individual problems. That would mean there are as many problems as there are people celebrating Christmas.

One person's problem might be how to fit the entire family around a small dining-room table. Solution: stand up and eat finger food; or invite fewer people; or have two parties, the second on Boxing Day; or if you're in a warm climate go outside and have a barbecue.

Another person's problem might be having no family, but even for this there are solutions. A woman I know always has a party for 'strays'. Unfortunate nomenclature, but good intention.

One person's problem might be not enough money to buy presents. Solution: only buy for the kids. Another's might be what to buy for friends who already have everything. Yet another problem might be what to buy that's thoughtful and inoffensive, without being too personal.

Solution: buy a plant from the garden shop and bingo, Christmas is solved.

FIELDS OF DISCOURSE

The more we poke around in matters linguistic, the more it seems apt to invoke the metaphor of Russian dolls – the further in you go, the more you find replicas in miniature. While the metaphor should not be pushed too far, we might think of language as our biggest Russian doll. Inside her we find the English language, and inside her a particular regional dialect; for example, Australian English. Going further in, we will find sociolects (ways of speaking marked by socioeconomic class), genderlects (ways of speaking marked by gender) and ethnolects (ways of speaking marked by the coexistence of a different mother tongue). Still further in, we will find that venues come with their own subsets of language codes. By a venue, I mean a particular combination of circumstances: place (where), people (who), topic (what) and mode (whether, for example, the language is spoken or written). A wedding venue, for example, is partly about a formal public event participated in and witnessed by family and friends. Likewise, the talk that engages dog-owners in a neighbourhood park is shaped by its own rules of where, who, what and how. This chapter contains ten such venue-based sections that explore the language characteristics of their particular circumstances.

Permanent fatal error

My screen is frozen.

With no warning, up pops a message from the dark depths of that place where messages live before they pop up. It's ugly DOS again, rearing his head through the user-friendly, Caribbean-blue waters of Windows: 'This program has performed an illegal operation. If the problem persists, please contact the vendor.'

'This program'? Does that mean me? Why do I feel culpable? Am I accused? Speak to me, Mr Gates.

'Has performed'? If ever there was a bald, harsh, existential assertion of non-negotiable fact, this is it. No history, no background briefing, no tracking of the problem. A world without a past. Just a problematic present and a questionable future.

What 'illegal operation'? Are we talking about corporate fraud? Or is it people-smuggling? Am I supposed to know? Will I ever find out? Notice how the insidiousness evolves: 'illegal operation' becomes 'the problem' and then it becomes mine. There's no talk of solutions except the seriously lame 'contact the vendor' (plus the vacuous 'please').

A swift washing of the hands of all responsibility. Like 'if the pain persists, please see your doctor'. (What if the doctor's on call, or away, or out of town, or unavailable, or over-booked, or out-of-action, or dead?) Contacting the vendor must be a joke. Is it being suggested that I go back to the be-pimpled boys on work experience at the computer store? Would they know? Or care? Or even see? (Women over fifteen are invisible to the young, testosteroned, electronically endowed.) I'll be passed from Spotty to Spotty in a macabre contest of resilience. It's a no through road.

My screen is frozen.

There's nothing accidental here. These messages daily remind me of the malevolence of the world. Their language is final in an unmitigated, absolute, back-against-the-wall kind of way. 'This message was undeliverable. The address has permanent fatal errors.' It's never 'temporary' and 'treatable'. Forget clemency. There is none. No one else speaks to me like this. Not the bank manager. Not the Tax Office. Not my periodontist. Not my ex. Not even my personal trainer.

I am besieged by the imminence of threat. Yet I remember when 'protection' used to be a TV euphemism and 'vet' meant animal doctor. Now vet is a verb and my virus protection needs regular upgrading. But who wants to know about viruses, worms, infiltration, aggression, malice, holes in the operating system's security, propagating payloads, with warheads and torpedos? Siege from without. A multitude of vicious enemy agents who attack and prey by stealth. In the wake of September 11, the language of bombardment takes on a new currency. It doesn't help to know that most viruses are hoaxes – the creative, sales-boosting handiwork of the software caste.

I wonder about the reflexive relationship of words to things referred to. Are computer viruses more viral for being called 'viruses'? Does one called 'Command Bomber' have a quality that it would lack if it were more benignly named? Are 'warheads' more invidious because they 'attack' in 'stealth' and 'propagate'? And what does it say that the opposite of an aggressive virus is termed 'coy'?

Primary master. Secondary slave. This is the language of feudal warlords, with power of life and death over their fearful underlings. The despicable life conditions of serfdom. It's a Schopenhauer universe where there are two kinds of feelings – that experienced by the animal eating and that experienced by the animal being eaten.

I know, I know. It's not personal. It's not my computer. It's the mail server, or the software, or Mr Gates. But these have all blurred into a corporate ideograph – a monstrous, monolithic, multinational male monopoly that's as invisible as it is omniscient. It's global corporations versus people-like-me. I bow, mute, humbled, dwarfed by the anonymity of corporate authority.

What kind of world is this, where the menace is invisible, help is unavailable and young pimply, uncommunicative boys constitute the new priesthood? All the possible diversity of life choices is straitjacketed into a *Yes*, a *No* or a *Cancel*. Errors come out of nowhere and are morally indifferent. You could be typing *Ulysses* or a shopping list. It doesn't matter. Remember to save.

My screen is frozen.

Real estate

Truth and falsehood are absolute extremes. They are the yes and no at the poles of the continuum. Between them lies a huge terrain of grey space where truth can be stretched, flexed, camouflaged, exaggerated, eroded, diluted – in some way acted upon. Especially when we are putting our best foot forward, we are expected to represent ourselves advantageously, albeit dishonestly.

Anyone who has ever bought or sold property knows, nay, expects, the associated rhetoric. The moment you're ripe for inspecting, you activate your metaphoric decoding dictionary. Even so, a friend of mine failed to recognise his very own apartment block when it appeared in descriptive newspaper print under the heading 'Tarzan's Tree-House':

Situated on the top floor of a boutique Art Deco building you will be seduced by the dappled north-easterly light, birdsong and lush forest surrounds. Stylishly presented with granite kitchen and modern finishes, there is still room to add your personal touch. From your balcony perched in the treetops . . . you may even spy Tarzan or Jane running on the forest floor below.

Here we have sixty-three words of recognisable real-estate-ese. The conventions are the result of an uneasy cohabitation of diverse elements. First, there's something which we might call Real Estate Code (REC), most notable for its hyperbole. In Tarzan's unit, 'green' becomes 'lush', 'park' becomes 'forest', the balcony is perched in the treetops.

Further, REC makes assumptions about the orientations of the prospective homebuyer. An old, small, dark-red-brick block becomes a 'boutique Art Deco building', aspect becomes 'dappled north-easterly light'. Here, the appeal is to seekers of a lifestyle to display, more than a home to live in.

The net effect of REC is a set of symbols that we adeptly interpret. We know from 'cosy' to expect cramped, from 'renovator's delight' to expect derelict. Now test your decoding agility with these: ideal starter; gourmet kitchen; priced to sell; fantastic potential; district vista; Euro appliances; summer breezes; spaciously gracious; graciously spacious; generously proportioned.

One of my favourites is 'affordable price range'. Given the absurdity of referring to affordability in absolute terms (I mean, Richard Branson's affordable is not mine), 'affordable price range' is meaningless.

What's included or excluded is also meaningful. Emphasis on lifestyle can focus attention on the environs rather than the property – hence a tiny stone cottage near the station becomes a 'superb first-home opportunity in the city's most exciting lifestyle precinct'.

We decode negatives that have been reframed as positives. Unfinished bits emerge as 'There is still room to add your personal touch.' 'Off-street parking' means no lock-up garage. 'Ample parking' means no lock-up garage or off-street parking. Similarly, absence or topic silence is meaningful. No mention of any kind of parking means start thinking about public transport options. The same conclusion can be drawn from descriptions that refer to 'walking distance to all amenities'.

In stark contrast to REC, there are instances of what-you-read-is-what-you-get. This is stand-alone, baldly descriptive language like: '2 bedrooms, 1 bathroom, balcony, lock-up garage, eat-in kitchen'. So distinct from REC is this language that increasingly it's being removed to outside the blurb's frame, and represented iconically by pictures of beds, bathtubs, etc. It's as if this 'real' information can't successfully be included within the hyper-blurb. Imagine this: 'You will be seduced by dappled NE light and birdsong in your two bedrooms plus one bathroom top-floor unit.' If these *must* intertwine, the language shifts to cute: 'a smart one-bedder for the savvy young exec'.

Another feature of this kind of language is the off-the-planet flight of fancy. Like the reference to Tarzan and Jane. I mean, really! Even the missing exclamation mark hints at semi-seriousness. So removed from reality is this, I'm calling it the 'What the...? factor'

(WTF). The use of 'birdsong' as a collective noun for the proximity of fauna, the sexual overtone of seduction – these all qualify as WTFs. Read any real estate adverts and the WTFs leap out at you: Renaissance terrace, just over a year young; seamless indoor–outdoor living; consummate residence to entertain international guests; easy living packed with panache.

One clue to this over-the-topness is the worrying absence of verbs. If you come across something like 'a stunning intersection of heritage and contemporary architecture', I suggest you give it a wide berth.

Fashion police

It'll please the fashion police that the totalitarian spirit is alive and well in the language that announces new season's styles.

Here's a sample of text. It appeared with a picture of an androgynous urban waif, homeless-looking, albeit scrubbed up for the photo shoot:

Saturday morning and it's time to dress down. Knits are slim-fit and worn on their own. Shirts are collared but untucked. Pants must be well-cut, loose but not daggy-baggy. Choose neutral or subtle colours. The daily male is relaxed, smart and sexy.

Look at the verbs. The favoured tense is the factual present – the kind of verb you find in statements like 'birds fly' and 'fish swim'. This is the world of fact, unencumbered by preference or taste. It's the language of encyclopaedia reference (Cairo is the capital of Egypt), environmental documents (Forty-six species of fish live in the river), real estate descriptions (The property has a private courtyard) and X-ray reports (The nodule is slightly enlarged but remains within normal limits). So 'Knits are slim-fit…The daily male is relaxed' has the comfortable certainty of the natural world.

It's a cowardly discourse. When verbs actually venture into territory that carries opinion, we still see no evidence of choice or personal taste. Who says that 'it's time to dress down'? Stand up and show yourself, I say. But no, in each case the command hides behind the syntax, confident in the knowledge that English allows a phrase like 'it's time to' without betraying the opinion-haver.

English also allows you to state obligations without credentials. It's not 'the surgeon general warns that smoking is harmful'. Rather, it's 'Pants must be well-cut, loose.' Again, says who? Imperatives slip in ('Choose neutral or subtle colours'), but why, and on whose authority?

Nothing is negotiable. Be there or be square. Do what you're told. At least in the army, you see who you're saluting. Here you just rush to the closest boutique and choose neutral. It would seem that no one minds being constructed as mindlessly compliant. Indeed, agency is camouflaged to the point of garments acting independently. Forget special effects. These clothes are alive!

Call it the quirk factor. The French do it well, and there's lots of it happening this summer. Denim gets dressed up and flirts with off-the-shoulder tops. Cute logo T-shirts and ruched blouses team up for a look that's part gypsy, part urban chic, but all in all, *très* exotic.

Denim has its own wild spirit; it can go with whatever, be petulant (It's my party and I'll cry if I want to), even flirt. Tops accept that they're team-players, can't act alone, but they're flexible, open to suggestion. New words or, rather, technical words (ruched) have moved into general parlance, having fallen off the back of a truck or the front of a catwalk. Does not an element of arrogance lurk in the assumption that 'ruched' is known (what, you don't?)? It means something like bunched up and frilly (thanks, *OED*). Perfect for size 0 anorexic – it means you can have a bit of substance without having to put on any weight.

The syntax, too, is meaningful. 'Ruched blouses' seems as conventional as 'experienced travellers', but in fact 'ruched' with 'blouses' is a new concoction. One has to travel quite some distance to unpack the coinage – blouses that have been ruched. If you dare to question if blouses were ever not-ruched, you're condemned to the blurred time boundaries of fashion, where the present is everything. Before-today is daggy (unless it's been earmarked for retro-glory) and after-today is, well, stay tuned.

Old words have meanings corralled. The part that's gypsy is the wild, dishevelled, 'freedom's just another word for nothing left to lose' kind of gypsy. Not the underclass, underwashed, underprivileged part. Urban chic is sexist but hints at sophistication. As for sexy French, well, we've moved into myth here.

Adjectives work hard. Some are transparent, mean what they say (off-the-shoulder). But how easy is it to identify 'well-cut, loose but not daggy-baggy'? Will Tom's 'loose' be 'daggy-baggy' on Dick? If Harry makes it work for him, does this guarantee he'll feel relaxed, be smart and seem sexy?

Hey, don't look for guarantees. Just go shopping.

Dogese

'Pop your panties off and pop up on the bed, there's a dear.'

This gently camouflaged command is the kind of language a well-intentioned doctor might use with a child, with someone very anxious, and (regrettably) perhaps with the elderly.

It's also the way a foreign-seeming patient may be addressed. Notice the friendly markers – phrasal verbs (various kinds of 'pop'), diminutives ('panties'), idiomatic terms of address ('there's a dear'). These are thought to be easier for a foreigner than formal language. Like, 'Please be so kind as to remove your underwear and then position yourself on the examination bed' – which sounds pompous and over-bearing. Ironically, being closer to the written form of English in which foreign speakers may be schooled, they find formal language more accessible than the rather bewildering pop-up-panty kind. 'Friendly' spells 'trouble' for someone new to the language. It renders contact with native speakers a trial.

There's one real-life, if unlikely, encounter that's ideal for the foreign speaker, and others to boot. I speak of Dogese – what dog-owners speak when they're out talking to People-Like-Them. Dog people, as I think of them, counting myself among them, constitute a strangely bonded and single-minded community with its own particular discourse conventions. But then any collective of people with shared interests and frequent contact will have connections that seem odd to outsiders. Below is a near-verbatim, authentic transcription of one such dog-owners' encounter, produced while the dogs were enjoying a mutual sniffy moment:

Pretty cute.
Yeah thanks. Yours is too.
How old?
Six months.
Oh just a pup! Will she grow much bigger?
Yeah, probably. Like a Lab but not as heavy.
Oh, OK …
What's her name?
Honey.
Of course. The colour.
Yeah. And yours?
Rufus.
OK.

In fact, Dogese is a training ground for anyone inhibited by the cut-throat world of fast, unaccommodated, authentic speech. It's a linguistic safe haven, especially for the shy and introspective among us, a group within the community who remain largely invisible.

I speak of they who are at their least comfortable in any encounter of talk-with-strangers. These are people who dread conversations on buses, trains and planes, at the office with unfamiliar staff, on blind dates, at any social venue. Even, perhaps especially, the annual Xmas party. They are the folk targeted by producers of self-help videos like 'How to have a conversation with a Total Stranger' or 'What do you say after you say "hello"?' I know about this undernoticed group of silent sufferers because for a long time I was one.

Dogese works. It's a predictably limited encounter, a linguistic sheltered workshop. All the complex processes and intersections characterising authentic conversation are reduced. Talk becomes manageable. For starters, it's mostly one-on-one which, as a speech event, is a breeze compared to coping with multiple speakers. While dog-owners congregate in little clusters of the like-minded, conversations tend to be between two. It *feels* friendly – by virtue of your dog, you're immediately welcome as an insider. If English had a *tu/vous* pronoun (see page 6), you'd slip into *tu* on approach, your dog as your entrée and I don't mean in the culinary sense.

Topics, too, are limited and predictable. Breed. Age. Name. Idiosyncratic behaviours. A basic rule is an equalising reciprocity. Something like this:

What sort's yours?
Labradoodle.
That's a mix of Lab and Poodle, right?
Yeah. Yours is a Kelpie, right?
Kelpie/Collie cross.

This closed, convergent discourse won't take a sudden trajectory into the unexpected. It's a strictly limited doggy semantic field.

Encounters are brief, a few minutes only. You might move along and have nearly the same conversation with someone else. Thus, walking the dog can afford any number of multiple practice opportunities.

For the shy, there is the bonus of minimal eye contact. Dog-owners tend to look down, towards the dog, as they speak. The averted gaze affects the turn-taking rules, and pausing becomes more generous and frequent. As you look benevolently towards your dog or theirs, silence is comfortable and comforting.

For the language learner, a paradox: because you're there for your dog not for your English, you may actually pick up more language, as you pleasurably lose yourself in the English-speaking moment.

Just remember to pick up the poo.

Taboo topics in public

Q: How do hedgehogs make love?
A: Carefully.

So, too, with taboo topics. How do we broach them? Carefully. Very carefully.

Think of those advertisements for bran... 'keeping you regular' – with not a hint of a mention of anatomy or physiology. It's up to the consumer to make the leap to 'bowel motion'. Think of the ads for pads (menstrual, not writing), where blue ink (the blue is blue because it's not red) is poured onto a pristine, snowdrift-white surface to indicate absorption and protection (see pages 169–72). Indeed one ad, on post-menopausal leaking of another kind, was so evasive, I initially had no idea this was another condition I could look forward to.

Those whose work revolves around taboo topics learn, through training or on-the-job experience, how best to manage the linguistic pragmatics. Increasingly there is more guidance in the research literature on the broaching of lifestyle questions during medical consultations. The AIDS epidemic is an example of a crisis compelling doctors to learn to ask questions they'd really rather avoid.

Technical terms are a salvation: you provide a urine sample, rather than piss in a cup. When talking to expectant parents, there's something about the polysyllabic 'contraction' (compared to 'pain' or 'pang') that's less likely to promote panic. Sometimes, though, the technical can block rather than assist. After the birth of my first child, I was wheeled to a room where I was left flat on my back, with an instruction from the nurse phrased thus: 'You'll stay here until you've voided. Then we'll take you down to the wards.'

Voided? The act of delivery must do damage to the brain because even my Latin didn't help. Yes, it signalled 'empty' and I was aware of the closeness with 'avoid', but I ended up in a no through road. I was stuck in this voiding room which was a limbo-land where people who were too shy to ask for clarification (yes, shy, even after the indignities of birth) would languish indefinitely. The nurse returned every so often to check on voiding results, of which, for an inordinately long time, there were none to report.

But you have to sympathise. Advertisements that broach taboo topics navigate a vertiginous collision of goals: they have to broach an unspeakable in order to sell the product.

Think of the newspaper ads for erection problems (EPs), where the campaign, featuring Brazilian football superstar Pelé – whose signature is in the corner, like a famous painting, atop 'Athlete of the Century' – so serendipitously (not) coincided with soccer World Cup fever. There he stands, in a respectable suit, in the centre of the picture, an upward shot to a smiling face, a now middle-aged, ex-sporting hero, an empty stadium behind him, a soccer ball at his feet, the whole scene cast in eerie blue (why blue?). A blurb over his thigh-to-knee area has the text of his rhetorical question: 'What qualifies me to talk about Erection Problems?' (*capitals lend legitimacy*). 'Simple, I'm a man.'

The message is clear. Any penis-owner can have this problem. Even Pelé. And 'simple' readily detaches itself and free-floats ... 'a simple man'...'a simple problem'...'a simple solution'.

On the facing page, the text continues. The inverted commas imply that it's still Pelé speaking, though there's no allowance for either the nature of spoken language or the natural intrusion of the Brazilian-Portuguese influence: 'Erection problems are a common medical condition but they can be successfully treated. So talk to your doctor today. Or for a confidential discussion or a free video and booklet, phone...or visit the website...I would.'

'I would'!! The distancing 'would' is such a giveaway, it jars. He doesn't say 'I did' (that would mean his owning up to the God-forbid EPs). All he's agreeing to is the hypothetical action that would follow his having the hypothetical condition. (It's still an awful risk, as he's likely to be damned by association, but they must have made it worth his while.)

Yes, it's an impossible circumstance. The fine print claims the ad is 'in the interests of good health' and the claim is alongside the reassuring 'your call will not appear on your telephone bill'. On the one hand, any man, even a vigorous, athletic black man with the world at his feet, can know about EPs. On the other hand, the evasive language and arm's-length distancing reflect respect for your privacy. And the taboo goes on.

Somehow, I don't remember them being quite so solicitous when they were pouring out that blue ink.

Weddings

More than a stretch limo separates 'wedding' and 'marriage'. The former is all over in one day, and usually triumphantly; the latter takes a bit longer, and 'triumph' may not always be the best choice of word. Despite the statistics giving couples close to a one-in-two chance of making it, weddings are back in vogue.

But perhaps 'making it' means something quite different today. We've lowered the bar. No longer an innings of till death do us part, it's more like as long as the 'for better' lasts. And who's to find fault with this? You don't go into it for the 'for worse', so it's as good a time as any to bail.

Weddings are intensely public; marriages are intensely private. Words spoken at weddings are laboured over in advance, ritualised, performed under public scrutiny. Words spoken in marriage, whether intimate, banal or acrimonious, are spontaneous and uttered behind closed doors.

Weddings are touted as a moment of magic. Of course, the magic is a carefully crafted, minutely choreographed kind. One that you can relive again and again, on video/DVD (do people really do that?). If you factor in a weekly viewing, say, forty-eight weeks a year, over four years, calculating what you're saving on a rental each time, you can reframe the wedding's bottom line in a more palatable way.

It's a sign of their buoyancy that weddings continue to generate their own lexicon. First it was 'Bridezilla' – defined as an ordinarily sensible bride-to-be who, at some point in the nuptials planning, lost sight of the value of money and the point of the celebration and began countering every sensible cost-saving suggestion with a teary, 'But it's my special day!' To which there is no rejoinder that works.

Now there's 'Groomzilla'. He's the bridegroom-from-hell, totally into every style-planning detail, *à la* the fab five from *Queer Eye for the Straight Guy*. He's a far cry from the commitment-shy, altar-phobic stereotype of yesteryear. Or at least yesteryear's myths about what women want and what men don't. The language says it all: while a woman used to 'catch' (think 'bait', 'ensnare', 'incarcerate'), men used to 'get caught'.

The wedding resurgence goes hand-in-glove with the new, soft, no-fault attitude to divorce. With the stigma gone, many 'return business' customers front up eagerly for their second or third go at the nuptials, this time better able to spend more (or maybe this time it's they, not their parents, who are paying the bills). Their marriages weren't 'broken'; their new families are 'blended'.

If it's your first divorce, you can even avoid the word. What you had was a 'starter marriage'. An oops-experience. You're young, it was brief, it's cut-your-losses all round, there are no assets or kids to argue over, the bail-out is usually consensual. Some of the gifts may not even have been de-boxed.

We now have 'destination weddings'. This is where you have your tropical island wedding away, spending the bucks you saved on the guest list on travel and assorted whatnot. Either way you're supporting the industry. See www.confetti.co.uk for a sample of what eloping used to avoid.

A staggering cluster of service specialists now congregates around bridal needs. Nails, fake tans, fat loss (8 kilos / 9 weeks), marriage education. It's busy, busy, busy. Celebrants have to be met, assessed, shortlisted. Vows have to be planned, agreed, practised. Rings have to be chosen, ordered, collected, safe-kept, not forgotten. Wedding wordsmiths help design the invitations (choose traditional, romantic, contemporary or creative). They also do speeches. Or hire your own wedding planner – a firm called 'Tantrums and Tiaras' sounds promising.

Then there's the wedding gift list, where good taste gets sacrificed on the altar of practicality. Gone are the days of double-up kitchen appliances. While you're troubleshooting, consider the prenup, or, if it's too late, the postnup, each of which tries bravely to keep assets and love separate.

It's not only assets and weddings that don't mix. The new 'love contract' is a document signed by co-workers who agree to stay romantically uninvolved with other members of staff, for the good of their work focus/productivity as well as all-round workplace hygiene. Legally, this is merely a statement of intention and maybe not even legal.

In any case, people may be less able than previously believed to defend themselves against Cupid's arrows. British doctor John Marsden argues that what we call 'love' is indistinguishable from a severe pathology. Behaviourally, it is reminiscent of psychosis, and biochemically not unlike substance abuse.

In the light of Marsden's research, the 'starter marriage' phenomenon makes a whole lot more sense.

Language of dieting

While I'm counting calories, measuring fat, notching down carbs or walking the dog, I'm wont to wonder whether the whole dieting trip would be easier if the language in which we do it were less destructive.

I kid you not. The major dieting metaphor is war and competition. The battle of the bulge is something that's won or lost. You need an iron will and inner discipline. You must be on your guard 24/7, staying focused on your goal. This is the kind of talk you might hear in the army or even the corridors of the Olympic Village where world-class athletes prepare for their moments of gruel and glory.

Another metaphor is mental illness. *Woman's Day* screams, 'Elle: The Secret Torments that Drove her to an Arizona Clinic'. We're told her obsession put her in rehab, warning of an imminent explosion. There's talk of her insecurities, the image having to crack, the halo having to slip. Closely aligned are metaphors of suffering. Paula Abdul's bulimia is described as a descent into hell.

Another metaphor is the yo-yo or see-saw, or any other thing that habitually goes up and down. The woman (it's usually a woman) is on a treadmill, out of control, her ups and downs governed by extraneous malevolent forces. As the queen of yo-yo, Oprah, if nothing else, has removed some of the enveloping language of secrecy.

Meanwhile, though, the public talk about private shame has legitimised the confession genre. Indeed, the verbal purging provides such a fitting congruence with the other kind of purging: Jennifer Aniston admits to diet addiction, conceding her skinny image may have contributed to fans' pill-popping and starvation diets. Accompanying pictures of her developing svelte-ness are placed alongside the details of her high-protein/low-carb Zone regimen, in case you too want to try it. All this despite the warning, in the small print, that taken to extremes, the Zone 'can deprive the brain of essential nutrients'. Say no more.

But a women's mag is just not a women's mag without a royal, a celebrity, a scandal and a diet. Fergie's a steal with her four-in-one. If it's not a sensational new diet (trim those thighs before summer), exercise routine or meditative mind-shifting mantra, it's news about some celeb's great new figure or maybe her former figure (check out before-and-afters) disappearing into anorexia or obesity. When big-happy-and-sexy Camryn Manheim (of the TV show *The Practice*) lost 35 kilos, the bets were on: was it a diet? an exercise routine? a secret stomach stapling? or a new man? The headline's ambiguity ('Camryn's staple diet?') encourages you to join in the speculation.

Yet the thinner we wanna be, the fatter we get. The 'lost language of fat' is the topic of an article in the monthly newspaper *Sydney's Child* on the growing obesity epidemic. Frightened of creating a ripe context for eating disorders, parents fear that 'fat' is the new f-word.

With fat and diet as no-noes, they're pushed into silent frustration, unable to enforce sensible eating habits without reinforcing the negative aesthetics and shame of being overweight.

We need reminding that aesthetic perceptions are cultural constructs, not absolute truths. They vary in time and space. The early childhood photos of a friend of mine who was born in Italy in the aftermath of World War II have the roundness of face and form that are testimony to the attitudes of the time. Signs of bodily health, perhaps measured in units of fleshy bounciness, were doubtless linked to the recent struggle to survive in war-torn Europe.

I'm not wishing a war on anyone. There's got to be a better way of shifting perceptions. Enough of 'you can never be too rich or too thin'. 'More' does not equal 'happy' (for evidence of this, see Clive Hamilton's book *Growth Fetish*). And thin is sometimes just too thin. Maybe a wallpaper print of Rubens women would let cuddly sit next to beautiful for a while.

Anyway, losing weight is the wrong metaphor sending the wrong mental message: after all, what you lose, you go and look for, and it's usually just around the corner.

Protection

Once upon a time, a sanitary pad was a sanitary pad. No longer. Now we have a New York deli of possibilities. You can end up lingering, nay, loitering, among the supermarket's female-hygiene shelves for an amazingly long stretch of time. You see there faces of people on the cusp of giving up and making rushed, random, desperate selections. Send a man to do the shopping and he may never return.

There's a tension here, and I don't mean the crampy, premenstrual kind. I mean a linguistic tension. On the one hand, we have a contemporary pursuit of niche-sensitive diversification, resulting in a plethora of similar products – closer, even, than Coke and Pepsi. On the other, in the naming of these products, we have a coyness that is far removed from contemporary permissiveness.

It's challenging. Remember, the big, bad word of female-hygiene discourse is 'wet'. You see it nowhere but sense it everywhere. Its opposite is 'dry', but even here we have dangers: there's good dry (that is, not wet), and there's bad dry (rough, abrasive, sore). That's Challenge Number One.

Challenge Number Two is to market the products under a larger umbrella: the promotion of protection. But note that the noun 'protection' hints at (though does not name) the thing from which protection is being offered – exposure. Exposure and its minders, embarrassment and humiliation, are there in the backstage. And all of this is so delicate that the collective noun – female hygiene – actually has nothing to do with the marketing ploy. So we have a name that is not a name, but rather a code or a cue for something else.

They have to come up with names that are meaningful in terms of the product differentiation; that promise protection while tripping the fear of exposure; modest names that offend no one, while giving women what they believe they want; thereby addressing the need the marketers themselves have helped to create. No mean feat.

Thus we have 'regular' standing against 'super' (or maxi) with regard to absorbency (leakage). But 'regular' also opposes 'slim-line' with regard to width and thickness (comfort). Of course 'slim-line' *à la* pad is qualitatively different from the 'panty liner' per se, the former having to do with menstruation, the latter with the more generally classifiable and awfully taboo topic of 'discharge'. Though, geographically, yes, we're in the same terrain.

Wingage is something else again, and comes as an option among all the others. The angelically named 'wings' have a dual concern – sideways leakage and non-slippage. Sideways leakage matters because, fluid being fluid, it will find its way out wherever it can. Non-slippage matters because if the pad (any pad) should slip, its putative qualities are rendered void. No point having a highly absorbent pad stuck fast halfway down your leg.

Then there are the non-menstrual liners, which start off thin (absorbency being less of an issue) and move to ultra-thin, invisible, barely there and breathable (don't ask). Liners tend to be marketed for where they're going to be kept (purse packs); or for under what garment they're to be worn (like G-strings and, I mean, what's a little black dress without a matching liner?); or for where they might be accidentally discovered. The last of these establishes the need to cater for discovery, by a range of discreet but attractive packaging (florals, stripes, geometric, etc.).

Lurking below all of this is the generalised threat of mattress stain. It's a fear subsumed in a nomenclature of all nights, good-nights, extra longs and curved. One type, called 'overnights', makes a heavy flow seem more like a recreational weekend away (hey, why not?). Some handy packs include a day-and-night set, colour-coded in case you forget.

Yet, ironically, product diversification driven by commercial considerations is actually congruent with what women know – that periods vary from woman to woman, from stage of life to stage of life, from month to month, from day to day. So the notion of heavy/light has some validity. (I foresee the day when pads will come marked with labels like 'Day 3, 1400 hours'.)

As if the fact of menstruation, catering for half the population between the ages of thirteen and forty-five, were not enough, manufacturers continue to chase the god of commodification. Leaking slightly into the menstrual pads section of the supermarket is a new breed of pads that hints at other dimensions of female functioning. Maternity pads are really afterbirth pads, but hey, who wants to know about that? And then there's the marketing around the image of 'poise' – which taps into other varieties of leakage. Promises of odour control, discreet bladder protection, and an active life suggest problems one may never have known about. Some taboos only come alive in a supermarket aisle.

The linguistic tension between the need to describe something for the purpose of selling it and the perceived obligation to avoid being explicit is only part of the story. Consider, too, the rather bizarre paradox of the perceived need to euphemise about 'feminine hygiene' within a broader culture largely qualm-less about depicting female sexuality. When it comes to the female body in media, art and advertising, the word coy wouldn't know what to do with itself.

Teen talk

Ecclesiastes tells us that 'to every thing there is a season, and a time to every purpose under the heaven'. There's birth and death, sowing and harvesting, but nowhere in there do they mention, or even hint at, the season of adolescence.

This is the season when nerdy equals dead. Gotta be like my friends. Would die before I'd stick out and be different. Arguably, the best thing about Hugh Grant's film *About a Boy* is the boy himself – the one with the strange clothes, weird haircut and mother stuck in the 1970s. She's afflicted with her own torpor while he daily dies a thousand deaths for being different. Thank you, school bullies.

Teenagers do the identity thing most visibly through their music and their accoutrements, including (but not limited to) their clothes. It's endlessly fascinating – the need to be different from (parent generation) but identical to (own generation).

Language, too, is a way for identity to be forged and it at least doesn't require a cash flow (phew). Teenagers' talk displays, conveys and consolidates their in-group solidarity. And that, of course, is the whole point.

The creativity is awesome. Most visible are the words that they take from the regular mainstream and then reframe, injecting new nuances of meanings (see 'random' and 'gay' in the examples below) before adopting them into their own lexicon. Then there are the words they contort grammatically. Like 'heaps', which morphed from a regular plural noun (one heap, two heaps) into an adverb (heaps good).

Another common ploy is fiddling with a verb's transitivity: like changing a transitive verb (to wreck + object) into an ergative (it wrecks, no object, like it rains). I made the mistake years ago of responding to my son's 'it wrecks' with a 'what?' (meaning, what does it wreck?).

Some of their words they think they invented (what do they really know?), like 'groovy'. Others they acknowledge have been around for ages (like 'cool') – but they still want them, and want to mark them as their own ('kul'). But then they think they invented sex too.

Often their words migrate into the mainstream (as 'heaps' did). Once this happens, it loses all appeal to its originators, who promptly drop it like a hot potato. Once it's moved on, it loses the very social markings it was invented for. Worse, it takes on others. Then continuing to use it is tantamount to sleeping with the enemy.

You can see why one's teenagers and their friends would offer ripe pickings for a hungry linguist. Indeed, the very prospect gives chauffeuring a whole new dimension. (As for the subtle art of eavesdropping – we'll save that for another time.) Here is a recent harvesting from the home crop:

Wanna go to the shops and get some chocolate?
Nah. Effort.

Were there any cool guys at the party?
Just randoms.

Really wanna see the new Mel Gibson movie.
Same.

I so don't want to get my hair cut.
Neither.

Did you see her shoes?
Weird-as.

Look what that dog's doing. That's yuk-as.
Fully gross.

I love this song.
Yeah, Nova's da bomb.

I got grounded this weekend.
That's so gay.
It so is.

Even from these random (sorry) samples, a pattern emerges. The most visible feature is a quality of minimalism, especially in the rejoinders. Crisp military responses, taut and elliptically spare. This is new-season trim lamb, all fat removed.

Yet, it's not only minimal, it's *ostentatiously* minimal. This is the soundbite generation. It's communication by snatches of talk. (Sustained dialogue? What's that?) If they ask for an explanation (on anything from gravity to gerunds), you've got less than a minute to put it out there. Otherwise, don't bother. It's one-line kingdom. Fast and pithy wins hands down every time.

Note, too, the unswerving orientation towards alignment. Speaker and listener line up together. Discord is a no-no. It helps that the talk is vague: this allows little substantial basis for conflict. After all, who in that demographic wouldn't see a Mel Gibson flick?

And there's a sustained infusion of the emotive. Topic, style, purpose: it's all about attitude and agreement. Semantics and precision are joyfully sacrificed on the twin altars of affinity and solidarity.

And that's how it should be. After all, it's their season to be different-from and same-as.

The beauty beast

'Remember', my friend said, her voice taking on the timbre of prophetic admonishment, 'Your face starts here.' She was pointing to a place just above an imaginary nipple-to-nipple line. 'Mmm', I muttered, looking down and feeling down, 'That's a funny place for a face.'

There we were on the ground floor of Hamods, the department store where the gleam quantum is overwhelming. All those shiny, sparkly Mr Sheen surfaces, the beautiful packaging, pastel shades, clean lines. Salespeople who are s-o-o well-groomed and blemish-free (do they get fired if a zit appears?) and s-o-o keen to see you, can't wait to serve you, just want to show you this teeny-weeny powdery-blue free sample of ultra-refined, filtered, air-blended sea-weed retrieved from the floor of the Mediterranean. Yes, it's yours, your own very special, tautological 'free gift' in its own matching bag, if you (just) buy £500 worth of product (easy to do, there's the tragedy) within the next thirty minutes…time…starts…NOW!

It's the site of big business. What won't you pay to 'get back what time took away'? To 'turn back the clock'? To allow 'the years to slip away'? No accident that Old Mother Time features prominently in the promotional language, and is reinforced in the product names. Anti-wrinkle, firming cream called 'plenitude' suggesting a combo of 'plenty' and 'attitude'. You can't forget for a moment that you have no time to waste; indeed, you have time to make up for (or time to make-up for).

The choices are in your face, as it were. It's clear vs dark bags, firm vs sagging, crows'-feet vs unlined. Which do you want? The cashier is down there. *Tempus fugit*. Gravity falleth. Youthfulness is expensive. You get what you pay for. Who needs Botox? Line up here.

New verbs appear, especially for the metrosexual market. I asked an amazingly coiffed and oiled hunkoid masquerading as a sales assistant what 'scruffing' meant. He said it was the same as 'clarifying' for women, but 'the boys need their own word'.

There's a narrative being constructed here. Responsibility is being given to us. It's our skin. Only we can achieve results. It's a contract between you and your face: respond positively to the challenge, spend big, invest time and commitment, and bingo – the skin they've been telling us that we always dreamed of will be ours.

If on the off-chance, dream skin does not unfold, don't blame the product or the promise. It is we who are to blame and the language helps us to see that. 'Should' becomes the great tyranny, the universal regret. We should've started the regimen sooner, should've spent more, should've used more product. We should've prioritised the face over…(what? the kids? the home? the job? the mortgage?

the dog?). We should go back for more, try again, change product, spend big (or bigger), and this time, we should have more faith.

I'm sick of being reminded of the ravages of ageing. Isn't it enough that we age? Why must we anguish in advance? I don't want to find out about 'the seven visible signs of ageing' – the words that fade off the screen too fast for me to note them down, thereby contributing to the rising angst. I don't want to hear about any more awful 'bl' words – blemishes, blotches, blackheads.

I know the ritual: cleanser, toner, moisturiser. Or does the toner come after the moisturiser? The sequence was my undoing. Why can't they mix them up and put them in one bottle? They do it with triple antigens and pizza toppings.

There's that cheap, no-frills jar of Sorbolene cream from Price-Right, Bi-Lo or Reach-Down, or any other place named after a phrasal verb. Your dermatologist, backed up by *Choice* magazine, will tell you there's nothing good in the big-bucks stuff that isn't in the Sorbolene jar. Plus bottom-line blockout (anyone buying up blockout shares?).

Homogeneity is people in the beauty product promotions. All happy, successful and carefree (a word which has lost some of its panache since the panty liner people appropriated it). Is it good skin that made them what they are? Or is their skin the glowing outcome of naturally high levels of happy, carefree success? Chicken or egg? Or both? Blended in a smoothy with soy milk and aloe vera.

Promises, lies, blame and recrimination. I'd rather point the finger at heredity. Sigh. There's always Extreme Makeover.

WORD BIOGRAPHIES

This section contains a collection of word biographies. I use the term 'biography' because, despite their patterned nature, words also tend to develop their own idiosyncratic features. The analogy to human biography – recognisably human, yet uniquely (in a DNA sense) individual – seems apt. Over time and through particular circumstances, words accrue their own habits of use (we might say 'baggage' if we wanted to move towards another metaphor). The biographies portrayed here were chosen relatively randomly because any word would probably lend itself to the same style of scrutiny. In each case, a word or phrase, seemingly straightforward and innocuous, is the centre of attention, and the exploration follows various pathways – semantic, etymological, grammatical and pragmatic. As will become evident, to be of service, dictionaries worth their mustard must reflect popular and current usage, while also providing historical information. It is in the daily marketplace of language use, messy as it is, that words work, and their meaning must always be calibrated against their context of use.

Aspirational

When I was a kid there was no Turkish bread, pittas, bagels or focaccia. You didn't eat rocket, artichokes, eggplants or sun-dried tomatoes. Cheese meant Kraft and there were no goats involved. Roast veggies were potatoes plus pumpkin. Forget kumara.

Language, too, has changed. We now have the word 'aspirational' which until recently I'd never encountered. Now it's everywhere.

There used to be 'aspiration', which is the noun denoting the fact of aspiring, which means the having of lofty or ambitious desires. I once wrote history essays about 'Italian nationalist aspirations' under Garibaldi. And somehow I associate it with Verdi. Maybe it's an Italian thing.

Then there's the verb 'to aspire' ('s/he aspires to greatness'), and the noun for the person who aspires, 'an aspirant' (the stress falls on the first syllable), which can replace 'candidate' when the position being aspired towards is itself lofty – Governor-General, Pro-Vice-Chancellor, UN Secretary-General. Rather like the difference between 'kill' and 'assassinate' – what matters is the status of the object of the endeavour. All of the 'aspire'-related words are connected to the Latin *aspirare* (to breathe upon), perhaps because it connotes a certain breathless anticipation.

One dictionary defines aspirational as 'showing that you want to have more money and a higher social position than you now have'. The example given is: 'Designer labels have become aspirational status symbols, especially among the young.' But it's been suggested that everyone wants to improve their lot, and no one wants to impair it. Perhaps then, because we're not supposed to feel envy, it's a euphemism for 'greedy'.

I doubt that there's a link to the trademark Aspirin, outside the lofty aim of pain removal. And 'aspro' as academic slang for 'associate professor' may have a link, unintended though ironic, to 'aspiring' in the sense of trying hard, but never getting there. You have to wonder, though, why the existing adjective (aspiring), for one who aspires to things lofty, somehow fell short, necessitating the creation of 'aspirational'. Is it that 'aspiring' has a certain uncomfortable wannabe sense? Perhaps what was needed was a word with the denotation of 'aspiring' but a more ... well, aspirational connotation.

Yet, the push may be grammatical rather than semantic. 'Aspiring' tends to be an attributive adjective, which means its place of preference is usually before the noun ('an aspiring actor' or 'an aspiring cook'). Predicative adjectives, by contrast, come after the verb ('the door was ajar', not 'ajar doors'). If 'the aspiring actor' tells us something about where the actor wants to be but has not yet arrived, 'the actor is aspirational' tells us something about how hard s/he is trying. Maybe it's a glass half empty-or-full situation.

I suspect the emergence of this word is not unrelated to the self-help industry. Thinking lofty thoughts, wanting lofty things, seeking to be better, different, other – through astrology, yoga, Pilates, previous lives.

Another context where 'aspirational' appears is as a pejorative description of a certain voter or consumer. I'm told that the descriptor fits a woman with a young family, who dreams of having more materially than her background would have led her to expect. She's consumerist, pragmatic, possibly naive.

There was much talk, last election, about 'the aspirational vote'. Mind you, talkback radio king Alan Jones, when asked if his lucrative move from 2UE would alienate his audience, said: 'I don't think so. My audience is aspirational. As I am, and I think they know I worked hard and I don't leave them behind in what I do.'

This is the nice cousin of nasty 'ambitious'. Roughly: wanting to better oneself; having lofty plans; being on the way up; admiring talent; being forward-thinking; not standing still; not marking time; restlessly yearning for more, bigger, better; feeling the need to upgrade quite often; not being afraid to be aggressively entrepreneurial.

Would-be romance writers are advised to write for an aspirational reader. Heroes and heroines need aspirational names. Not Suzie but Selene. Not Craig but Creighton. Further, aspirational first names perform better when in an unequal relationship with the surname. So Coralie Lane works; Cora Lane doesn't. Rule of thumb: a three-syllable first name + a one-syllable surname (try Dominique Moss) for maximum aspirationality.

Not sure where that leaves Tom, Dick or Ruth.

Faux

Our preference for 'abattoir' over 'slaughterhouse' is quite transparent. To English ears, the French sounds more benign, certainly less bloody. 'Abattoir' allows one to be a carnivore a while longer.

Why borrow a foreign word when we have our own in the pantry? Consider the appropriating panache with which the French *faux* has launched into English. Certainly, 'faux' wins over all its rivals – 'false', 'imitation', 'replica', 'fake', 'artificial', 'inauthentic', 'simulated' or 'synthetic'. But then, we're not averse to positively connoted neologisms when it suits us. We have 'illusionist', in the visual arts, for a master of the technique of imitation. How then can we explain our wholehearted embrace of 'faux'?

I once spotted a bag in an el-cheapo mail-order catalogue (don't ask). While the bag in the accompanying picture was definitely plastic, the finish was described as 'leather-like'. Now 'like' is notoriously slippery – and I don't mean the teenage 'like' used more or less to punctuate. 'Like' as in a hyphenated suffix, tacked on as an afterthought almost, offers a potent *mélange* of associations. These exploit the multiple functions of 'like' as verb (to like) and as preposition (it's like leather). At a pinch, a wafting symbiosis seeks to blur appearance and reality – so, you like leather? Maybe you like to think this bag is like leather? Maybe not.

'Faux' plays havoc with our notion of value. Faux marble looks like marble, faux *bois* looks like wood. Do we go for faux because we want the look but not the expense? Do we hope no one will notice? Apparently, George Washington got away with using painted pine to look like mahogany on his house at Mount Vernon. Then again, here we are, centuries later, passing comment, so perhaps in the long term he didn't quite get away with it.

When the great unwashed go faux, will the value of the genuine article increase? Or will the snob value of 'real' drop when faux becomes the flavour of the month? What will happen when production methods so streamline the faux as to make it superior – more real-looking, more durable, more economical than the real thing.

Is the day coming when faux will be the pricey option? Perhaps it already is.

'Faux' remains a word replete with inner tension. On the one hand, like 'abattoir', it serves an aesthetic, camouflaging function. On the other, it has a reverse-snob effrontery: yes, I know I'm not the real thing, but I'm proud of who I am. I may not be real, but I'm totally open about being fake, which makes me pretty real. If there's nothing wrong with a pretend-real, then there's everything right about a transparent faux. All told, you've got to admire faux. In one sneery, dismissive syllable, a sleight of hand no less, made the more condescending by the silent 'x' ('faux' rhymes with 'go'), faux wipes the slate clean, moves the goalposts, sets up new rules and comes out the winner.

These days you can get faux fur, faux lawn, faux antiques, faux pearls, faux pets, faux body parts. A company operating out of Las Vegas at www.faux.com specialises in faux finishes (one presumes for the kitchen) and faux tools (yes, I wondered, too). There's the faux-hawk hairstyle, where a strip of hair across the top of the head is longer and higher than the rest but somehow it can magically normalise in time for work on Monday morning. There's the faux-mosexual (you work it out) and the fauxhemian (or pretend-grunge). There's a Faux Faulkner contest where entrants are invited to par-ody the style of the original William Faulkner. I wonder if they had originally wanted to go for Hemingway but the name didn't have the same alliterative ring as the double-effed Faux Faulkner.

Now, we have faux kidnapping – a fake four-to-six-hour kidnap staged as real. It costs between $500 (econo-deal) and $5,000 (top-of-the-range) to have agents from Extreme Kidnapping abduct you. Optional extras (payable in advance) include sensory deprivation, verbal abuse and mock torture. The line blurs between client and victim. You can also arrange for a faux rescue. Some bored couples do it for the 'rescue sex' alone.

The postmodernist sculptor Ron Mueck constructs artworks of the human body with a grotesque verisimilitude, but usually with one variable askew – such as the body made larger or smaller than life – a reminder that reality perhaps needs a touch of the fake to make it bearable.

Get

Some words attract enemies. Take 'get'. There's a story, which I don't think is apocryphal, about a schoolteacher who annually initiates her little charges in the same ritual. It's perhaps their first introduction to serious writing. The children each write 'get' on a small square of paper which they then fold into a smaller square. The class then traipses outside to a plot of soil where the children solemnly bury their 'gets'. The message is clear: 'get' has no place at school.

The Swiss psychologist Jean Piaget would be delighted at this act of concretisation. Reify, bury, then ban. Not an abstraction in sight. It's neat and doesn't take long, but what other messages slip through? If a child believes her 'get' is dead and buried, how does she account for its popping out of her mouth/pen, rogue-state style? How come 'get' is OK outside the classroom, but not OK inside?

I mourn those little 'gets', languishing in their earthy graves, their little lights hidden under multiple bushels. They never knew the warmth of day. Perhaps the word's foul reputation derives from its prominence in expletives, like 'get fucked'. But why limit our appreciation of 'get' to the boundaries of an expletive? 'Get' is like cooking with mushrooms or tofu – bland but versatile, adopting the flavour of its surrounds, becoming whatever one wants. How else could it accomplish the diversity of 'get' + 'married', 'lucky', 'lost', 'stoned', 'rid of'? And what does this illustrate? That there's more than one kind of risotto, one shape of pasta. And there's more than one 'get'.

Those who condemn and ban 'get', and have their little charges bury their 'gets' in school soil, have missed the point. They have made three assumptions. First, that 'get home' is a lazy version of 'arrive', 'get dinner' a lazy version of 'cook'. As well as this assumption of indolence, there's the assumption of equivalence, as if the two are identical in meaning. But the choice of 'arrive' over 'get home' is a function of context and purpose. We have them both; we use each according to the circumstance. And third, there is no inherent superiority in the (usually Latinate) verb as distinct from the (usually Anglo-Saxon) phrasal verb.

Furthermore, purists mistake the slippery quality of 'get' for sloppiness. In fact, it is this very imprecision that gives it such mileage. A recent campaign by Mercedes-Benz – 'some people just don't get it' – makes its classist point by exploiting the slippery quality of 'get': 'get' as in 'grasp' or 'understand' and 'get' as in 'receive' or 'acquire', a subtle, blurred intertwining of brain power and income that is ignorant and arrogant. Slippery 'get' is infinitely flexible, as evidenced in an ad for a holiday resort in which a woman massages a man's back over the caption 'Let the pressure get to you'.

Everywhere you look, 'get' is doing diverse things. It appears in a few different structural patterns, each associated with a particular set of meanings. One is 'get' + direct object (the thing being got) as in 'Did you get my letter / the milk?' or 'Can you get me from the airport?' Here 'get' means something like 'receive', 'obtain', 'fetch' or 'take'.

It has a metaphorical use, too, like 'getting a joke' (understand) or 'I'll get you for this' (revenge). Then there are the odd word combinations that signal a change, shift or movement: 'get old', 'get to know', 'get going'. Verbs based on phrases, in particular, carry a strong sense of this: 'get away', 'get back', 'get up'. We have hyperactive 'get' where change is made to happen, as in 'get someone up / moving', 'get your hands warm', 'get your elbow out of my face'. And there's the one I think of affectionately as 'rude get', where attention focuses on a completed end point, like 'get lost' and 'get a life'.

Colloquial 'get' has various manifestations. 'Get with' (teenspeak for 'kiss') has recently morphed into a noun ('Was he a good get?'). And an increasingly popular pattern is 'I didn't even get to dance', as spoken by my daughter after a failed Saturday night. This construction carries a certain goal-oriented striving. Witness the

celebratory energy of 'Wow, we even got to scuba dive!' The colloquial is often evanescent: many such verbs enjoy their fifteen minutes in the sun, the way 'do lunch' did for a while, before vanishing.

A newish subclass of 'gets' forges a middle path between active
and passive. If 'being stoned' refers to the state of being, then 'getting stoned' refers to one means by which that state is reached.
While both are passive, 'get' somehow has more gumption. Which
brings us back to 'rude get', which also has a hint of being between
active and passive. Telling someone to 'get fucked' actually wishes
on them the ignominy of being the agent in their own destruction.
Neat.

The teacher who gets her pupils to bury their 'gets' suffers from
UBCS (Unwitting Blanket Condemnation Syndrome). As I've said,
judging 'get home' and 'get dinner' as unacceptable synonyms of
'arrive' and 'cook', respectively, falsely assumes these words are
equivalents. In fact, acceptability is a function of context and purpose. The choice of the formal ('to bathe') over the less formal
('have/take a bath') relates to the why / where / with whom of its
use. Nothing to do with the inherent quality of the one compared
to the other.

After all, the results, in terms of cleanliness, are the same.

Random

Speech is different from writing. Here I am referring of course to
spontaneous everyday speaking, not the studied, re-drafted, nicely
choreographed speaking out loud which is formal speech. After all,
formal speech is really written language read / spoken out loud.

In most forms of writing (excepting shopping lists and postcards),
we try harder to choose our words. We look for logical development.
We interweave cohesive links so as to ensure that each bit follows
the earlier bit nicely. By contrast, when we speak we're granted less
encoding time, the upside of which means we're also granted more
licence.

Or so I thought until recently. My teenage daughter found a particular remark I'd just made quite non-sequitural (I just invented that adjective). Her comment was, 'That was a bit random.'

Perhaps I should have been grateful to have a stray thought so swiftly and neatly classified. But the 'random' caught me unawares and led me down a track of its own making. This wasn't the first time I'd heard the new-random. I distinguish it from old-random because it is different.

Old-random nests comfortably in a domain called research, being found alongside companions like sampling or selection. It means an absence of definite or prearranged order. The *Collins Dictionary* says it well: 'chosen without regard to any characteristics of the individual members of the population so that each has an equal chance of being selected'. Thus 'random breath testing' is supposed to be just that – though when you're chosen, of course, it never feels very random.

Another dictionary cites 'random' in the building-trade context of paving stones, or the method of laying them. It denotes an irregularity of size or arrangement, the absence of a discernible pattern. In buying pebbles recently for a Japanese-style patio, my choice was among small, medium, large, polished or random. I went for medium, finding small too piddly, large too big, polished too expensive, and random, well, too random. Yet, while 'random' wasn't my choice of pebble, I cast no aspersions on the word itself. Such usages are neutral and unemotional.

Etymologically, 'random' dates back to the fourteenth century and the Old French *randir* (to gallop), which is connected, apparently, to the Old High German *rinnan* (to run). As for links to 'randy', use your imagination: perhaps running/galloping out of control?

The *Collins Dictionary* suggests an informal meaning of 'unknown', giving the example: 'Some random guy waiting for a bus'. Yet the new-random moves a step beyond 'unknown'. It seems rather to mean 'unconnected'. Thus my earlier non sequitur was random, I am led to infer, because it didn't explicitly and recognisably link up with anything textual or contextual.

Snippets of overheard teenage telephone discourse have featured 'random boys' at a party, referring to the odd groupings of unconnected young males appearing unexpectedly. It's a short jump, of course, from 'unexpected' and 'unconnected' to 'weird'. Yet, despite their randomness, I sense a ubiquity about the party boys, and a concurrent low-lying compliance among the girls. Perhaps, built into the semantics of new-random, is an acceptance of an underlying and implicit social chaos. Perhaps, once the unexpected is allowable, even predictable, then 'random' may have more to do with the boys' whatever status than with the fact that they showed up uninvited.

New-random is not only a semantic shift. Where old-random was largely neutral, its contemporary cousin can carry shades of negativity – from, most mildly, 'people I don't know', to, more judgementally, 'peculiar' or 'strange'. At its worst, it's a denigrating of otherness within the all-important adolescent identity stakes.

New-random has also roamed away from its adjectival status. It now works as a noun: 'A few randoms dropped in later.' It's also turned up as an exclamation-*cum*-interjection of surprise, rather like 'wow': 'Random! Where did you come from?!'

I sense that 'random' is nowhere near the point of having exhausted its morphing potential. Meanwhile, I'm aware that the car industry is close to exhausting its stock of potential names for new models. Witness bottom-of-the-barrel scrapings like Echo, Laguna, Tribute, or the faux-foreign Sportivo. Indeed, on the upturn are numbers – less emotively imbued if somewhat sterile. Before 'random' becomes too negative, now might be the time, perhaps, for one of those jeepy vehicles that purport to work on bitumen and unbeaten track. That sounds pretty random.

Actually

A reader wrote to me about 'actually'. She said it was everywhere and getting worse.

I could tell she was gritting her teeth. It was driving her to distraction, she said. Even well-known current affairs commentator George Negus is doing it, she wrote. What about an 'actually'-free day, she proposed. A welcome interlude when we could all self-deactualise. She warned that we were in the midst of an epidemic; she foresaw no natural abatement; she ended with a capitalised 'HELP!'

But what help is to be had, I thought. Banning a word is like banning anything. It's complicated. Think Prohibition in 1920s USA if you have any doubts. What's the point of a ban if it can't be policed? Doesn't language move, morph, mutate, multiply on its own terms, out of reach of the language police? Is the answer re-education?

Perhaps the solution is understanding, and for that we need analysis. How does it work in a sentence? What does it mean? What purpose does it serve? Why does it get some people's goat? All good questions, worthy of the probe.

It turns out that 'actually' is not a menace. It's an adverb. The 'ly' tells us that and any grammar book confirms it. But of itself this is empty – the question is, what do we learn by knowing that it is an adverb?

It depends on how deeply we delve. If we skip across the literal surface – for example, 'Actually, George Negus uses the adverb quite often' – and milk it of its semantic content, the sense we derive is a statement of actuality (what Negus does), which clearly doesn't need 'actually' to work. Delete it here and the meaning remains (mostly) unaffected. The perception of a tautology may account for the irritation factor.

If 'actually' adds anything, it's a sense of 'contrary to what you might have thought'. A signal that expectations may not be met:

I better take my brolly.
Actually, the rain's stopped and the sun's out.

So, you can identify the man you saw?
Well, it was actually quite dark at the time.

But the main function of 'actually' is not to contribute to the propositional content of the sentence. 'Actually' is what we call a 'stance adverb'. It signals the attitude of the speaker/writer towards an aspect of the idea being expressed. So 'Actually, George Negus uses it a lot' registers the speaker's surprise that this would happen with someone of Negus's something (insert: class, education, reputation, position, age, height, etc.). It conveys information about what the speaker thinks of Negus – and not only Negus, but Negus-like people. So, far from 'actually' being redundant or empty, it quite reverberates with meanings.

'Stance' literally means the way you stand. Metaphorically, it suggests the way you position yourself ideationally, or in relation to the ideas or propositions you are uttering. Beyond actuality, there are other stance adverbs. For instance, you can insert your stance on the reliability or otherwise of the source of information ('Apparently, George Negus does it all the time'); or on the notion of certainty or likelihood ('George Negus can probably get away with it'); and on distribution of use ('Typically, Negus says it when he's chatting with someone'). You can even use the offices of a stance adverb to comment reflexively – for instance, to comment on your own style of conveying the message ('Quite frankly, George Negus gets my goat'). Stance adverbs are handy items, worth not leaving home without.

But the notion of stance is not restricted to adverbs. Grammar actually (there we go) affords us many opportunities to insert our stance. Depending on context, purpose and audience, our choice of words will vary. In formal and written contexts, typically the personal quality is suppressed or distanced and the phraseology changes. We're more likely to express our position thus: 'It has been noted that George Negus has a tendency towards a hyper-use of "actually".' Or 'Regrettably, George Negus has been reported dabbling in the actuarial [sic] pond.'

The formal context signals its particular relationship between user and receiver in the choice of words. But, while an unfortunate degree of prestige accrues to the one and not the other, it's not a case of the city-slick cousin (written/formal) being superior to the sloppily inept country cousin (spoken/casual). One should not be judged in terms of the other. Actually, they're just different.

Bored

'Teacher, I'm tired of this grammar. I'm boring.'

I doubt there's any teacher of English as a second or foreign language anywhere ever who hasn't heard this construction, or a version thereof. It is as unremarkable in its ubiquity as it is remarkable for its irony.

Actually the ironies are multiple and embedded. First off, there's the irony of the student's self-diagnosis alongside the error. Clearly she needs the grammar, notwithstanding the boredom. Second, there's the ironic unwitting self-disclosure: who among us freely admits to being boring, the more so when it's done unawares? Third, there's the pedagogic irony that the teacher, no doubt warm, fuzzy and caring to the end, will probably not let the student in on the gaffe. This is despite the fact that until such time as the student discovers that it is a gaffe, the confusion will continue – dare I say it – *ad* (boring) *nauseam*. Sadly, this is a by-product of the 'benevolent conspiracy', that cloud of positive approval by which language teachers, in the quest to build confidence, pretend to their students that their level of competence is a great deal higher than it is.

Another irony is that, as long as students persist with the complaint, they will indeed be boring, and remain so, albeit unintentionally. And there's the final crowning irony which is that, if indeed there's any boredom to be had by anyone, it rests with the teacher who for so long has been reteaching the same grammar point, in a grotesque classroom parody of the burden of Sisyphus.

But back to the homepage. 'Boring' and its sibling 'bored' started life as verbs. From there they developed into participles (active/present in the case of '-ing'; passive/past in the case of '-ed'). Depending on the direction, we either create the boredom or receive the boredom. Same with these: amazing/amazed, amusing/ed, pleasing/ed, worrying/ed. Not hard. Learn the rule. Problem solved. Go to the movies. Film's a dud. It's boring. You're bored. Bob's your uncle.

Hold on. Not so fast. Whose responsibility is the boredom? I contest the notion that it's as simple as give/receive, agent/recipient. Borees, if you will, surely bear some responsibility for their condition. We're not talking chickenpox – you can't just blame the person you got it from.

I confess to an ideological bent here. I banned the use of the 'b' word when my kids were growing up, calculating that, without a naming mechanism, they'd be less prone to the condition. Years later, my well-honed-with-leisure-skills son said: 'You know the "b" word that we don't have in our home?' ('Y-e-s', I said, gingerly.) 'Well, if we *did* have it – I know we don't, but just imagine for a minute that we did – well, I'd very probably be using it now.' Partial success on that front.

I tried the same ban at work, in the classroom. 'Learning a language', I'd tell a captive class, 'is not like tanning. You don't just lie there and then turn over after thirty minutes and expect it all just to happen. In learning a language, you actually have to bring something to the party, actively engage, use cognitive processes you never knew you had. So . . .' (I'd conclude with hapless, death-defying logic), 'if you find me boring, ask yourself – how hard have YOU worked? What responsibility have YOU taken?' It's my little version of 'ask not what your country can do for you . . .' And, I have to say, quite some success on that front.

You see, I am ideologically opposed to the way English constructs boredom. I rather prefer the Romance language approach where the verb 'to bore' is reflexive (Spanish: *me aburro*; French: *je m'ennuie*); for instance, *me aburro en el cine* (I'm bored at the movies). Instead of the passive construction ('I am bored'), the Romance form is 'I bore myself'.

I'm attracted to the suggestion that the self is at least partially complicit in the processes by which boredom is generated. Perhaps, freely decoded, the meaning is: 'I am so boring that I bore myself.'

I figure that if the bored had to suffer the stigma of also being boring, there'd be far fewer people going around using the 'b' word.

Flotsam and jetsam

In a recent national newspaper column, a reader sought clarification on how 'flotsam' differed from 'jetsam'. I mean, they're always together, you never see them on their own, and 'flotsam' always comes before 'jetsam', as if the order were fixed in concrete. So it was a good question.

One respondent, Lillian Andre, offered an admirable explanation, citing maritime law: 'flotsam' was the name for wreckage that continued to float after a ship had sunk, while 'jetsam' was what had been thrown overboard to lighten a distressed ship, and had sunk or washed ashore. This being the origin of the words, she said that the phrase 'flotsam and jetsam' today had come to refer collectively to things found floating on the ocean or washed ashore. Easy to remember too – the 'flot' suggests floating and the 'jet' suggests jettison. Nice. This has an intuitively satisfying ring to it.

Another respondent, Frank Tovell, created an Aesopian tale of two beach scavengers, perhaps previously shipwreck survivors themselves, or FedEx-style wash-ashores in the Tom Hanks tradition. In any case, they were called Flotsam and Jetsam: Flotsam was the proactive one, who rowed out to find the goods thrown overboard, while Jetsam was the clever, if indolent, one who waited on the shore for said goods to arrive.

Of all the explanations published in the newspaper, my favourite was from Fred Menz, who said, simply and elegantly: 'Flotsam are the bits and jetsam are the pieces.'

Menz's response is brilliantly pithy. His sentence deftly achieves multiple functions. It conveys the answer, in the sense of carrying a propositional load. It also illustrates his point by seeming to be an example of it. Menz appears to be drawing a semantic distinction between what counts as flotsam and what counts as jetsam.

But there's a twist in the inferential backwash: the dissonance between the apparent message (namely, the semantic difference between the two words) and the real message (itself induced from the realisation that his own illustrative example is as semantically imprecise as 'flotsam and jetsam'). With 'bits' and 'pieces' being interchangeable, Menz's point is that his definition is pointless. Neat.

A larger point is floating here (sorry) and it's related to the nature of what might broadly be called 'lexical bundling'. Superficially, 'flotsam and jetsam' might be considered the same linguistic genus as 'bits and pieces', a category described as common phrases, often noun + noun combinations, linked by a conjunction. Other examples might be 'over and above' and 'neither here nor there'. All are rather vague semantic lumps that are not meant to be decoded in any tightly technical or literal sense.

There is one important distinction, however. In the contemporary use of 'flotsam and jetsam', the phrase is indivisible. As already observed, we don't find 'flotsam' without 'jetsam'. They're joined at the hip, as it were. 'Bits and pieces', on the other hand, may be uncoupled and used separately if one wishes.

Aside from bits and pieces of flotsam and jetsam, another category of phrasal combinations exists. This is where the meaning of the whole is not easily derived from either the individual parts or their sum. In 'kick the bucket' we have the idiomatic equivalent of a lexical verb ('die'). As well as the non-literal meaning, there's the rule that when you opt for the idiom, you can't tinker with the formula: it has to be 'bucket', can't be 'pail'; it has to be 'kick', can't be 'trip over'. Knocking the bucket over with your foot doesn't work. You might lose a lot of milk and make a mess, but if it is to mean 'die', it's got to be a fully fledged kick.

English is replete with such gems: 'bite the bullet' (to put up with), 'build a fire under someone' (to provoke someone to do something), 'by fits and starts' (irregularly, unevenly, with much jerky stopping and starting), 'hell-bent' or 'hell for leather' (heading somewhere fast and recklessly), 'keep the home fires burning' (ensuring continuity of custom).

All languages have these and they become a regular stumbling block (there's another one) for foreign language learners, for whom the 'logic' is often counterintuitive. My Polish-speaking mum would frequently admonish me about doing things in good time and not missing life's trains. I puzzled for years. She meant 'boats'. Bottom line: if you choose to use the idiom, get it right.

Hygiene

Hygeia was the Greek goddess of health and, apart from keeping herself scrupulously clean at all times, she gave us our word 'hygiene'. Dictionaries tell us this word denotes both the science and the practices of preserving good health. So far so good.

When I was little, hygiene was a word primary school teachers used when they meant 'body odour' (BO). It was a formal-occasion word – the kind that, in the first ten years of your life, you're much more likely to hear than use. You learn early that it's an iceberg word. By this I mean that you know there's more to the meaning than that which is visible up top. You know real meaning is submerged below the surface but that you're too little as yet to know what it is. This kind of thing tended to happen at school assembly – making you look down, keep very still and wait for the moment to pass.

Later, at the dentist, the word reappeared. 'Dental Hygiene' was written on those plastic freebies containing brush and micro toothpaste tube. These days, add floss. Toothpaste was to bad breath what soap was to BO. Then, in my teens, some quiet inferencing enabled me to discover that 'feminine hygiene' had a particular meaning, of which the logical counterpart, 'masculine hygiene', did not exist. Mmm. Big dollops of iceberg there.

But yesterday, talking to a web designer about an idea for my website, he shook his head, muttering, 'Nope, not a good idea – poor web hygiene.' Aha! I thought. The H-word has spread. It's not so much that the underwater berg has been exposed, as that the semantic range of the word has broadened. Think of it as a lateral rather than a vertical shift. We're no longer talking about the body's smelly spots. In fact, we've left the body behind entirely, apart from a tangential metaphoric connection.

Think of it as a colonisation. As we move away from the body, the word becomes more prophylactic than remedial. It's not 'wash those smelly bits and you'll be all right'. More like 'wash them regularly and the problem won't appear'.

I went looking for other newly colonised zones. There's sleep hygiene – advice for the sleep-challenged, a set of pro-sleep practices (like going to bed at the same time) and a set of no-noes (coffee, cigarettes before bed; laptops and worry in bed with you). Tranquil music is OK, as is a drop of warm milk and a smear of peanut butter on toast.

And there's workplace hygiene, which goes further than post-loo hand-washing. It's 'think preventatively at all times' – don't smoke near hazardous products; wear protective spectacles in the presence of vapours. Very Occupational Health and Safety.

There's computer hygiene, a term that plays on the metaphor of viruses and suggests good practices – like not opening email from unknown senders. But why, in a professional environment, would you open something that says 'I love you'?

Camp hygiene is about community-spirited outdoor practices. A website about it includes the line – 'Before camp hygiene, there was bubonic plague.' A little Baden-Powellesque.

A Christian book company offers a title on keeping your body 'neat and clean'. No mention of the soul, or other soap-inaccessible parts, but the inference is that cleanliness and godliness are still in bed together.

There's classroom hygiene used in the context of good group-management skills for teachers – what once would have been termed 'control' or 'discipline'. The focus is on what to do before there's an outbreak, rather than how you mop up afterwards.

A website dedicated to hygiene for verbal viruses has a stern-looking man warning us about 'excessive progressivism' (overusing continuous tenses) and 'egophilia' (starting sentences with

'I feel'). This passion for the defence of the language is not uncommon among a contingent of people who see good grammar as a metaphor for good morals. Bad grammar sets you on a slippery slope.

Such attitudes provide Deborah Cameron with a database for her book *Verbal Hygiene*, which is about people who, if they could, would legislate about language like the French do. Or bring back the lash.

Something to think about while soaking in the bath.

Special

Life isn't fair. We know that, don't we? When God was handing out the goodies, some people (and cities, countries, continents, etc.) got more/better/nicer than others. No explanation for disparity or inequity. That's just how it is. You can rail against the inequities or resign yourself to them.

In language as in life, some words work much harder than others. They sing more songs, and more sweetly, for the same supper. No explanation. They just do.

'Special' is a word that works its little butt off. It's an adjective (I cooked a special dish for you); a noun (a pre-Christmas special; oysters are our specialty); an adverb (divorce especially hurts the children; you'll need a car specially for long-distance trips); a verb (to specialise). Notwithstanding its grammatical diversity, it is in the semantics – specifically the social functions – that 'special' is, well, special.

'Special' is able to accomplish both general and imprecise meanings on the one hand, and specific and precise meanings on the other. The *Oxford English Dictionary* tells us it means 'of such a kind as to exceed or excel in some way that which is usual or common'. But exactly how it exceeds is a function of larger concerns, accessed through some hardcore inferencing.

If a fellow worker is given 'special privileges', it's not the same 'special' as that bloke last month who was relentlessly 'singled out for special treatment'. 'Special delivery' suggests a service that is outside the normal business hours and therefore comes at a price. The UN 'special envoy' to the Middle East is someone outside the regular diplomatic circle of traffic and therefore suggests 'crisis'. 'Special forces' suggests an elite unit outside the ranks of the regular military. 'Special effects' in film has come to mean whiz-bang computer-generated visual effects, *à la* the film *Spiderman.*

'Specials' at restaurants are dishes not on the regular menu. But the label camouflages a more complex *raison d'être.* Specials might supplement or complement the standard menu. They might showcase the chef's creative outbursts, or just as easily resurrect leftovers, the spices artfully disguising use-by-ness. They might address an oversupply or exploit seasonal buy-ups. In research and development terms, they might actually be auditions for prospective main meals.

Take 'His love for her was special.' This is not your usual, run-of-the-mill love. It's outside the ordinary and that's what makes it special. But precisely how, only the context will tell. It might be the stalker's obsessive *über*-infatuation, or a cloying and needy kind of love, or it might be special by virtue of its romantic intensity. Ultimately, the meaning of 'special' will be one that we ourselves (as listeners or readers) collude in – we will invest it with meaning that we draw from context. Both the immediate, explicit textual context (technically, the co-text) and the larger, extra-textual implicit context.

Paradoxically, there are times when 'special' serves precisely because it is imprecise. In other words, hiding behind the camouflage are other, perhaps less pleasant or worthy nuances. In these cases 'special' cues us to look behind the imprecision and infer what is really meant. What does it mean that the United Kingdom has a 'special relationship' with the United States? What do we mean by children with 'special needs'? 'Special Ed' at Teachers' College used to be the politically correct way of referring to teaching children whose physical, intellectual or behavioural characteristics marked them out as different ('special'). A patient requiring 'special care' is likely to be a whole lot sicker than one who doesn't. In thousands of instances, imprecision is not so much a matter of sloppiness as it is a deliberate strategy serving any of a range of functions, from camouflage, evasion and polite hedging to obfuscation and denial.

Yesterday, with 'special' on my mind, I passed a greengrocer. Next to some large, purply greenish grapes was a sign – 'Special Grapes'. Time for some hands-on data collection. I took a small bunch to the counter:

These grapes are special, are they?

Oh yes, very special.

What makes them special? (*Hint of a friendly smile*)

The price.

Ohhhh, so they're actually ON special. (*A gentle English lesson, in situ*)

Yes, yes, of course, special grapes, very special, on special . . . You try. You like. You see? You want?

I did. And they were.

WORLD ENGLISHES

More people today speak English as a second or foreign language than speak it as a native or ancestral language. This means that, for most English speakers, the language is not their first. It's one that they have acquired or are still acquiring. Over time, this fact alone will be responsible for massive changes in the language. Mindful of these developments, linguists today tend to speak of English in the plural – as 'Englishes'. In general terms, the language's development reveals two competing pressures – to diverge (and be different) and to converge (and be the same). The local variety inevitably takes on its own colour and shape, resulting in massive dialectal differentiation. At the same time, globalisation and the internet mean that people increasingly are in contact, creating a need for a common standard English (English as an International Language) to which all speakers of English can relate. In fulfilling this need, English has quickly become the first truly global language or lingua franca. Each piece contained in this section addresses a particular implication of the fact that the world's Englishes have to satisfy the identity needs of their speakers as well as the pragmatic need for wider communication.

Migrant headache

The middle-aged student waited patiently for the teacher to catch his eye. He had a foreignness about him. Maybe it was his quiet patience, his willingness to wait for the moment to present itself.

Eventually it did. He apologised for leaving class before the day's lessons were over. He couldn't stay, he said, as he had 'a migrant headache.'

Now every English language teacher has one or two of these priceless phrases tucked away. It's part of the reward. Mine is the message on a multiply signed farewell card. It read: 'We wish you were the best teacher in Australia.'

Correcting students' errors is a delicate business. They need to know, of course, but they also need to stay confident. Attitude is everything – well, nearly everything. Certainly, the moment of error utterance is the least appropriate time to correct. In some circumstances, it is 'riding roughshod', to say the least:

Teacher: What happened over the weekend? Any interesting
   experiences?
Student: Um, mother ...er ...dead.
Teacher: Careful now. Watch your tense. It's 'my mother died.'
   Died. Not dead. Repeat please.
Student: Mother ...er ...died.
Teacher: Very good ...Does anyone else have something to add?

Of course the migrainous student was excused, his teacher understanding, better than most, why learning English might be the stuff of migraine. The script runs in the wrong direction; the letters are alien, the sounds even more so. In both a literal and a metaphoric sense, one's foreign tongue intrudes everywhere. And in any case, how's it possible to concentrate on learning when you have a family to relocate and support?

For the ignorati, taking on a new language is a simple matter of swapping labels. A chair used to have a different label. So did dog and kitchen and unemployment. Would that it were quite so simple!

One reason it isn't is that languages carve up the universe – and ways of experiencing it – in uniquely different ways. Italian has a verb for doing integrity; English doesn't. Nor do we have a phrase for making too many familiar assumptions and being out of line as a result, or a term for knowing your social position/station, both of which exist in Italian. There's a Melanesian language that doesn't distinguish between blue and green. German, I'm told, has one word for 'aimlessly twiddling your hair' for which English has 'aimlessly twiddling your hair'.

As well, syntax and intonation operate differently and serve different purposes in different languages. The Yiddish-influenced 'I should be so lucky!' or 'For this we worked so hard?' are windows onto the reality that people do things, including language, differently.

The Russian-accented trainer at my gym said to me, 'You maaast put your hand straight and you maaast lean back, abdominals in, breath out, eyeline down, thaaaat's it, gooooood gell.' She's sweetly well intentioned (I tell myself) and she's successfully swapped almost all her linguistic labels, yet she still has a long way to go. She's yet to learn that giving instructions can be done gently in the imperative (lean back). She's yet to learn that 'you must' is for obligations and responsibilities (you must wear a uniform/vote, etc.), not for recommendations wrapped inside instructions. Further, when it is pronounced 'maaaast', the obligation is even more knuckle-rapping. Lastly, calling a woman (me) twice her age 'girl' is off-puttingly inappropriate. (What does she say to a man of the same age?)

I stop thinking about her English. I concentrate instead on my abdominals. Now that English is the world's lingua franca, it has disconnected, rather pre-eclamptically, from the native uterine wall. It's become the language by which people who don't share a language nonetheless communicate. English as an International Language (EIL). Japanese earthquake engineers helping out in quake-rocked Turkey speak English to the Turks. An Israeli agronomist advising on irrigation in Cambodia does it in English.

EIL is fast becoming the most populous English spoken. Enormous changes are afoot. 'Babysister' in many places is the accepted term for 'babysitter'. I suspect it started out as a non-native version which was appropriated by a whole nation and then fossilised. This may be the way ahead for 'migrant headache'.

Meanwhile, if the migrant headache strikes, seek out a quiet room, draw the curtains, gently place a cool eye pillow on the throbbing. This will do wonders for your English.

Bananas and sausages

The first thing I ever failed was first-year French at Sydney University in 1966.

Until then I'd scored well in typical school grammar-translation-style tests. The kind that had me rote-learning word lists until the early hours of the morn. For me, the learning of vertical lists of foreign words meant the said words were stored in similar fashion – altogether, in one long vertical list, in a file, in a filing cabinet, on a dusty shelf in my long-term memory.

The problem with this style of learning is that it assumes that when you ask for some onions in French, you will also be wanting to ask for potatoes, pumpkin, corn, asparagus and cauliflower. Years later, in France, actual shopping would mean I'd re-encounter my stale list of vertical veggies – which I'd go through, in order, till I landed on the one that best accompanied the planned dish. Call me inflexible but I couldn't get to the cauliflower without traversing down from potatoes.

In the light of such a non-generative learning style, perhaps I should have expected university French to present me with a new kind of difficulty. But I didn't. I was stunned to discover that what had served me well in the past had now let me down.

Failure left me numb and bewildered. My written paper, though grammatically perfect in form, had earned a fail. Summoning courage I barely had, I went to see the Professor. 'Pfff', he spluttered with Gallic disdain. 'It might be grammatically correct, yes? But no French person uses language like that.'

The old native-speaker put-down. Duly dwarfed and dismissed, I crept from his office and put French classroom learning behind me for good. After that, it was the streets for me.

I was reminded recently of the French debacle when an unsolicited text arrived by internet pigeon. A gem of non-native perfection, it was attributed to a Japanese schoolboy in Swann and Sidgwick's *The Making of Prose*:

The banana are a great remarkable fruit. They are constructed in the same architectural style as sausage, difference being skin of sausage are habitually consumed, while it is not advisable to eat wrapper of banana. The bananas are held aloft while consuming; sausage are usually left in reclining position. Sausage depend for creation on human being or stuffing machine, while banana are pristine product of honourable mother nature. In case of sausage, both conclusions are attached to other sausage; banana on the other hand are attached on one end to stem and opposite termination entirely loose. Finally, banana are strictly of vegetable kingdom, while affiliation of sausage often undecided.

This is a painstakingly constructed text. Indeed, the pain resonates in every line. It's a work of art in foreigner-speak, which, if put to the test would fail just as my French failed.

Many are the ways in which the banana text is non-native-like. And mostly the sins are ones of omission. The most important absence is one of social purpose. The text dangles in space, unconnected to any speech community or social participants or social goals. Who is writing this text, to whom, for what purpose? The closest is likely a Japanese schoolboy, for the teacher, in English class, to display linguistic devices for managing comparison and contrast in a sustained text. Where else, pray, would one ever want to write a critical comparative analysis of the properties of bananas and sausages?

There are grammatical problems – again ones of omission. The writer has some difficulty managing the plural markers for his main nouns (banana, sausage). Mostly in English, we mark plurals with a final 's' (one dog, two dogs). There are some oddities that

Scrabblers know well (ox/oxen, foot/feet, criterion/criteria). In rare cases (sheep/sheep; fish/fish), singular/plural share the same form. An oddity of the banana text is that its composer places both bananas and sausages in the fish/fish category, not the dog/dogs one.

To compound things, the writer mixed the rules for making general statements. We can say 'Bananas are yellow' (no article + plural noun + agreeing plural verb) or 'The banana is yellow' (definite article + singular noun + agreeing singular verb). Instead, this writer invents 'The banana are' and 'sausage depend'.

Perhaps the most prominent non-native element is found in the word combinations that are grammatically correct but situationally inappropriate. We simply don't use architectural and building language for describing qualities of fruit or food manufacture. Bananas have skins, not wrappers. Holding aloft is more dramatic than bananas generally warrant, and reclining position is more suitable to the outdoor banana chair than to sausages. The ends are neither conclusions nor terminations. And sausages don't get affiliated, unless they take up an academic post, which, granted, is not unheard of.

Japanese schoolboys, however, are not alone. The former Italian Prime Minister Silvio Berlusconi suffered from comparable bouts of non-native-ese. His website, apparently, was replete with examples according to *The Sydney Morning Herald* (of 11 December 2001). It includes 'America's Goblet' (for America's Cup), the 'Forehead of Youth' (for Youth Front), megaphone (for spokesman), 'Minister for Atmosphere' (Environment) and 'Minister for the Inside' (Interior).

I return to learning styles. The culprit here is surely the student's word list derived from the bilingual dictionary – that silent but malignant sponsor of cross-lingual one-to-one correspondence in word meaning/use. This will resonate with anyone who has tried to decipher Danglish instructions so as to assemble Danish furniture.

Come to think of it, I should have simply told that Gallic sod he was off his noodle.

Kaput

My local dry-cleaner has an ancillary repair and alteration service. A Chinese husband-and-wife team, they're whizz-bang at fixing anything. Believe me, over the years I've had many occasions to test their expertise, and nearly always they pull through.

Imagine my disappointment, then, when I took them a favourite pair of black pants that were letting me down. The husband checked them out disdainfully, his utterance punctuated by condemnatory grunts. The ultimate pronouncement was delivered thus: 'He no good. He no work. Zipper kaput.'

Distancing myself emotionally from the bleak destiny of my favourite black pants, I'm able to recognise that the man's pronouncement furnishes an enlightening example of the gap between linguistic and communicative competence. Clearly, there's a lack of linguistic competence, evidenced mainly by verb failure – which is a bit like heart failure, with less dire consequences. The first verb (which should be 'is') is simply omitted, suggesting that this man has little use for grammatical chess.

This opinion is confirmed when in the next sentence the verb, which appears this time ('work'), is crudely denuded of any of the compulsory accoutrements that verbs need. It is unmarked for the singular subject (which itself is incorrectly gendered), for, of course, the complexity of negation has been sidestepped by the simple, never-varying, preceding 'no'. The third verb again is omitted. Or perhaps 'kaput' has been appropriated to do the work of an uninflected verb. If we wanted desperately to think it's a verb, we perhaps could ascribe its meaning as 'having been reduced to the state of being broken', although strictly speaking such an explanation would require us to accept the simple form as 'to kaput' which, really, is a bit rich.

'Kaput', in fact, is a predicative adjective. This means I can say 'my pants are kaput' but I can't say 'my kaput pants' – though the latter is certainly within my dry-cleaner's realm of possibility. According to the *Collins Dictionary*, it means 'ruined, broken, not functioning', and it entered English in the twentieth century. Yet a favourite resource of mine, John Ayto's *20th Century Words,* has no listing between 'kamikaze' and 'karaoke'. There's a link to the German *kaput,* meaning 'done for'; and also the French *être capot* (to be hoodwinked), from *capot* (hooded cloak); and the Latin *caput* (head).

My dry-cleaner's 'kaput' is certainly handy. It's easy, economical and effective. It just isn't very, well, English. But it is communicatively competent. I went away with no illusions about my pants' future.

It struck me as I walked home, sadly, how much of the hurly-burly world of commerce has to do with things not working well, being in the need of upgrade, repair, alteration. Just plain fixing.

One would expect there to be loads of ways to express such meanings. The dictionary confirms this. Something can be broken, bust or busted. It can be out of order or out of action. If it's engine-related, it might have cut out, broken down or failed. If it's computer-related, we might say it's crashed or down. Increasingly, as computers infiltrate our lives we'll be borrowing computer language, like 'crashed' and 'down' for non-computer-related malfunctioning. Handy, say, at the doctor's.

If we're being formal, we might go Latinate and say 'not operating' or 'defective'. More informally, we're likely to use 'done', 'finished', 'through', 'over it', 'on the blink', 'playing up', 'had it', 'packed up' and, of course, the ever-graphic, if somewhat sexually bleached-out 'fucked'. Idioms are found in 'end of the line', 'over the hill', or 'up shit creek without a paddle'.

A cheque can be a 'dud'. A car, or even a date, might be a 'lemon'. This marks it for disappointment, suggests that the hype, as well as the expectation, outstripped the reality. Perhaps it's a metaphorical extension of a lemon's sour tang, applied to human experience. The taste of disappointment.

I googled 'kaput' and reaped 75,200 results. One was at www.kaput.com. The website simply said:

Sigh. I can't keep up with the disasters…the unprecedented solar activity…rise in earthquakes and volcanos, freak weather, the Middle East, North Korea, three new potential plagues, high-risk near-earth asteroid activity, geomagnetic faults…UFO sightings, and the…media blackout regarding all of the above…kaput.com will go away until I think of what to do.

All things considered, I think my dry-cleaner said it better.

Ego permeability

Ever had a friend return from travels abroad speaking somehow differently? A year in Sydney can do serious harm to your vowels. In South Africa, even less time is needed. Most destabilising of all is the impact of a cross-lingual relationship. Marry a Swede and your intonation may be changed forever.

It happens. Our experiences of other ways of speaking influence us. Even accents you might have thought were set in concrete can shift. Take the Queen – hard to believe but yes, the royal vowels have travelled discernibly over the last decade and, what's more, in a non-snooty direction. And that's not anecdotal; it's research-driven.

It's not just the monarch who's lost a bit of plum. British dialecticians have been noticing some Australian vowel-creep in British-speak. They attribute this to two phenomena. First, the popularity of Australian TV serials – apparently, there's only so much *Neighbours* and *Home and Away* you can watch without your vowels going wobbly. Second, the returning peripatetic British backpackers. These travellers have their Oz experience and then return home – tanned (or burnt), broke and slightly vowel-shifted. The burn will heal, the pocket will refill, but will the vowels ever be the same again?

It's unlikely the Queen stays up watching Australian soaps, or that she sneaks out to consort with young British backpacker types. (If she did, a butler would surely already have told us by now.) And she's understandably cautious about her offspring. So surrounded by minders was Prince Harry during his visit to Australia, and so insulated from ordinary local influences, it's likely he went home with the royal accent intact. This is neither good nor bad. It's a neutral observation: our experiences can leave their footprint (soundprint?) on the way we talk.

You can hear it in Nicole Kidman and Elle MacPherson. There's variation, of course. Depending on where they're speaking (locally or overseas), who they're being interviewed by (an Australian or not), and what mood they're in, the accent will fluctuate. In other words, the influences on accent are both long-term (where you live) and short-term (who you were with when you had those drinks the other night).

But whether it's long- or short-term, the imprint of experience on accent is all bound up with affect and attitude. We can open ourselves up to the influence of the outside and lap up the exposure. Or we can pull up the drawbridge, close down the receptors, defend the psyche, and refuse to be influenced.

Some people mop up accents the way tofu mops up curry sauce. Others can live in another speech community for years (think Indian Raj) and maintain their lingual identity with nothing short of Mel-zeal (I'm thinking Gibson).

Whether you do or don't soak up accents is partly linked to a concept called 'ego permeability'. This lovely notion describes the strength or confidence of your sense of self. A person with a low self-conviction is said to have low ego permeability (LEP). A person with high self-conviction is said to have high ego permeability (HEP). LEP suggests high defensiveness and low receptivity to outside influences. HEP suggests low defensiveness and high receptivity to the same outside influences.

Perhaps that's too simplistic. Just to open up a little more complexity, it's possible to have HEP in relation to one foreign language but LEP in relation to another. Consider a foreign-born Francophile who loves anything to do with France, associating 'French' with sexy, stylish and sophisticated. He or she may be as open and receptive to French as they are closed and resistant to, say, German, associating 'German' with things harsh, guttural, abrasive, like tanks and factories. In other words, this is very subjective – you can see, I'm sure, how biography, education and association shape, even pre-determine, particular levels of permeability.

People who seem to have a natural talent for learning foreign languages are giveaway high-permeables. They're wont to warm to the accent, rub along with native speakers, feel comfortable in the culture, not worry about looking or feeling stupid. Generally, they're satisfied that near-enough is plenty good-enough.

Meanwhile, their disambiguating, low-permeable cousins are back at the hotel, rechecking the bilingual dictionary to ensure they can faultlessly ask the concierge about the timetable and route of the local bus. LEPs have their skills too, just not in language learning.

Leaky showers

It's amazing what you think about in traffic. Extended thought sequences must be the only positive by-product of vehicular overcrowding.

On this occasion, I was behind a van, the kind that tradesmen or handymen drive. The company name and phone details were written on the back and along the sides. Underneath this was the line: 'I fix leaking showers without disturb tiles.'

Ring him up, I thought, and tell him about your leaky shower. When he shows up, give him a lesson on verb forms, specifically the non-finite '-ing' form used after 'without'. Check to see that he understands. Go over any bits that may seem fuzzy to him. Set him homework to email to you.

Or be more direct. Ring him up and ask him, nicely, whether he knows or cares that his van displays bad grammar. Be nice. Always be nice. Suggest he would make many grammatically retentive types happy with the simple addition of the inoffensive '-ing' to his 'disturb'. Hint that there may be oodles of prospective leaky-shower owners who need his services but are put off by his grammar. Exaggerate if necessary. It's a good cause.

Or – and here's a novel approach – just back off. Lose the judgemental attitude. If the meaning is clear, where's the law requiring perfect grammar? Realise leaky shower man (LSM) may have no interest in this matter. After all, how much do you know about leaky showers and no one's hammering on your door demanding that you upskill.

Perhaps what's needed is a wider consciousness. Contemplate getting your own van with the inscription: 'I fix leaking grammar without disturb tiles.' Or if that's deemed too in-your-face, rethink the inscription, going for something less parodic. Maybe 'Grammar help available without pain'.

Maybe it's you who needs greater understanding. Feel sympathetic thoughts about the complexity of learning another language, the illogical rules, the stupid exceptions, the general all-round craziness. Reminisce about how foolish you used to feel when your Argentine ex-father-in-law corrected your Spanish, emphasising that you'd got the gender wrong for *vestido*. Well, why not? What is there, from an English-speaker's perspective, about *vestido* that makes it more inherently masculine or feminine? Remember how that prickle of irritation travelled down your spine and came to rest in the small of your back, where it languished sullenly, until the next onslaught.

Keep trying for the empathy. Recall how awful it was, failing first-year French without a clue about how to improve. Think about all the survival skills needed in a foreign culture. Remember how creative foreign learners can be, like the student in a test situation who was searching about for a word like 'irreplaceable' and came up with 'uninsteadable'. And the other student who was searching for a word for 'people with mobility problems' and constructed 'dismoveable'.

Maybe we need a government department that takes in suggestions from the public. It might be called the Ministry for Lexical Invention. They'd need a website, an electronic newsletter, and a TV programme to boost exposure and encourage participation. The *American Idol* people might be consulted about hype creation. Schoolchildren could have a 'jump rope for words' campaign. And there could be marathons where contestants wear their favourite word (instead of a number) on their back. We could have 'New Word Day' – which might later graduate to 'New Word Week' – when you'd buy a little letter to pin on, for solidarity. Anything to raise public consciousness.

But wait, what's that? Is the traffic moving? No, false alarm. The LSM vehicle remains stationary in front of mine, its leaky sentence mocking me, as if to say 'Get a Life!' Hey, wait a minute – should that be 'leaking' showers or 'leaky' showers? After all, he made a mistake with 'disturb' – what's the bet there are more leaks in this sentence? Hmm, I wonder what the difference is between a 'leaking' shower and a 'leaky' one. Maybe it's a quantitative versus qualitative thing. Maybe one refers to the volume of water leaked while the other refers to the pattern of leakage. No, hang on, maybe...

Hold on, the lights have changed, the traffic is moving, the van is turning, 'without disturb tiles' is nearly out of view.

Out of sight, out of mind. No more disturbance, to tiles or anything else.

Red-faced tomatoes

'You shall know a word by the company it keeps', said linguist John Firth, referring to the tendency of words to behave in predictable ways. 'Blonde' goes with hair, 'flock' goes with sheep, 'cute' goes with puppy and 'cantankerous' goes with old man.

'Lukewarm', however, doesn't go with faith. This is a discovery made by the elders of a church in New Mexico. It seems a bereaved family there has sued its local Catholic church over a funeral Mass in which the priest allegedly called the deceased a 'lukewarm Catholic'. Bad choice. Most would agree, I think, that 'lukewarm' goes much more happily with bathwater, or even audience reaction, than it does with 'Catholic'.

Collocations – or word combinations – are embedded in languages and that's where they like to stay. They resist moving out of their comfort zone and shun cross-language expeditions. This means that learning new collocations becomes a major challenge for those in the business of language learning. The temptation always is to translate from the mother tongue.

My Polish-speaking parents, for instance, were forever 'opening' and 'closing' lights, rather than turning them on or off. It's pointless to indulge in cross-linguistic comparisons, comparing logic or finesse, for instance. Different is as different does. In English, we 'face' problems and 'interpret' dreams. In Hebrew, we'd 'stand in front of' problems and 'solve' dreams.

These word combinations are conventions of use that have hardened into habit over time. But some sectors of society are given greater dispensation to frolic at the boundaries of convention. Children are deemed cute when they mix things up; not so the elderly. Poets and comedians have *carte blanche*, but it's a *carte* that's shredded when it comes to foreign speakers. Asked what kind of funeral he'd like, Bob Hope said: 'Surprise me.' Try that in a foreign accent and no one would laugh.

As we move from the conventional centre to the perimeters of language use, we become more inventive and inferential. Increasingly, we call on our listeners' interpretive skills. The linguist Geoffrey Leech demonstrated this with the word 'ago'. Moving from the mundane towards the weird, we have: several hours ago, many moons ago, ten games ago, several performances ago, a few cigarettes ago, two wives ago, a grief ago (thank you, Dylan Thomas), a humanity ago. Now you can argue about the sequence, but it's clear there's a linear move away from the literal and towards the bizarre. It gets harder and harder to imagine a plausible context.

Great poetry hovers on the perimeters. It's strange enough to be striking, but not so arcane as to defy interpretation (well, depends on your poet).

In a country of immigrants like Australia or Canada, you're more likely to meet non-native accents than poets. It's a safe bet that these non-natives occasionally do strange things with word combinations.

My mother's contribution to this bottomless well of weird combos was 'good tomatoes'.

Most afternoons, she'd send me to the fruit shop to get provisions – typically, 'five good tomatoes'. How I hated the 'good' in the phrase 'good tomatoes'. Being shy, I'd sooner have died than ask for good tomatoes. But I was as obedient as I was shy, so I was looking for a way out of my quandary. I found that by dropping my volume on the 'good', I could have it heard as 'five + (*pause*) + tomatoes'. From my perspective, it was better to be perceived as having a minor speech defect than ask the man for quality tomatoes.

Mum would inspect the tomatoes and invariably say: 'These aren't "good"! Did you ask for good ones?' And, being as honest as I was obedient and shy, I'd think literal and I'd say: 'Yes.' Strictly speaking, it wasn't really a lie. She'd shake her head and mutter. I'd slip away. We'd have squishy tomato salad – again.

Forty years later, I worked out what she meant. Tomatoes don't come in one binary good-or-bad container. Different tomatoes serve different purposes. Salad tomatoes need to be 'firm'; cooking tomatoes need to be 'soft'. So it's not good as in opposite of bad (as in rotting). She wanted 'good' as in 'firm' – somewhere between 'soft' and 'green'.

But for me, the aha moment came too late for action, only reflection. Looking back, it would seem I've taken the squishy-tomato path in life and that has made all the difference.

Un-English

What do pyjamas, jodhpurs and shampoo have in common? What about sofa, safari and algebra? Yes, they're all loan words (foreign borrowings) from other languages – in these cases, Hindi and Arabic respectively.

Yet in a language as mongrel as English, what does 'foreign' mean? When does a loan word cease to be a recent arrival? How long before it can apply for citizenship? Certainly, the French borrowings from the Norman Conquest are long established, as too is the second-round Romance intake of the Renaissance, and even the colonial loans from days of Empire.

Understandably, borrowed words take different amounts of time to feel at home in English. And some stay foreign to differing degrees forever. It's like the accent acquired when you learn a foreign language after puberty. Chances are it'll be there, albeit perhaps softened, till you die and will be buried with you. I recently recognised the Belfast in a sixty-year-old lift operator, who told me, when I checked my intuitions, that he'd arrived in Australia at age eight.

My mother never forgot that a cop on New York's Brooklyn Bridge in 1960 asked her, after hearing her speak, if she was from Down Under. She had no illusions that the Polish was still somehow 'in there', but for her to be taken as an Aussie abroad was akin to the award of an Honorary Doctorate. Whenever she was teased about her accent, she'd quietly remind people about the Brooklyn cop who took her for an Aussie. His throwaway line was held close to her heart on the other side of the world for another twenty-five years.

Some words have been around for ages but remain inalienably alien – and I mean that not in any pejorative kind of way, but purely phonologically. Sounds something 'other than' English. Un-English.

Take 'hoi polloi'. I first heard this from the mouth of my own foreign-born, polyglotted mother and until I re-encountered it, years later, from an Australian of long local lineage, I assumed mother had code-switched into a different tongue, which she did whenever her English let her down. But it turns out 'hoi polloi' is English, derived from Greek, meaning 'the many' (literally), or 'the common people' (free translation), or, more snidely, 'the great unwashed', because, of course, it's so value-laden you can almost touch its looking-down-the-nose quality. Strangely, it's often confused with (the quite opposite) 'hoity-toity', which, funnily, is housed nearby in the dictionary (along with two other value-ladens – 'hogwash' and 'ho-hum'). Must be something about 'h'.

Another import is 'brouhaha'. Now, how un-English is that! Meaning a noisy, unruly commotion (a bit of a kerfuffle, in fact). The jury remains out on its origins. One suggestion places it in the French *rabrouer* (to taunt); another links it to noisy bull-baiting and the Spanish *bravo*; a third, to the Hebrew *barukh habba* (blessed be the one who comes; or, in shorthand, 'welcome'), though why this should suggest a commotion only makes sense if the welcome is particularly boisterous.

Another foreigner is the rather strange phrase 'to put the kibosh on' (+ object), meaning to mess something up and finish it off. Theories abound: it's derived from Yiddish slang, meaning 'suppress'; or Gaelic, meaning 'cap of death'; or German, meaning 'carrion'. The jury is still out on its pedigree; meanwhile it remains in English, if startlingly un-English in flavour.

Yet another example is 'hunky-dory', which means something like 'everything's fine, now', with the implication things were not always hunky-dory. Again, origins are unclear, though the various threads date back to the mid nineteenth century. One thread points to a Japanese connection, where *dori* means 'road', and 'hunky' seems linked to a street in the port area of Yokohama which catered, as you might say, for the 'special needs' of sailors. Another thread points to a Dutch word (specifically, from a Frisian variant of the game of tag), meaning being OK or safe or in a good position. Either way, we're left with a very 'up' kind of word, as foreign-sounding as it is handy.

And that's the paradox – that we can actually perceive the characteristic of 'un-Englishness' in a language as fundamentally borrowed as English. And while it may not be hunky-dory that the hoi polloi tends to make a brouhaha, colourful it surely is.

Something about Mary

It wasn't long after the engagement of Mary Donaldson, of Tasmania, Australia, to Crown Prince Frederick of Denmark, that the Mary-and-Fred jokes started circulating. An Australian cartoon appeared with the caption 'Great Dane Meets Tasmanian Devil'. A newspaper columnist mocked Mary's linguistic efforts by calling her 'completely multilingual' – as well as speaking Australian, Tasmanian and (a bit of) Danish, she also, allegedly, speaks 'Supermodel, that rare dialect where in a transatlantic accent, one appears to struggle for certain words'. That of course is why we have *je ne said pas* – for those pauses when the words stubbornly refuse to oblige.

It's not fair, of course, but where in the rule book does it say anything about 'fair'? No doubt, from the stance of an Australian republican, you're asking for it the minute you start to drive around in those fuel-efficient carriages, engage in the royal wave (which has to be specially learned) and marry men in funny uniforms.

Coping with public scrutiny clearly is something you can get private lessons for in Denmark. So far Mary's topping the class. But it's early days, they're still in love, the honeymoon's barely over, and the gown's not even mothballed. What poor Mary has to look forward to is more of the same scrutiny, for the term of her (un)natural life.

Personally, I can think of only one thing that might be worse for Princess Mary than the public spectacle of her wedding, and that is learning Danish under the national spotlight. Well, actually it's two spotlights. In Denmark, the Danes will be watching her acquisition of Danish. In Australia, we'll be watching her English, noting any accent-creep.

No one should have to learn a new language in the public gaze. Not only because it's unpleasant, but also because the only thing that public scrutiny will enhance about Mary's Danish is her own self-consciousness, and this, ironically, will impede her progress. In his seminal work *The Inner Game of Tennis* (which is about winning at tennis, and so much more), Timothy Gallwey describes how a heightened Critical Self is counterproductive to the success of the Performing Self. In fact, the best thing you can do for yourself when you play competitively is start out by praising your opponent's backhand (or whatever). This judgemental comment energises your

opponent's Critical Self which will then interfere with their performance, and you'll win hands-down (or that's the theory).

The other thing about Mary being in the spotlight is that it's a
win/lose situation. The more Mary's linguistic prowess pleases the
Danes, the more likely she is to displease us with an eroded Aussie
accent. This is because of a process called 'communication accommodation', which has nothing to do with hotels and overnighters
and everything to do with the instability that characterises the early
stage of learning a language. Loving Frederick, wanting to please
him and by extension her adopted homeland, it's likely that Mary's
Danish-learning will exhibit a strong convergence pattern, at least
in the early stages.

Communication accommodation is not always convergent. It can
also be divergent, as when a speaker deliberately, albeit not necessarily consciously, chooses to diverge away from the ways of speaking they hear around them. Young Australians in London were once
(and perhaps still are) known for their attempts to maintain their
Australian speech identity, perhaps motivated by an anti-cultural-
cringe urge. I suspect that when Kylie, Elle and Nicole are back
home Down Under, their speech identity may more consciously converge with the local home accent, only to diverge again when they
cross the Equator going northbound. Accent is intimately bound up
with identity and easily malleable for the purposes of impression
management. Some speech identities are so invested with prestige
value – a sexy French accent, for instance, or a smoothly seductive Spanish one – that bearers of such identities hold onto them
with great tenacity. I don't see Antonio Banderas changing the way
he speaks any time soon – it's indivisible from his charm and has
taken him too far to consider a backtrack now. One might even
venture the hypothesis that without his distinctive way of speaking
(in English), Antonio Banderas would really no longer be Antonio
Banderas.

So Princess Mary is hell-bent on converging with things Danish.
She'll want to be like them and sound like them. Just as her clothes,
her gait, her smile, her wave are morphing into those appropriate to

a Danish royal, so too will her vowels, consonants and intonational contours. As she converges vocally with the sounds of Danish, she will almost necessarily have to diverge from her former identity, which, while only ever quite mildly Aussie, is still distinct enough to be remarked upon.

With time and patience and much less scrutiny, Mary's likely to master Danish and regain an Aussie-flavoured English – especially when she can get away at Chrissie and come back to Tassie to visit the rellies.

Saddam's English

Not long after Saddam Hussein was captured by US forces in Iraq, a report circulated that he'd been learning some English. Allegedly, he knew the words 'surrender' and 'rubbish'. On this basis, a reporter conjectured, Saddam had been learning English in preparation for giving himself up.

Not a lot of evidence, really, to make the leap to the conclusion that Saddam had had his head in the books. What kind of scenario is being conjured?

US trooper: What do you want to do now?
SH: Surrender.
US trooper: What is your comment on the location of your
    weapons of mass destruction?
SH: Rubbish.

Unlikely, for lots of reasons, but let's be fair. Every field has its folk beliefs, and language learning is far from being spared.

Two primal myths spring to mind. The first is that you can learn a language from a phrasebook. This belief is so pervasive that a whole industry (of phrasebooks, in every language you could imagine) is founded on it. It's something you wish were true rather than actually believe. Oh to march into a French bakery, inquire if they have any fresh olive-and-sundried-tomato twist buns, find out they don't, listen to what they do have, and then make an informed selection.

It's a good belief. Not only would it get you breakfast, it would remove all the drudgery from language learning, along with the boredom of rote learning and error correction. It also removes the anxiety and embarrassment that hover around language-learning classrooms where students are required to wrap their mouths around very strange sounds – and do so, mind you, in public. It minimises both the time expenditure and the upfront cost. On the other hand, a phrasebook is available for under £10, so, for the price of a light bistro lunch, you can wrap up your language needs, and carry around the solution in your pocket.

There are so many reasons why phrasebook pedagogy is dodgy. Let's stick to one very basic point: language interaction is a two-way event, requiring both speaking and listening. Even assuming you choose the right phrase for the circumstance, inflect it appropriately for the person you're speaking to, deliver it in a comprehensible accent, it all counts for zero if you can't understand the response. And there's nothing in the phrasebook that will prepare you for the automatic gunfire rapidity of natural speech, where word boundaries fade into nothingness and 'how was your weekend?' morphs into one long 'howuzyerwigend?' – manageable in English to an English speaker, but not when the exchange is between a native-speaker and a non-native.

A second myth is that you can learn a language by gathering up all the words you need (like 'surrender' and 'rubbish'), then add a generous portion of grammatical rules, mix in a few prefabricated phrases, garnish with an appropriate accent, and there you have it. A Bob's-your-uncle kind of foreign language flair.

The reality, sadly enough, is quite different. It's rarely the predictable language that causes problems. Rather it's the unpredictable, unrehearsable part. When you go to check-in with your phrasebook language in tow, and they tell you there's no room with a view, what would you like instead? Or you're ordering lunch, and you don't understand the specials, and you ask, and at the end of the explanation, you still don't understand the specials.

Spontaneous, unrehearsed, unpredictable language is always the hardest to manage. I recall a class of overseas-qualified doctors that I once taught. They had not a smidgin of trouble with the predictable language of medicine, nor the predictable subset of speech events peculiar to the medical profession, like taking a medical history from a new patient or writing a letter of referral. The only thing that caused them serious difficulty was the language they needed to chat with other doctors and staff in the hospital canteen at lunchtime. Here the unpredictable, plus the natural accent, plus the casual banter that characterises informal interaction in Australia, had them stumped. It also raised important pedagogic concerns, like how do you prepare for the unpredictable?

It's not known whether Saddam had an English phrasebook with him or an L–Z volume of a dictionary. If indeed his two words were evidence of preparation for what lay ahead, perhaps he'd have been better off hiding in his hole a bit longer.

Dialect borrowings

George Bernard Shaw famously wrote: 'England and America are two countries divided by a common language.' I say throw Australia in there too, to add to the divisions. Years ago, a visiting American actor was described as 'homely' by an Australian newspaper. It was an allusion to her girl-next-door style of unpretentiousness and was intended as a compliment. But to her, 'homely' meant something like 'wallflower' used to in Australia. She was very 'not happy, Jan'.

Many have commented on the dialectal differences among the Englishes, especially British (BE) and American (AE). Just think biscuit/cookie, footpath/sidewalk, petrol/gas, cashier/teller. In fact such couplings as these have served the transatlantic stand-up comic very well over the years. Of course, there are other categories of difference – like accent and grammar – but it's differences in word choice that more often than not capture public notice

The lay intuition is that, as English goes global, the lingua franca will blur over the differences, because users will opt for intelligibility rather than for carving out their own identity. In fact, however, the more English goes global, the more local variation proliferates and develops. We're moving towards a core centre of standard English which is increasingly less culturally hinged to a particular people. The standard core continues to be surrounded by massive differentiation and dialectal variety.

And there's plenty of lateral seepage – or cross-dialectal word borrowings – between/among dialects. My word-watching colleagues at Collins Dictionaries in Glasgow report that some recent Americanisms to creep across the pond are 'no-brainer' (noun), 'kick-ass' (adjective), 'leverage' (verb), along with the comparative construction 'is so not' (as in, 'that dress is so not you').

And it's a two-way street: the traffic goes the other way as well. An article, by Ben Yagoda in the *Chronicle Review*, remarked upon the unusual number of Briticisms creeping into AE. Yagoda is referring to new-arrivals like 'go missing' (in AE, 'disappear'). He points out a common wisdom in lexicography, that is, the role of the mass media in catapulting a word to prominence. Typically, a news medium makes an uncharacteristic, even odd, choice of word and *voilà!* – the word is launched into mainstream usage, if initially self-consciously. For example, the noun phrase 'wardrobe malfunction' was coined subsequent to an incident (choreographed to appear accidental) involving the attire of pop singer Janet Jackson. When, a few months later, Miss Universe Jennifer Hawkins lost her skirt in public, the incident was quickly called 'a wardrobe malfunction', whereupon it would seem handy enough to be considered a new term.

The electronic media enable lexicographers to monitor usage – or, put more militaristically, to track the infiltrations. In 1983, according to Yagoda, 'go missing' was not mentioned once in *The New York Times*; then it appeared twice in 1993, twenty-four times in 2001, and fifty in 2003. Yagoda tracks the process by which a borrowing becomes acceptable and unremarkable. By 2004, 'go missing' was being used everywhere, and with a straight face. If you watch the TV series *Without Trace,* you'd be hard-pressed to know that 'go missing' didn't come across on the *Mayflower.*

The acceptance process may be fast-tracked when a word is adopted metaphorically. An example is 'sell-by date' (BE), for AE's 'expiration date' or the Australian 'use-by date'. At first, the new 'sell-by date' in the USA was applied only to spoiled food. Then it did a lateral leap into the world of ideas (for example, 'communism reached its sell-by date'), much as Australians might talk about 'shelf life' for things that don't normally sit on shelves.

Yet, how to account for the sudden popularity of Briticisms in the USA? One explanation is an Anglophilia born of shoulder-rubbing within the Coalition of the Willing. Another is the belief (or if you prefer, aspirational prejudice) about sounding British in the USA, accounting perhaps for their interest in the Royals, and for Weight Watchers' success with the newly thinned Duchess of York. Yagoda calls it 'the eternal appeal of sounding classy without seeming pretentious'.

REFERENCES

Arnold, A., *How to Visit America and Enjoy It*, London: Putnam, 1964.

Ayto, J., *2oth Century Words: The Story of the New Words in English over the Last Hundred Years,* Oxford: Oxford University Press, 1999.

Bettelheim, B., *A Good Enough Parent*, New York: Vintage Books, 1987.

Bierce, A., *The Devil's Dictionary*, Oxford: Oxford University Press, 1911.

Burridge, K., *Blooming English: Observations on the Roots, Cultivation and Hybrids of the English Language*, Sydney: ABC Books, 2002.

Burridge, K. and Mulder, J., *English in Australia and New Zealand: An Introduction to its History, Structure and Use,* Melbourne: Oxford University Press, 1998.

Cameron, D., *Verbal Hygiene*, London / New York: Routledge, 1995.

Carter, R., Goddard, A., Reah, D., Sanager, K. and Bowring, M., *Working with Text: A Core Introduction to Language Analysis*, London: Routledge, 2001.

Chaucer, Geoffrey, Prologue, *The Canterbury Tales,* Parallel Texts, Fordham University Center for Medieval Studies, www.fordham.edu/halsall/sbook.html.

Collins Australian Dictionary, 5th edition, Sydney: HarperCollins, 2003.

Coren, S., *How to Talk Dog: Mastering the Art of Dog–Human Communication*, New York: Simon & Schuster, 2001.

Courtier, J. and Rogers, R., *The No-Garden Gardener: Creating Gardens on Patios, Balconies, Terraces, and in other Small Spaces*, London: Marshall Editions, 1999.

Craig, W. J. (ed.), *The Oxford Shakespeare*, London: Oxford University Press, 1914.

Crystal, D., *The Cambridge Encyclopedia of the English Language*, 2nd edition, Cambridge: Cambridge University Press, 2003.

    The Cambridge Encyclopedia of Language, 2nd edition, Cambridge: Cambridge University Press, 2007.

Eliot, T. S., *Four Quartets*, London: Faber and Faber, 1959.

Gallwey, W. T., *The Inner Game of Tennis*, Pan, 1986.

Gay, P., *My German Question: Growing up in Nazi Berlin*, New Haven and London: Yale University Press, 1998.

Glazier, S., *Word Menu*, New York: Random House, 1997.

Goffman, E., *Forms of Talk*, Oxford: Basil Blackwell, 1981.

Good News Bible, Canberra: The Bible Society in Australia, 1976.

Grambs, D., *The Describer's Dictionary: A Treasury of Terms and Literary Quotations for Readers and Writers*, New York: W. W. Norton, 1995.

Grice, H. P., The Logic of Conversation (unpublished ms.), Department of Philosophy, University of California, Berkeley, 1967.

Hamilton, C., *Growth Fetish*, Sydney: Allen and Unwin, 2003.

Heller, N., *Why a Painting Is Like a Pizza: A Guide to Understanding and Enjoying Modern Art*, Princeton, NJ: Princeton University Press, 2002.

Hoeg, P., *Miss Smilla's Feeling for Snow*, London: The Harvill Press, 1995.

Hollender, J. and Catling, L., *How To Make the World a Better Place: 116 Ways You Can Make a Difference*, New York: W. W. Norton & Co., 1995.

Homer, *The Iliad,* trans. Richmond Lattimore, New York: Perennial Classics, 1999.

How to Write and Speak Better, Sydney: Reader's Digest, 1989.

Huddleston, R. and Pullum, G., *The Cambridge Grammar of the English Language*, Cambridge: Cambridge University Press, 2002.

Johnson, Samuel, *A Dictionary of the English Language*, London: printed by W. Strahan, 1755.

Joyce, James, *Ulysses*, Paris: Shakespeare and Co., 1922.

Kacirk, J., *The Word Museum: The Most Remarkable English Words Ever Forgotten*, New York: Touchstone, 2000.

Kafka, Franz, *The Trial* (1925), New York: Schocken Books, 1998.

Keats, John, 'Ode on a Grecian Urn', A. Quiller-Couch (ed.), *The Oxford Book of English Verse: 1250–1900*, Oxford: Oxford University Press, 1919.

Koenig Coste, J., *Learning to Speak Alzheimer's: A Groundbreaking Approach for Everyone Dealing with the Disease*, Houghton Mifflin, 2003.

Kundera, M., *The Unbearable Lightness of Being*, New York: Perennial Classics, 1999.

The Longman Essential Activator, London: Longman, 1997.

The Macquarie Dictionary, 3rd edition, Sydney: The Macquarie Library, 1998.

Macquarie Learners Dictionary, Sydney: The Macquarie Library, 1999.

Marlowe, C., *The Tragical History of Doctor Faustus* (1604), in W. W. Gregg (ed.), *The Complete Works of Christopher Marlowe*, 1950.

Mawter, J. A., *So Grotty!* Sydney: HarperCollins, 2004.

Menendez, A., *In Cuba I was a German Shepherd*, New York: Grove Press, 2001.

Milton, John, *Paradise Lost* (1667), Renascence Edition, University of Oregon, 1997.

Nafisi, A., *Reading Lolita in Teheran: A Memoir in Books*, New York: Random House, 2003.

The Oxford Dictionary of the English Language, Oxford: Oxford University Press.

Partridge, Eric, *The Gentle Art of Lexicography*, London: Andre Deutsch, 1963.

Peters, P., *The Cambridge Australian English Style Guide*, Cambridge: Cambridge University Press, 1996.

Phillips, A., *On Kissing, Tickling, and Being Bored: Psychoanalytic Essays on the Unexamined Life*, London: Faber and Faber, 1993.

Phillips, E. and Pugh, D., *How to Get a Ph.D.*, Philadelphia: Open University Press, 1996.

Ponafidine, P., *Life in the Moslem East*, New Jersey: Gorgias Press, 2003.

Quinion, M., *Ologies and Isms: Word Beginnings and Endings*, Oxford: Oxford University Press, 2002.

Rayson, H., *The Inheritance*, Sydney: Sydney Theatre Company, 2003.

Robbins, Tom, *Fierce Invalids Home from Hot Climates*, New York: Bantam, 2000.

Ross, A., *The Language of Humour*, London: Routledge, 1998.

Rostand, Edmond, *Cyrano De Bergerac* (1897), New York: Bantam Classics, 1950.

Rushkoff, D., *Coercion: The Persuasion Professionals and Why we Listen to What THEY Say*, London: Little, Brown and Co., 2000.

Salmansohn, K., *How to Succeed in Business without a Penis: Secrets and Strategies for the Working Woman*, New Zealand: Pan Books, 1997.

Shields, Carol, *Unless*, London: Fourth Estate, 2002.

Sontag, Susan, 'Fascinating Fascism', *Under the Sign of Saturn*, New York: Farrar Straus Giroux, 1975.

Swann, R. and Sidgwick, F., *The Making of Prose: A Guide for Writers*, London: Sidgwick and Jackson, 1949.

Tuchman, Barbara, *The March of Folly: From Troy to Vietnam*, London: Abacus, 1997.

Underhill, R., *Khrushchev's Shoe and Other Ways to Captivate an Audience of 1 to 1000*, Cambridge, MA: Perseus Publications, 2002.

White, Edmund, *The Flâneur: A Stroll through the Paradoxes of Paris*, New York: Bloomsbury, 2001.

Woolfe, Sue, *Leaning Towards Infinity*, Sydney: Vintage, 1996.

Word Finder: A Dictionary of Synonyms and Antonyms, Sydney: Reader's Digest, 1979.

Wordsworth, William, *The Complete Poetical Works* (1888), London: MacMillan, 1999.

Zuckermann, G., 'Israeli (Modern Hebrew)', Keith Brown (ed.), *Encyclopedia of Language and Linguistics*, 2nd edition (14 volumes), Oxford: Elsevier, 2005.

Websites

www.faux.com

www.i-do.com.au

www.kaput.com

www.schwarzenegger.com